THE new CLIENT

THE new CLIENT

paul HOFFERT

how customers shape business
in the information age

VIKING
CANADA

VIKING CANADA
Published by the Penguin Group
Penguin Books, a division of Pearson Canada, 10 Alcorn Avenue, Toronto, Ontario,
Canada M4V 3B2
Penguin Books Ltd, 80 Strand, London WC2R 0RL, England
Penguin Putnam Inc., 375 Hudson Street, New York, New York 10014, U.S.A.
Penguin Books Australia Ltd, 250 Camberwell Road, Camberwell, Victoria 3124, Australia
Penguin Books India (P) Ltd, 11, Community Centre, Panchsheel Park, New Delhi –
110 017, India
Penguin Books (NZ) Ltd, cnr Rosedale and Airborne Roads, Albany, Auckland 1310,
New Zealand
Penguin Books (South Africa) (Pty) Ltd, 24 Sturdee Avenue, Rosebank 2196, South Africa

Penguin Books Ltd, Registered Offices: 80 Strand, London WC2R 0RL, England

First published 2002

10 9 8 7 6 5 4 3 2 1

Printed and bound in Canada on acid free paper.
Manufactured in Canada.

National Library of Canada Cataloguing in Publication

Hoffert, Paul
  The new client : how customers shape business in the information age / Paul Hoffert.

Includes bibliographical references and index.

ISBN 0-670-04352-4

1. Electronic commerce. I. Title.

HF5415.5.H568 2002a   380.1'0285'4678   C2002-904335-2

ATTENTION: CORPORATIONS
Books are available at quantity discounts with bulk purchase for educational, business, or sales
promotional use. For information, please email or write to: Penguin Books, Special Sales, 10
Alcorn Avenue Suite 304, Toronto, Ontario, Email ss.corp@pearsoned.com. Please supply: title
of book, ISBN, quantity, how the book will be used, date needed.

Visit Penguin Canada's website at **www.penguin.ca**

For Quinton, Serena and Jorel

CONTENTS

PREFACE

My father ran a small manufacturing business. He taught me that a good deal is one from which both parties emerge feeling upbeat and victorious. But what makes both the client and the supplier feel good? How high must a profit margin be to make a supplier feel good? And what constitutes good value for the client? These are difficult questions, since what makes a good deal depends on the expectations each party brings to the deal. What's more, these expectations vary from culture to culture and from time to time. And in the new millennium the times and culture are changing—a lot.

Today there is a new framework. It has many names—the digital economy, the information society, the knowledge-based economy, and a host of other terms that imply the use of computers, the Internet, wireless connectivity, and electronic commerce. Internet-related technologies and applications have changed how organizations manage, procure, manufacture, distribute, and sell products and services. And since the new digital supply networks are bi-directional, clients can also be suppliers, sending information and content through the same distribution channel from which they receive it. Consequently, clients are more empowered than ever before, and this empowerment has changed their expectations and perceptions of a good deal.

Who are these clients? They are any person, organization, or country that enters into a client–supplier relationship. Consumers are clients of companies; citizens are clients of governments; students are clients of schools; developing countries are clients of the World Bank; and so on. At the beginning of the twenty-first century, many of these clients feel that they are getting a raw deal from their suppliers.

As the Digital Age takes over from the Industrial Age, the older transactional framework is no longer providing the win–win feelings that my father spoke of. The scandalous and cavalier practices of executives at companies like Enron and WorldCom have caused investors to lose faith in the integrity of public equity markets, depressing stock prices by hundreds of billions of dollars. Why? The answer to that question is the subject of this book. It is a recipe for rectifying the imbalance between suppliers and clients; a new framework within which suppliers are more responsible to their clients and both sides get what they want—a good deal.

THE END OF THE
INDUSTRIAL FAIRYTALE

Once upon a time, there was a land with riches beyond compare. In this land, wondrous machines performed miraculous feats that freed the people from the daily toil of their ancestors. Mammoth mining machines replaced laboring miners, drilling deep into the ground and piling up mineral-laden rocks. Motorized conveyor belts with the power of hundreds of horses moved the crude rock to crushing machines, where powerful mandible-like teeth ground it into bite-sized chunks. Other machines separated the sludge into its essential nutrients and wastes. People used the valuable metals, minerals, and hydrocarbons that were extracted from the ground to build and fuel a cornucopia of other machines that performed every imaginable task. Farmers no longer tilled their fields directly, but rode atop mechanized oxen, pressing a button here and pulling a lever there, as powerful mechanical claws tilled the earth, planted seeds, harvested crops, threshed grains, and baled hay.

Traveling, once time-consuming and dangerous, was now commonplace and effortless in amazing vehicles that traversed the land, sea, and sky. Voyages that had once taken years now took less than a day in vehicles fueled by the hydrocarbons that were mined from the earth.

As people were freed from laborious tasks, they were able to concentrate on improving human health and longevity. Fewer mothers died in childbirth, fewer children died from illness, and people lived longer than ever before. In fact, more people were now engaged in keeping others alive and well than in producing food and shelter.

With greater lifespans and fewer deaths, the population grew. Villages expanded into towns, then cities. The cities grew too, fattened by the influx of rural folk who no longer needed to work the farms. Cities expanded until they encroached on other cities, then merged into huge megalopoli, the edges of which sometimes touched, forming an unbroken mass of humanity.

Huge factories manufactured primary materials, such as textiles, plastics, metals, and chemicals. These materials fed other factories that manufactured clothing, appliances, and every type of tool to make life easier and more enjoyable.

Generally the people were very happy. Unlike their ancestors, who sweated endlessly for the benefit of despotic kings and queens, people were now allowed to keep the fruits of their labor. They owned land, homes, and even businesses. They measured their wealth by the number of months of wages they needed to buy a home, a vehicle, or an entertainment appliance.

Compared with their forebears, the people lived a fairytale existence. But people being people, they eventually became dissatisfied with their lot. No matter how much wealth they had, they wanted more. No matter how much free time they had, they wanted more. No matter how much control they had over their natural environment, they wanted more. At the same time, it became clear that there was a limit to the expansion of their wealth, because the natural resources upon which it was based were being used up, leaving insufficient raw materials and fuel to build and run their machines in the future.

The people had come to imagine themselves frolicking at a grand ball, dressed in luxurious clothes, dancing to fabulous music, and impressing their friends. But, as is frequently the case in fairytales, midnight was approaching and there was a foreboding that the good times were about to vanish. There was the nagging problem of nonsustainable growth. It became apparent that the natural resources that had supported the great Industrial Age were finite, while the greed of the people was infinite. Sooner or later (and many feared sooner), the people's opulent coaches would turn into pumpkins, the bubble of progress would burst, and wealth would begin to disappear.

Just when it seemed like disaster was imminent, wise people proclaimed that they had found a solution to the problem of industrialization. A new value system, based on information, could be introduced using a new nonindustrial technology called digitization. The new measure of wealth would lie not in the acquisition of material goods, such as minerals, fuels, food, or tall buildings, but in acquisitions of the mind, such as knowledge and human experience.

The new measure of wealth would lie not in the acquisition of material goods, but in acquisitions of the mind.

People began diverting their spending from jewels to entertainment. They increasingly watched television, went to movies, and surfed the Internet, gathering information and reaping enjoyment.

The world's financial systems were altered so that the quantification of assets and savings was no longer based on quantities of precious metals like gold. Companies were no longer valued by their physical assets but by their ability to produce information and entertainment that others would pay for.

This new way of measuring value was truly a revelation. For years, poets and saints had decried the elevation of the material over the spiritual, but the people had never taken these warnings seriously. After all, tangible things—bars of gold, land, buildings, jewels, and the like—had always measured value. But now, for the first time, even wealthy people and political leaders began talking about the new measurement of wealth and the new economy based on it. The new wealth, they said, could be found in a person's mind—the information, knowledge, wisdom, and enjoyment that sometimes passed through and sometimes lodged in the consciousness of a person.

This new wealth could not be easily measured by suppliers because it was no longer based on the cost of the raw materials or the labor required to produce it. The new wealth could not be counted as easily as diamonds or dollars. It was best measured by those who consumed the information and the entertainment, since the new value now resided in their minds.

The burgeoning wealth of information and entertainment became the new currency. This information currency was universal and could be created by anyone with a modicum of intelligence or creativity. More important, the creators of information could distribute their works at almost no cost to anyone, anywhere in the world, who had access to the information routes. The dawning era was called the Information Age.

Needless to say, the Information Age threw a monkey wrench into the older business culture of the Industrial Age, which had developed around the mining of natural resources and manufacturing of physical goods.

There was great confusion in the realm. On the one hand, the new way of measuring value and wealth seemed to alleviate the problem of dwindling natural resources, which were no longer the necessary ingredients for creating wealth. But on the other hand, the two currency systems seemed incompatible since there was not yet a framework for converting the old currency into the new.

Hundreds of years of business practice and culture had been handed down from generation to generation based on Industrial Age frameworks for calculating wealth and value. Yet these practices would now have to be discarded. The mandate was clear: Every person or company that engaged in transactions, as a supplier or client of a product or a service, would now have to reconsider how to evaluate the bargain.

All of a sudden, it seemed, a near paradise had been turned topsy-turvy.

The New Technology: Changing Everyone

As much as we might wish the story of the Information Age to have a fairytale ending, with everyone living happily ever after, there is no indication that it will. In fact, the next few decades will be characterized by continuing clashes between legacy Industrial Age economic interests and the new economy, which is based on creating and manipulating information and entertainment.

What's more, these clashes will affect everyone and every business, whether they are online or not. Like the Agricultural Age and the Industrial Age before it, the Information Age touches absolutely everyone and every organization, and affects every business and every business transaction.

When a fundamental change in technology occurs, one that revolutionizes the way people work and play, it also revolutionizes the way they think, what they expect out of life, how they communicate with each other, how they balance their personal desires with the needs of their community, and the way they trade with each other. In business, the new digital technology is causing a shift in power and control from suppliers to clients, and that shift has infiltrated every aspect of every business, from transactions between customers and suppliers to interactions among employees and business planning. All are subject to a new set of business rules.

When a fundamental change in technology occurs, one that revolutionizes the way people work and play, it also revolutionizes the way they think.

Legacies from the Industrial Age include big factories, big unions, and big governments. One by one, these took control of our communities in the nineteenth and twentieth centuries, dominating our culture, politics, and livelihood. And one by one, they are losing control and mind share in the twenty-first century.

Steelmaking: An Example of Change

Take steelmaking, an icon for the industrial era. Andrew Carnegie built the Carnegie Steel Company into a corporate powerhouse in the late 1800s. Its factories produced one-quarter of all the steel in the United States. In 1901 Carnegie sold the company for $400 million (US), an unimaginably huge sum in those days, to New York banker J.P. Morgan. Morgan transformed the company into U.S. Steel, the first business enterprise in history with an authorized capitalization of more than $1 billion (US).[2] Because of its immense, unprecedented size, financiers on Wall Street nicknamed it "the Corporation." U.S. Steel was, for a long time, the largest company in the United States by a wide margin. But as the Industrial Age waned and the Digital Age waxed, the steel industry faded and lost its dominance over the economy.

Today, in fact, a third of the U.S. Steel capacity is bankrupt, tens of thousands of jobs have been lost, prices have fallen to a twenty-year low, and in March 2002 the United States had to impose a 30 percent tariff on imported steel to try to save the remaining steel companies from going out of business. The United Steelworkers Union, formerly a stalwart of the trade union movement, is also on the ropes. Leo Gerrard, president of the Pittsburgh-based union, faces a declining membership in a declining union movement within a steeply declining sector of the economy. There are ten retired steel workers for each active steel employee, and the cost of providing the 600,000 steel-worker families with retirement and health benefits is more than $10 billion (US).[3] In these circumstances, the union is a shadow of its former self, and is waging a rearguard action to prevent further erosion of jobs and benefits.

The problems in the steel industry are not unique to the United States. In April 2000, I attended a conference on community informatics (transforming communities using new media infrastructure) in Middlesbrough, England. That area had been the center of the British steel industry in the mid-twentieth century and had produced about a third of all the steel supplied to the Allied forces in World War II. But at the turn of the twenty-first century, Middlesbrough's steel industry was dead. Unemployment had reached 80 percent, the coal mines that had fueled the iron factories were closed, and there was no longer any heavy manufacturing in the region.

In the local pubs, however, there were computers at the bar and on the tables where local citizenry could log on to acquire new skills training in computer programming, online marketing, and the like. I witnessed this transformation from old to new economy as I shared a few pints with some ex-miners, whose rough hands and hard accents belied their sophisticated knowledge of digital networks. One middle-aged gent told me he flew to Silicon Valley, California, every few months to meet face-to-face with his clients, for whom he was managing a software project. The relatively cheap and eager labor pool in his town, coupled with the distance-erasing communications technology of the Internet, provided the grease for the wheels of his new career.

As for the remaining steel industry, it too is undergoing Digital Age transformations.

This old steel town and others like it are in the midst of a difficult transition from the old to the new currency. As for the remaining steel industry, it too is undergoing Information Age transformations, lowering costs and bringing up efficiency. The e-STEEL exchange, launched in 1999, is an online marketplace for the exchange of steel components and products. Like other true markets, e-STEEL does not own any of the products traded on the system and is not affiliated with any industry participant. But unlike traditional markets, it is instant and global, erasing regional business networks and replacing them with territorially agnostic transactions.

The e-STEEL exchange has quickly become the leading global marketplace for steel, enabling buyers and sellers to negotiate, transact, and conclude business with increased efficiency, fewer errors, and reduced costs. The online exchange boasts more efficient trades and auctions, reduced transaction costs, and a wealth of information to enable smarter procurement decisions. The online steel portal provides automatic conversion calculators for imperial and metric equivalents of area, energy, flow, length, pressure, temperature, velocity, volume, and weight. This tool brings a greater pool of buyers and sellers together from all parts of the world, dramatically decreasing transaction costs and simultaneously providing better margins and lower prices.

In 2002, NewView Technologies (e-STEEL Exchange's parent company) partnered with IBM to transform the global steel-supply chain into a giant collaborative supply network. Instead of the traditional supply chain, in which each supplier in turn delivers its product or service to the next link without any knowledge of what's going on a few links removed, all levels of the newly networked suppliers share their information across an integrated communications system that translates each company's business processes and schedules into a common shared database. The network-wide system enables many companies to operate as if they were a single integrated organization. This virtual organization behaves just like a real one, eliminating duplicated efforts, greatly streamlining processes, and responding rapidly to changes in the specification, ordering, manufacturing, marketing, and sale of steel.

A Time of Transition

If these radical changes have taken place in an industry that was the poster-boy of industrialization, it's not hard to imagine the sea changes that are rocking every other industry, particularly those that are tied more directly to information infrastructures. The changing environment is so profound that wordmongers have added "new" before just about every noun you can imagine. We have "new media," a "new economy," and (*mea culpa* for having joined the parade) "new clients."

But the new will not entirely replace the old. You can't run your car on information. It still needs gas (or electricity). We will continue to rely on many natural resources and manufactured products for the foreseeable future.[4] Consequently, the underlying industrial and digital frameworks will continue to scrape against each other, causing sporadic stresses and disruptions, clouding the atmosphere with destructive fumes, and radically changing the landscape.

As information becomes more available to clients, they become more powerful in transactions.

One fundamental disruption is the relationship between suppliers and clients, brought on by the rapid ascendance of digital and information technologies. As information becomes more available to clients, they become more powerful in transactions. One adage still holds true: Knowledge is power. And today's clients are dramatically more knowledgeable than they were a few years back.

It is relatively easy for a customer to go online and find web portals that display recent transaction prices for injection-molding machines, trucks, heart surgery operations, legal services, or antique music boxes. What's more, in many cases, the websites include client ratings of the various suppliers. Still other websites detail the cost structures of providing the products and services, enabling clients to do quick calculations of their supplier's gross profit and by extension their maneuvering room on price.

Access to Information

The Information Age is aptly named.[5] Everywhere you look, there are new sources of information. The World Wide Web was invented in 1993, yet less than a decade later it provides ordinary users with more information than was ever available before to professional researchers. According to a Cyveillance study, there were 4 billion unique, publicly available webpages in 2001, with a growth rate of about 10 million webpages a day.[6] Each of these pages, on average, contains 10,000 bytes of information, 14 images, 23 internal links for easy navigation on the site, and 6 links to webpages on other sites.

In 2002, there were about half a billion users of the Internet.[7] The number is significant because each one of these users is both a supplier and a client of online information through the empowering architecture of the Internet that lets every user contribute to the body of publicly available information. The Internet has transformed the nature of personal and corporate research, allowing anyone online to access unimaginable stores of information that were previously closeted in inaccessible databanks, corporate vaults, government ministries, and filing cabinets. And much of the information is new, having been created by volunteers whose personal interests, hobbies, or work encourages them to spend time creating, cataloguing, and collaborating on meaningful online information.

The information resources available to ordinary people today are enormous. The first Canadian census of the new millennium was also the first to be made available online—free, instantly, to everyone—by Statistics Canada (www.statcan.ca). The census profiles the number of people and dwellings in every province, region, city, town, and neighborhood in Canada. It includes 400 thematic tables and more than 8,000 maps of geographical areas, right down to the size of a city block. Users can type a street name into their browsers to see its location on a map and find out how many people live on it.

Mike Sheridan, Statistics Canada's assistant chief statistician, notes, "We made an effort to put it out online so more people can make use of it. Until this census, anyone interested in the data had to purchase a CD-ROM or order customized data."[8] That meant ordinary Canadians did not generally have access to the information. But all citizens are greatly affected by the data, not just academics and government officials. At stake, for example, is $47 billion (Can) in federal transfer payments that flow according to the population distribution in the census numbers. The chief electoral officer also uses the numbers to redraw federal election boundaries, a reallocation that occurs every ten years.

Knowledge Is Power

Access to information, which used to be controlled by intermediary government and industry gatekeepers, is now available universally and instantly. An important consequence of this shift is the sense that instead of *them* (faceless government and business interests) keeping tabs on *us* (ordinary people), *we* are now watching *them*. The change is profound, deraling the expected Orwellian scenario in which Big Brother would control every aspect of our lives and replacing it with a scenario in which governments, businesses, and suppliers of all sorts are accountable to clients.

Access to information, which used to be controlled by intermediary government and industry gatekeepers, is now available universally and instantly.

Perhaps the most miraculous aspect of the Digital Age is not the mountain of information available to us, but our ability to filter it quickly to get what we're interested in. Search engines such as Google return addresses of webpages related to a query in a fraction of a second, correcting spelling mistakes and translating the pages into our language of choice along the way. Although we complain when the catalog of "hits" or the translation is imperfect, the wonder is that it can be done at all. A decade ago, this type of automatic data mining was in the realm of science fiction. There is no doubt that a decade hence we will be able to speak into a microphonic piece of apparel, like the ones depicted in *Star Trek,* and request any information we are interested in. The response will be instantly forthcoming in text, pictures, sound, and video, on appliances distributed throughout our homes and offices. Now that's empowerment!

The New Client

Remember the last time you bought a refrigerator or washing machine? If it was a few years back, you probably shopped at a few stores, trying to gauge the differences in makes and models. Basically, they all looked about the same, so you relied on the salesperson to help you make your choice based on functionality, features, reliability, and price.

Today, customers browse the Internet for information about appliance brands and models, getting detailed information about features and technology that would be too time-consuming for a salesperson to explain in a store. They check out consumer-run websites that rate the reliability of appliances and industry websites that quote recent market prices and detail industry trends. Other websites post customer satisfaction ratings of retailers, with a combination of quantitative (usually one to five stars) and qualitative (signed email) reviews.

Customers also can get quotes online from appliance dealers. Some websites use software agents to provide quotes from dozens of dealers, listed in order of increasing price. This kind of information makes customers much more powerful when they walk into an appliance store to negotiate a purchase. And it has changed the way suppliers need to deal with their clients.

But the concept of new clients goes far beyond the older stereotype of business customers. The term "customer" is too restrictive in this context, because it implies a commercial transaction in which a product or service is exchanged directly for money. While business customers are certainly clients, the world of the new client encompasses a much broader range of transactions, in which the delivery of products or services can be much less direct.

Citizens see themselves as clients of government. In the past, the masses had little choice but to blindly accept government pronouncements and activities. Only those few individuals who were willing to devote a lot of time and energy to voice their opinions would be heard by their representatives. The process was lengthy and not very responsive: Constituents had to send letters to their elected officials and wait for their replies. Only organized interest groups with the money to hire professional lobbyists could break through the governmental bureaucracies, which acted as barriers to direct communication.

Today, within minutes of a political speech or news bulletin, thousands of emails stream into government offices.

Today, within minutes of a political speech or news bulletin, thousands of emails stream into government offices, warning of dire consequences in the next election if the sender's point of view is not heeded. Citizens expect quick replies, with explanations of how elected officials will respond to their concerns. The term "political masters" is losing relevance as the idea of "political servants" becomes more plausible. Citizens set their expectations of government in commercial terms: "I pay my taxes and I expect good value for my money."

Students and educators now also see themselves as clients and suppliers of education products and services. In the age of lifelong learning, almost everyone is engaged in some form of learning activity, whether by attending classes at traditional schools, upgrading skills at work, taking correspondence or distance education courses, using CD-ROMs, or learning through the Internet. In each case, today's learners demand and gain more control over all aspects of their learning.

Patients see themselves as clients of the health care system. Hospitals are phasing out the term "patient" and speaking instead of health care "clients." The change in terminology is not just business-speak but reflects a deeper change in the way we view our culture and environment. Doctors, nurses, clinics, drug companies, HMOs, and government health agencies are all feeling the wrath of patients who want more and better services for their money. Patients now have access to all the minutiae of their ailments, diagnoses, and treatments. They know how much each service costs, and how it compares with others in neighboring communities and around the world. In response, the health industry is shifting its emphasis from satisfying health care professionals and institutions to satisfying client/patients.

That's the new client—a person or organization empowered by the Information Age to deal more knowledgeably with suppliers.

The client metaphor has extended to many areas not normally associated with transactions. Parishioners see themselves as clients of their churches. Like other consumers, they shop around (in this case, for congregations), looking for the best deal in religious services. Caught between the divine inspiration of their rigid organizations and the reality of mostly dwindling flocks, churches today must be more responsive to the changing demands of their congregants.

Members of trade unions, formerly content to leave the driving to their bosses, are now taking the wheels of power, sometimes overturning the negotiated settlements of their leaders and more frequently asking, "What value am I getting for my union dues payment?"

Whether they are businesses, governments, schools, hospitals, churches, or unions, organizational suppliers need to re-evaluate their relationship with their clients. Without exception, their clients are emerging from these re-evaluations with more control than they had in the Industrial Age because they are now more informed. That's the new client—a person or organization empowered by the Information Age to deal more knowledgeably with suppliers. And that's what this book is about.

1

THE NEW AGE OF
INFORMATION

There's a reinvention process going on

right now with customers: They are more

empowered, and companies have not

yet caught up to that empowerment.[1]

KELLY MAHONEY, CHIEF MARKETING OFFICER, STAPLES.COM

The invention of printing led to an ever-increasing availability of books, newspapers, magazines, and journals. By the middle of the twentieth century, the application of word processors and automated typesetters to the printing process enormously increased the proliferation of information. The democratic access to education, which had produced millions of new writers, further accelerated the trend. By 1970, the amount of information had become overwhelming and disheartening, leaving us over-stimulated by mounds of new facts without the time needed to read and make sense of them. The situation prompted Alvin and Heidi Toffler to write *Future Shock*, just as our brains went into overload from too much data and not enough capacity to analyze it. At the time, we all recognized the problem but were unable to come up with a viable solution.

A decade later, the Tofflers predicted the rise of the Information Age as the third wave of the technology revolution, after agriculture and industrialization. They argued that industrial civilization was based on social conformity and machine power, which would be replaced by a new culture of information technology and human creativity. They reasoned that, somehow, this change would solve the problem of the surfeit of facts and paucity of understanding.

But not even the Tofflers could foresee the almost accidental invention of the World Wide Web in 1993 by a group of cloistered scientists in a European atom-smashing compound. Like the introduction of the automobile, which enthusiasts thought would simply replace the horse but eventually became the agent for replacing towns and rural communities with suburbs, the Internet, created to increase information flow, has become the instrument for filtering its seemingly infinite expanse, actually decreasing the amount of information we need to process. Seemingly miraculous search engines can be set to winnow the amount of information received, so that we now spend less time tossing out the chaff and more time chewing on the intellectual wheat. In fact, one of the most popular Internet games in 2001 was to devise search words for Internet search engines that would return only a single website address.

Search engines dramatically reduce the time and effort required to do research—a task that no longer implies academic pursuits but more frequently relates to finding a telephone number or email address, locating the pet shops in your neighborhood, choosing the perfect vacation resort, or reading about the life of your favorite movie star.

The purveyors of research used to be librarians, archivists, and academics. They still are, except that those appellations can now be applied to each and every one of us, since we've gained access to the catalog system of the largest repository of information ever assembled. It's like being in charge of the Library of Congress ... times a gazillion. Instead of the older two-step process of finding the desired title in a catalog and then having to locate the physical book, journal, recording, or video, we now click to find a title and then click again to get the content. Even a decade ago, we could never have imagined how well informed ordinary people would be today.

The new client was born in the maternity ward of the Information Age.

Want to search the archives of the *New York Times*? the *London Financial Times*? the *Chicago Tribune*? the records of the House of Commons, House of Lords, or Congress? *Ba-da-bing ba-da-boom!* Done. Here are the matches to your query. Time taken? Less than half a second. What did the candidate in your riding (or district) have to say about the environment? How did she vote? *Ka-ching!* The result comes up on the screen of your tiny Blackberry wireless Internet device, right in the middle of an all-candidates' meeting.

Armed with powerful, previously unavailable facts and arguments, accessible at a moment's notice, ordinary people have begun to take control of their former masters. The realization that individuals are more empowered than ever before has nurtured the growth of the new client psyche. The new client was born in the maternity ward of the Information Age.

The Impact of Information Technology

The new client and the new economy are consequences of great stores of information from which targeted material can be searched and retrieved almost instantly. Information technology (IT) refers to the tools that enable the storage, processing, and retrieval of information. IT makes possible a broad range of commercial activities, from electronic data interchange (EDI) to data mining (finding useful relationships in collections of data). IT powers private digital networks (intranets) in business, government, and education, enabling myriad applications that help organizations run more efficiently.

Although the IT sector accounts for only 5 percent of the workforce, it generates about 10 percent of the gross domestic product (GDP). According to the U.S. Commerce Department report, *Digital Economy 2000*, the IT sector has been responsible for one-third of all economic growth over the past decade, outpacing every other sector by a wide margin.

IT also makes the Internet work. And the Internet has been working extremely well. In 2001 almost three-quarters of Americans went online regularly for an average of ten hours each week.[2] No other modern technology, including telephones, radios, phonographs, and television, has achieved this level of penetration and usage so quickly. The main reason people go online is to obtain information quickly. Internet users watch five hours less television per week than their nonconnected peers. The online trend is even stronger for children, who use the Internet more and watch television less than their parents.

E-commerce is also growing rapidly. Internet users rate their online purchasing experiences as 3.7 on a scale from 1 to 5, a surprisingly strong endorsement, given that on average it takes new Internet users about eighteen months of online experience before feeling comfortable enough to make their first online purchase. According to the U.S. Census Bureau, in 2001, after only half a dozen years of availability, online sales in the United States totaled $35 billion (US), out of $800 billion (US) total retail sales, an annual increase of 20 percent over the previous year.

Pan-Nationalism of Digital Networks

International commerce has always depended on territorial licenses. A company that has the rights to sell a product in Britain, for example, might not have the rights to sell that product in the United States or Canada. Each territory has its own political, cultural, and business contexts, and these must be factored into the local business plans. Even multinational companies tailor their operations to the individual countries in which they operate, since production, marketing, advertising, and other costs in one territory are different from those in another. Each country and region has its own duties, sales taxes, certification processes, and transportation charges that result in different local prices.

Today, a website in South Africa is just as close to a client in Halifax as the store down the road.

However, these differences become irrelevant when trade moves to the global Internet. The fact that there are no customs booths to intercept digital data as it travels from country to country is a bonanza for clients. They can shop for the best deal anywhere in the world and even avoid taxes if the product or service can be delivered online. Today, a website in South Africa is just as close to a client in Halifax as the store down the road.

But web sales can be a disaster for traditional distributors and retailers who depend on local protected markets for their client pool. These suppliers are threatened with losing their territorially exclusive lines of merchandise and their advantageous proximity to local clients by the pan-national aspect of digital networks, with their global marketing, sales, and distribution channels.

Since digital services and products can circumvent regional and national protective barriers, they encourage free trade. The effects of free trade vary greatly from one organization to another. Some gain and others lose. So on the supplier side, one may say that pan-nationality is globally neutral, with some winners and some losers. But on the client side it's a win any way you look at it. There are more suppliers, more competition, and lower prices.

The Internet: Equalizing Suppliers and Clients

Digital computer networks such as the Internet are essentially symmetrical, meaning they provide users and servers equal access to the distribution channel. The interactive digital technologies encourage two-way control, in a back-and-forth seesaw between suppliers and clients.

In the era of mass communication, clients (television viewers, radio listeners, newspaper and magazine readers) could only *receive* information from their suppliers. There were channels through which they could send information to suppliers, such as letters to the editor, but the old distribution channels were biased in favor of providers. In the Information Age, however, a client on a web browser, chat line, or email service can also be a supplier of information. Many companies now solicit detailed information and opinions from their clients, using formats that range from online questionnaires to focus groups. Increasingly, clients and potential clients are paid for their participation in cash, rebates, or free goods and services, including frequent-usage points (air miles, and so forth). This new environment places clients in a similar role to their suppliers, equalizing the relationship and power structures.

With the proliferation of business and personal websites, more clients are also becoming suppliers, and vice versa. This switch further blurs the formerly distinctive mind-sets of these previously separated groups. The new perspective is closer to a partnership than were the older, more adversarial roles. The new supplier is more apt to build a pitch around the theme of "Let's get together and find the best way to deliver what you want (excellent value in a product/service)" than "Help me make a profit."

Most new computers come preconfigured with web servers as well as web browsers, allowing users to easily publish online information that is indistinguishable from that in large suppliers' websites. This duality erases the psychological barrier between *us* and *them*, since they are us and we are them.

It is now the user who drives the interactive flow, not the supplier. The user clicks on a link or types in text to control the flow of a session. The new ability of users to control interactions comes at the expense of suppliers. Jakob Nielsen, in his biweekly column for useit.com, notes, "The web is the ultimate consumer-empowering environment. He or she who clicks the mouse gets to decide—EVERYTHING."[3] In our parlance, the online user is a newly empowered client, controlling the place and pace of interactions with suppliers of information and products.

The online user is a newly empowered client, controlling the place and pace of interactions with suppliers of information and products.

This experience, repeated online millions of times a day by people throughout the world, is conditioning us to accept clients as being in control. Consequently, clients are much more forceful when they deal with suppliers and expect them to respond to their requests instantly with a list of options, so that clients can decide to their best advantage.

An Example: Buying a DVD Player

Here's an example of a newly empowered client—me!

The 2001 Christmas season for retailers turned out better than expected. One of the key contributors was consumer electronics, which registered a record number of DVD sales. The DVD sales bonanza was driven by very low retail prices—less than the magic price point of $100 (US).

Most of the DVD machines that sold for as little as $70 (US) in discount chains (such as Target and Wal-Mart) were manufactured in China by companies with no consumer brand awareness (no-names) and no history of aftermarket support. Customers bought these machines because they were typically half the price of name-brand DVD players. But many customers wondered whether the quality, features, and service could be as good as those offered by Sony, Panasonic, and other known brands. So did I. I had begun a collection of DVD titles and was wondering whether I should buy a second player for the bedroom.

By early 2002, the verdict was in from those who had bought the cheap machines. I was able to easily sample their opinions by logging on to websites such as amazon.com for a sampling of reviews. I checked out the Apex DVD player, which was the second-best-selling brand (after Sony) during the Christmas season. A typical write-in reviewer to amazon.com noted, "You get what you pay for. Very few options, and the quality is poor. For just a little more cash ($149 to $199) you get a much better product with lots of options. If you do get this DVD player, in just a few weeks you will wish you spent the extra $60 to $110 bucks!"

A few clicks later, and my Google search engine found a *New York Times* article that reported the results (some positive, some negative) of comparative tests between the no-names and the name-brand DVD players.[4] The subhead of the *Times* article read, "The Apex AD-1500's DVD tray sometimes refuses to open." The article went on to quote other online reviews: "About a third of the ratings are 1 star [lowest, with comments such as] 'Dead on arrival' [and] 'Tray won't open.'" The article also revealed that "the no-name companies can save up to $28 per player by not paying the proper royalties to the patent holders for DVD-player technologies," an issue that is relevant to me, as an author and a composer who relies on royalties for my livelihood.

Finally, in blind comparison tests, the picture and sound quality of the no-names were found to be inferior to those of the known brands.

This information, which took me ten minutes to find on the Web, made me a much more knowledgeable consumer and enabled me to make an informed decision about which DVD player I should choose.

Could I have done this before the Web? No way! If I had gone to an electronics store, a salesperson would have told me to stick to a name brand. But I would have been suspicious about her motives because her store only sold name brands and she earned higher commissions for higher-priced items. At a drugstore or discount store, there would have been no knowledgeable sales staff to answer my questions. Ads in the newspaper mention only basic features and price. And magazines such as *Consumer Reports* would only review these units months or years after I had made my purchase.

Online transactions are mimicking mail-order catalogs, which give customers the benefit of buying through one channel (the catalog) and servicing through another (the store).

I made my purchase in a retail store. I could have bought my DVD player online for a lower price, but I was concerned about future servicing and the potential hassle of returning the unit in the event that it was faulty. For me, the primary value added by my retailer was aftermarket convenience.

That situation is beginning to change as online retailers increasingly make deals with bricks-and-mortar stores to handle their product returns. Online transactions are thus mimicking mail-order catalogs from retail chains, which give customers the benefit of buying through one channel (the catalog) and servicing through another (the store). Every week, it seems, there's a strategic alliance, acquisition, or merger aimed at bringing together the advantages of web-based commerce and traditional business outlets. As that trend continues, millions of consumers may well re-evaluate their purchasing patterns and move more of their buying online.

Symmetrical Networks and P2P

One of the least-understood aspects of digital networks is the symmetry of their distribution channels. In "one-to-many," or asymmetrical, distribution systems, economies of scale apply for mass production. The cost of distributing an item by truck, train, boat, or plane is much lower if you can distribute many of the same items to the same destination at the same time (mass distribution). But in electronic distribution systems, the cost of distributing a single digital item is almost nothing and is not lowered by sending many digital items to the same destination. There is no digital parallel to filling a truck or container with the maximum load of a single product in order to reduce human handling costs because there are no human handling costs in digital transport. Furthermore, the cost of digital distribution has no relationship to the distance traveled or number of borders crossed.

Unlike physical distribution costs, which rise quickly when customer interaction is factored into the process, digital processing and distribution costs are almost independent of the number and level of electronic interactions with customers. Consequently, it costs no more to treat each digital transaction as a unique and personalized ("one-to-one," or symmetrical) interaction.

Symmetrical connections enable very different kinds of distribution patterns and client–supplier relationships. Perhaps the most novel is peer-to-peer (P2P) distribution. The term "peer-to-peer" generally refers to activities for which users (clients) contribute (supply) files, computing time, or other resources to other users who generally share an interest or a project. Even more interesting than P2P's technical underpinnings is its social potential, as it gives content, choice, and control to users.

The most publicized use of P2P is the distribution of computer programs, music, video, and books as digital files, most of which are available commercially but are circulated as "pirated" copies among interested users. These Napster-like distribution systems are also used, however, for activities that are perfectly legal and have the blessings of businesses. For example, demo files of all sorts of software, entertainment and otherwise, are distributed by P2P methods at almost no cost to companies and with positive effects on sales, as the companies' e-commerce website addresses are included in the sample offerings. The demos are usually excerpts (of music, books, or movies) that are partially functional or functional for only a limited time (known as "try and buy").

There is freeware—computer programs or other intellectual property for which the author does not wish to be paid. More frequently, offerings are made as shareware—applications for which payment is encouraged but voluntary. Shareware authors are the most client focused because their income depends entirely on making a customer satisfied enough to dig into his wallet. To date, the amount of optional shareware payments has been generally disappointing, except in a small percentage of cases for which the optional payment is small but the utility is high, such as computer software programs.

One of these applications, New NotePad (see www.hisadon.cup.com), is the software I use for organizing my professional writing. This text-organizing program, originally written for the Japanese market and later made available in English, is perfect for pasting research articles from different sources in different formats because it supports only plain text. Thus, when I paste text from a website into my New Notepad, it automatically strips out all the unwanted Web formatting, leaving nice and clean unformatted text. In more capable word-processing programs, this process usually takes several manual steps. Moreover, New Notepad lets me organize my text notes hierarchically in folders that parallel sections of my essays or chapters in my books and allows me to move these around easily, like an outline processor. The voluntary payment of $20 (U.S.) is a small price to pay for this utility, so I (and thousands of others) sent my money in, resulting in enough income to encourage the author, Hiroki Hisaura, to make numerous updates and upgrades to the product.

P2P has proven to be the hottest new tool for savvy business marketers who wish to promote their products and services to a large audience at low cost.

But P2P has also proven to be the hottest new tool for savvy business marketers who wish to promote their products and services to a large audience at low cost. They seed a few influential clients or potential clients with compelling information. These clients forward the information to their friends, and, in the viral nature of Internet communication, it quickly reaches a large audience that is self-selected by the seeded peer group. This viral marketing, as it has come to be known, is one of the most important tools of business today. The key, of course, is making your organization's message compelling enough to warrant forwarding to others. Each target group will have different criteria for a compelling message. For some groups, it need only be advance information that is not yet available to the general public, so those who forward it are seen as insiders. In all cases, it is important for viral marketers to have a good sense of what information will push the emotional buttons of their target clients.

Although newer technologies may eventually eclipse digital technology as the Information Age progresses, digital technology, like the steam engine before it, will have permanently altered the way we perceive the world around us and how we relate to things.

Convergence in the Information Age

Until recently, most recording and storage systems were analog; that is, they used signals that corresponded to physical variables. The squiggles on a phonograph record and the waveforms of a television broadcast are examples of capturing sounds and images in analog format. Digital technology, on the other hand, reduces phenomena to simple numbers. The expression of the world around us by these standard numbers has been the key to convergent digital networks.

In digital technology, every type of information can be expressed in the same number system, a system so simple that it has only two numbers: zero and one. For example, a single microchip component interprets zero as off and one as on. Being able to describe everything in the same system creates a lingua franca that allows all manner of hitherto incompatible systems to interoperate. This means that digital systems are intrinsically open to access from an increasingly wide range of suppliers and clients.

The new interoperability leads to many types of convergence. *Media convergence* is the ability to express formerly different products within a single new product. For example, before digitization, the manufacture and distribution of audio recordings (LPs, audio cassettes), photographs (paper), cameras (film), computer data-storage devices (floppy disks), and rental movies (videotape) were distinct for each industry. But when the first digital medium was introduced—the music compact disc (CD)—the same technology and manufacturing plants could also produce photo CDs, CD-ROMs, recordable CDs, and digital video discs (DVDs). As a result, the number of CD plants mushroomed, the price of a manufactured CD came down, from about $1.50 to $0.50 (Can) within a few years, and the suppliers of the older analog media were, for the most part, put out of business unless they switched to the new digital media manufacturing.

Channel convergence is the ability to distribute products that formerly required separate channels (truck and warehouse systems, rail transport, shipping, air cargo) through the same single channel of the Internet. Digital distribution is cheaper and available to more distributors than physical distribution systems because digital transport requires no warehousing, no human handling, and hardly any energy for transportation.

Digital transport requires no warehousing, no human handling, and hardly any energy for transportation.

The older physical distribution channels are frequently an expensive component of product costs, while the new digital distribution networks are usually a small cost factor. For example, books and music CDs are very different physical products, but they are now both available through new products such as Palm Pilots (PDAs) and MP3 players. The book or music content is mostly distributed over the Internet but will be increasingly available on wireless networks that reach cell phones and other portable devices. These developments will further erode the traditional distribution businesses.

Business convergence is a result of media and channel convergence. Businesses that formerly had distinct geographic and product markets now find that their markets have converged with those of new competitors that use the same media and marketing channels. For example, in the travel industry, the former advantage a travel agency had in being located nearby clients (to deliver airline tickets and have a personal chat) has been eroded by the advent of online electronic booking and ticketing, which allows airlines, websites, and distant agencies to compete with local agencies.

Finally, *industrial convergence* is the bringing together of formerly separate industries—such as communications, broadcasting, cable television, computers, entertainment, and culture (books and other media)—that enables each to encroach on the clients of the other, resulting in market chaos and disruptions. The content and communications industries, once separated by incompatible technologies, distribution networks, and laws prohibiting cross-ownership, are now merging and thus being serviced by just a few large suppliers. Digital convergence allows a customer to receive television programs through telephone company cables and to receive telephone and Internet service through TV company cables.

The convergence of content and communications companies is still in its early stages, and the ultimate competition between these major industrial stakeholders has not yet taken effect (see Chapter 5, "The Anti-Clients"). However, when convergence brings the telecommunications, computer, and television industries into full competition, we can expect the same results as when the long-distance telephone industry was deregulated, bringing more competitors to the marketplace. In that case, the increased competition brought dramatically lower long-distance telephone prices and greater choice to clients.

Since online services can be delivered across territorial boundaries while circumventing regional and national protective barriers, digital technology encourages free global trade. The digital revolution increases freedom of choice of suppliers and decreases the ability of nations to regulate. The centrally controlled industrial giants that had tight control over Industrial Age distribution channels now find themselves unable to control access to the interoperable digital channels that are open and available to all. Thus, digitization is a motivating force for disintermediating the Industrial Age's distribution networks.

The Vanishing Middle: Disintermediation

The term "disintermediation" was first used in the finance industry to describe a customer's ability to "go direct" and buy money market instruments, such as Treasury bills and notes, from governments and issuing companies rather than through sales agents for financial institutions. The phrase was quickly picked up by the rest of the

It turns out that clients aren't the only ones who want to go direct. Suppliers are just as keen to deal directly with their clients.

business community, which was struggling to deal with the new marketplace, where Internet customers were buying direct from primary suppliers and cutting out the middlemen sales organizations. It turns out that clients aren't the only ones who want to go direct, however. Suppliers are just as keen to deal directly with their clients. In his book *Customer Relationship Management*, Stanley Brown notes, "It has always been the marketers' deepest aspiration to be able to ... get rid of all these barriers and distortions created by the non-value adding intermediaries placed between the supplier and the customer, disintermediating or *selling direct* to the customer."[5]

Many types of resellers—distributors, stocking reps, jobbers, and retailers—no longer add the same level of value to the system. The tension in business today lies in determining which of the intermediaries between supplier and client will be done away with because they do not add value to the product or service and which will survive because they do add value.

The Bagel Effect

In 1994, my colleagues and I at CulTech Collaborative Research Centre, part of Toronto's York University, concluded that the introduction of digital networks was changing the balance of power in society. Everywhere we looked, massive shifts were disintermediating traditional power holders and empowering new ones. In 1995, I came up with the term "bagel effect" to describe the phenomenon of disintermediation, which cuts out the middle portion of systems, leaving a hole.[6] The shape looks like a bagel (minus the poppy seeds). As the middle in organizations (the middle managers) diminishes, transactions that were formerly concentrated at the center move out to the edges. Consider the following examples:

- City centers, the financial and business hubs of commerce, are no longer the office locations of choice for most companies. Instead, companies increasingly locate in suburbs and exurbs (commuter communities) at the edges of cities. More than half the North American workforce (both employees and senior management) now work at least part time from their homes, close to the suburban and exurban corporate offices.
- Broadcast television networks, the small group of companies that centrally control television programming and scheduling, have lost ground to television viewers at the edges of their networks, who increasingly select their own programming and scheduling using VCRs and PVRs (personal digital video

recorders) built into set-top boxes from such companies as TiVo, Replay, and Bell ExpressVu. The short-term consequence is more specialty channels at the edges (or fringes) of broadcasting. The long-term consequence is the marginalization of broadcasting in favor of narrowcasting and client-controlled programs delivered through Internet-like digital television.

- Old-style telephone networks that switch circuits in a central facility are being replaced by Internet-style computer-compatible routers, located at the edges of the telephone system near clients. The cost saving is about 100:1. The short-term consequence is chaos in the telephony industry. Looking long term, you'll be making your telephone calls through your Internet connection, not your analog telephone, cutting out your local phone company (the middleman), unless that company becomes your Internet supplier.

- The central regulations imposed by federal, provincial (state), and municipal authorities to control commercial activities in energy, transportation, telecommunications, and broadcasting (to name a few) have been crumbling as part of general demands for fewer intermediaries between clients and suppliers, a gutting of "red tape," and a reduction in the size and cost of government. The consequence? A continued move to freer markets, deregulation, and free trade in place of protective tariffs and onerous regulations.

- Health care facilities—hospitals and mental institutions—are now regarded as sometimes unnecessary and too costly interventions between health care suppliers (doctors, nurses, alternative health professionals) and clients (patients). The short-term consequences are shorter hospital stays and the outsourcing of medical procedures to out-patient facilities. Over the long term, the sector will redirect resources to focus on the more client-centric and much less expensive aspects of health care, including illness prevention (wellness) and home care.

- Educational institutions—primary and secondary schools as well as colleges and universities—are now seen as being administratively heavy and having poor outcomes. Students, parents, and educators agree that the huge resources applied to the educational system are not preparing graduates well for work opportunities. There is little connection between formal schooling and lifelong learning. The short-term result is stress and chaos in the schools, which are underfunded by old metrics and viewed as too expensive by current public funders and students. The long-term consequence is that students and parents (the clients) will take greater control of the educational system (the supplier) and will rely less on existing schools and more on placing students directly in industrial and organizational settings (for example, students might learn microchip design from Intel).

In business, supplier focus (central control) has shifted to client focus at the edge of the organization. Although disintermediation is still rampant, organizations have begun to come through the transition and are desperately seeking ways to reintermediate themselves within Digital Age infrastructures. The best of the old are not satisfied with going the way of the dinosaurs and want to transform their organizations into the new.

Changing Relationships

In business, supplier focus (central control) has shifted to client focus at the edge of the organization. In 2001 I interviewed John Sheridan, president of Bell Canada,[7] and asked him about changes in the power relationship between Bell and its clients. He indicated that the digital revolution had altered every aspect of Bell's relationships with its clients: how it communicates with them, the types of products it develops, the aftermarket support it provides, and the control that clients are given to design and operate their own custom networks.

He noted that Bell has been refocusing its business model from supplier-centric to client-centric. "You might think that this would be an obvious move, but it hasn't been easy," Sheridan said. "I've got over 50,000 employees, $7 billion of earnings, but when a residential customer emails me on a specific issue I email back and we have real-time communication that is very powerful, very quick. It's how we operate and how companies need to operate today."

I asked him who filters his email. Sheridan replied, "No, no filters! I'll be working at home, or on my laptop on the weekend, and I'll see an email from a customer about a security issue, throughput on their high-speed service, a firewall question, content question or whatever. In most cases, I can give them an answer. I'll say, 'Thanks for the query or complaint, I do understand your point, let me get so-and-so involved and I'll be talking to them on Monday.' Typically, customers come back with a 'Thanks.' Sometimes they say, 'Gee, I didn't know that you answered your own email.'" He continued, "If you go back a few years in Bell, there would be an office of executive complaints, and there would be a relatively junior business office-type manager with a mini-army of good client-reps, dealing with, quote, irate customers. And part of their success metric was how many of those customers could they satisfy, or at least close off, without those customers talking to a senior executive of the company. In other words, the goal was to get rid of those pesky client complaints and keep them away

In business, supplier focus (central control) has shifted to client focus at the edge of the organization.

from the executives whose time was too valuable to deal with the clients." Sheridan continued, "All this was counter-intuitive, because the customer is supposedly calling in to the executive complaints group."

John Sheridan's comments are emblematic of the shifts taking place among suppliers who are learning how to focus their companies more strongly on their clients.

Which enterprises will live and which will die? The number-one question facing most organizations today is "Will we lose our place in the new scheme of things, or can we find a strategy to survive and increase our importance?" The answer to that question is the latter, provided the proper steps are followed with a commitment to staying the course. The next chapter provides the beginnings of such a strategy.

2

THE NEW BUSINESS RULES

Important [online] intermediaries have

emerged rapidly in virtually all industries,

providing new places for buyers and sellers to

meet, allowing a variety of pricing schemes

to flourish, altering the roles of traditional

intermediaries, enabling complex transactions,

and, by making vast amounts of information

available at very low costs, shifting the balance

of power among market participants.[1]

U.S. DEPARTMENT OF COMMERCE

Why do we need new business rules? Because the game is changing. We are in a period of transition from the introduction of a new technology to its transparent acceptance and utility. This sort of transition takes two generations, or about fifty years. The first generation invents the tools and builds the necessary infrastructure, and the second generation grows up using the tools without the baggage of old ways of thinking. This second generation is better able to comprehend the true impact and opportunity of the new environment and to use it instinctively, as part of the culture.

In the first generation of change, the emphasis is on the new technology. That was the case when the steam engine ushered in the Steam Age. The technology of heating water to expand it and using the resulting steam to power machines was revolutionary. It enabled the construction of factories such as lumber mills and vehicles such as steam locomotives and steamboats. As a result, the technology brought about a new way of looking at production, communities, and human control over the natural environment.

The outcome of the Steam Age was industrialization. By the time industrialization took hold, the technology that had enabled it—steam—was being superseded by newer technologies such as electric and gasoline engines. By then, industrial mass production was well established, and the newer technologies were absorbed into the larger movement known as the Industrial Age.

Marshall McLuhan, the communications and technology guru, charted the stages of introducing revolutionary technologies. He noted that the first stage always echoes the functionality of the previous technology. For example, steam-, electric-, and gasoline-powered automobiles were called "horseless carriages" during their introductory phase, connecting the utility of a car to the earlier mode of transportation, the horse.

The same holds true for digitization. In the current introductory phase, email is regarded as the new mail, and the same (one-to-many) marketing, advertising, and selling techniques used in the Industrial Age are being applied to the Internet because the methods are well established and familiar.

The first phase also focuses on educating the general population about the differences between the old and the new technology. For example, at the turn of the nineteenth century, the media were filled with articles about electricity, ohms, volts, amperes, AC power, DC power, batteries, and the like. Nowadays, it's hard to avoid articles about digital networks, bits, bytes, routers, and microchips.

In the second phase of transition, the emphasis moves to social, political, and industrial change. The technology-based terms "Steam Age" and "Digital Age" are replaced by terms such as "Industrial Age" and "Information Age," which refer to new frameworks for living and working.

The World Wide Web, the defining technology of the Information Age, fits the two-decade time frame for transition. Although it was invented in 1993, the infrastructure necessary for its optimal operation has not yet been built. In order to deliver television-quality video, top-quality sound, and quick access to graphic information, the Web needs high-speed communication links to every home and business. Most of these links will be fiber-optic cables,[2] and the rest will be high-speed wireless networks. As neither of these infrastructures has yet been made available to a sizable fraction of the population, we are certainly still in the first generation of transition. Consequently, the true impact of digital networks and ubiquitous information will not be known for perhaps another thirty years.

The true impact of digital networks and ubiquitous information will not be known for perhaps another thirty years.

The lasting impact of digital technology will be a new era in which the creation, manipulation, and distribution of information will continue to define the ways we think, interact with one another, and transact business. Fifty years hence there may be new technologies that replace digital electronics (biological computing, optical computing, nano-technologies, and molecular-spin electronics are all good candidates), but the Information Age will be with us for a long time to come.

Access to useful information is therefore the most important outcome of the current transformation. The availability of information everywhere to everyone at almost no cost has been the agent of change that is empowering the new client. And it is the new client who is defining the new business rules. Consequently, it's paramount that suppliers understand the motivations and needs of these new clients. All the rest, as the saying goes, is window dressing.

The New Business Rules

Organizations that are responsive to the new client have been very successful, while those that stick to the old business models have been unable to mine the gold in the new territories. An example of the former is eBay. It has been one of the most successful ventures in recent times, enjoying phenomenal growth of more than 50 percent annually since its 1995 founding by Canadian Pierre Omidyar, and has had a major influence on the entire commercial environment for selling, creating a worldwide marketplace for millions of products worth billions of dollars. In 2001, 42 million people were registered eBay users, double the number from the previous year.

eBay ascribes its success to its almost fanatical focus on its clients. User comments drive all the functions and features of the website. The original business plan called

Each of the new business rules is rooted in structural change brought about by the Information Revolution.

for creating an online experience that matched the friendliness of a flea market with the information-processing power of the CIA. Like other successful web ventures, eBay builds on the interactivity inherent in digital networks to engage visitors and let them drive their own sessions. The eBay.com website enables buyers and sellers to conduct their transactions with the most complete and up-to-date information available.

Unlike previous markets, eBay provides identical information to both buyers and sellers, equalizing the power of each party to the transaction. Powerful companies using eBay have no advantage over individuals who buy or sell only once.

When we examine the implementation strategies of eBay and other organizations that are thriving in the new environment, commonalities emerge that can be stated as guidelines for encouraging success, whether an organization uses online or traditional delivery channels. These new rules of business are shaped by clients.

Each of the new business rules is rooted in structural change brought about by the Information Revolution. The rules are driven by clients but need to be adopted by suppliers—businesses, governments, and other organizations—that wish to thrive in the twenty-first century.

The new business rules are:

1. Shift from internal to external focus.
2. Give clients more input and control.
3. Base pricing on client valuation.
4. Motivate clients with emotion.
5. Put yourself in your client's shoes.

Let's examine each one in turn.

1. Shift from Internal to External Focus

Organizations are forced to be more responsive to external factors—including clients—as a result of downsizing, decentralization, deregulation, and increased competition.

Downsizing

Downsizing swept through the public and private sectors in the last decade of the twentieth century like wildfire. Industrialization had produced companies, unions, and governments that were overstaffed and bulging with middle managers. Organizations had become less efficient and were more concerned with avoiding labor unrest and generating high profit margins than with encouraging high productivity. Tariffs and duties protected domestic industries from cheaper competition from countries with lower labor and production costs, and it was the clients who suffered because they paid higher prices.

When governments began to embrace freer trade and globalization, the bubble burst. Japan, Taiwan, Korea, and other Pacific Rim countries caught up with the West's industrial technology and were able to produce and market goods more efficiently. Western economies began to feel the competitive heat in industries ranging from automobiles and high-tech equipment to fabrics and clothing. Consumers rejected higher-priced local products in favor of less costly and sometimes better-made products from abroad.

Consequently, there was great pressure on industries within every sector of the economy to increase their productivity and competitiveness. So they downsized, cut their workforces dramatically, and contracted out work that could be done more cheaply outside the corporation. Middle management, in particular, was decimated, and, in the end, many companies reduced their labor forces by one-third. As companies shed employees, they contracted out work as needed. The result was a redistribution of corporate workforces from full-time employees[3] to contract workers and suppliers, a shift that, in turn, has prompted a refocusing of corporate attention from internal to external factors—contracts and clients.

The internal cost cutting and efficiency boosting that drove the agendas of administrators for the past decade have now pretty much run their course. By and large, the fat has been cut from organizations, and there are diminishing returns for squeezing out the last ounces of excess. With productivity back at good levels, the watchwords have become "increasing sales" and "retaining clients," both elements that are external to organizations.

The watchwords have become "increasing sales" and "retaining clients," both elements that are external to organizations.

Decentralization

Decentralization, the shift from central organizational control to distributed control, has been a powerful and parallel trend to downsizing. In governments, decentralization has resulted in a movement of power from federal to state and provincial governments. In companies, it has meant a move from central office to local branch control and from senior management to staff who are closer to production and clients.

Decentralization got a huge boost when the Soviet Union, the hallmark of central planning and control, collapsed. The shock wave was immense, flowing to every nook and cranny of the globe. The Berlin Wall fell and with it crumbled notions of powerful central control that abrogated individual freedom of choice. The Soviet system had stood for upsizing, centralizing, regulating, and denying its citizens access to information and communications technologies such as fax and digital networks. Its demise caused a corresponding backlash in favor of downsizing, decentralization, deregulation, and better access to information.

At the same time that communism fell, the Internet arose. And the contrast could not have been stronger: The Internet is a completely decentralized and disintermediated system, with power and control lying at its edges, with its users. This supposed anarchic network of networks has no center and no central controls, yet it has exhibited unbridled growth and success. It has done so without any central administration at all, *because* it has no center.

Decentralization has been one of the best predictors of an organization's performance and success in the past decade, even better than the acquisition of information technology. In a major study, "Beyond the Productivity Paradox," Erik Brynjolfsson and Lorin M. Hitt compared the impact of introducing IT tools with decentralizing corporate controls.[4] They found that decentralization was more closely linked to high productivity. Most important, companies that combined decentralization with the use of information technology had the best results, while firms that were highly centralized and spent little on IT fared the worst.

Deregulation

In the 1980s Ronald Reagan headed the U.S. government, Margaret Thatcher was in charge in the United Kingdom, Mikhail Gorbachev led the Soviet Union, and Deng Xiaoping ran China. Each of those leaders, within their very different national contexts, began deregulating their economies.

Deregulation was fueled by the desire of companies and individuals to get Big Brother governments out of their businesses and lives. The movement from regulation to free markets also means a shift from internal to external focus.

Federal regulators such as the CRTC (Canadian Radio-Television and Telecommunications Commission) in Canada and the FCC (Federal Communications Commission) in the United States have been ceding their regulatory controls. Although they maintain a stranglehold on licensing traditional broadcasting and communications, for example, they have allowed the Internet to evolve without intervention.

In many respects, the Internet's lack of regulation is a return to the free-wheeling capital-friendly environment of the late nineteenth and early twentieth centuries.

In place of international trade barriers that regulated trade between nations, we now have free trade agreements that reduce government regulations and promote open access to markets. The North American Free Trade Agreement (NAFTA), the European Union (EU), and the General Agreement on Tariffs and Trade (GATT) are replacing tariffs and other regulatory impediments to free trade in Canada, Europe, and the United States. When protective tariffs are replaced by free trade, clients get a wide choice of products and services and lower prices, both supportive of new clients.

Increased Competition

The overabundance of information, products, and suppliers available to clients today brings many more competitors to each transaction. A company or a person shopping for any type of product or service now has a world (literally) of suppliers to choose from and many e-commerce websites provide automatic language translation and currency conversions.

Express delivery services such as FedEx and UPS, which are external to supplier companies, have become essential parts of their businesses. These old-economy delivery services have successfully crossed over into the new economy and are now a crucial link in the distribution chain, allowing a supplier to sell from a website based anywhere, while delivering from a warehouse located anywhere to customers in all parts of the world. Old-economy businesses that relied on their proximal location to customers for competitive advantage must now compete with companies world-wide. And as competition goes up, prices go down, adding yet another benefit for the new client.

Patricia Seybold, founder of a customer-centric consulting firm and author of *Customers.com* and *The Customer Revolution*, agrees that organizations need to concentrate more on what's happening outside than inside. In her books, talks, and consulting practice, she emphasizes that organizations must shift from being product-centric to being customer-centric. She notes that "the old economy was characterized by force-feeding goods and services to clients while the new is about making it easy for clients to do business." [5]

Organizations that redirect their focus to the external—to their clients—frequently need to alter their internal practices. This may mean modifying management structures and business models, contracting out labor, and rethinking profit margins, objectives, and strategies. Thus for suppliers, it's a whole new ballgame. Although the game is still in the early innings, the bigger the lead a supplier can build now, the further ahead it will be in the later innings, when the winners and losers are decided. In

For most organizations it's a question of change or die. any period of disruptive change, not every organization will survive, so those who don't get it—the need to focus on external competition and clients—won't get the business. For most organizations it's a question of change or die.

2. Give Clients More Input and Control

Organizations need to give their clients more control over interactions and transactions. This shift can be painful, since most corporate executives have been trained to control client interactions and transactions as much as possible. But just as the Industrial Age empowered organizations with one-to-many tools, the Digital Age empowers clients with one-to-one tools. Therefore, clients expect and need to be given more input and control.

Henry Ford had this to say about mass production: "I can produce the highest quality automobile with the lowest maintenance cost and sell it for an incredibly low price. And you can have it in any color you like, so long as it's black." The wealth of industrial nations has been built on making many of the same item. Mass production is an essential byproduct of industrialization, as there are relatively few suppliers and many consumers (few-to-many supply). The positive consequences are economies of scale and much cheaper products that are available to a wider range of consumers. The less positive consequence is forced conformity of products, meaning customers no longer have the individual choices that were available when craftsmen hand-built each product to order.

Personalized Products

The Information Age is the antidote to the depersonalized uniformity of mass production. Digital technology supports personalization, individualization, and target marketing, the exact opposites of the industrial model. Whereas the industrial tools of mass communications (newspapers, radio, TV, books) and mass marketing (advertising in broadcast and print media) are aimed at the broadest common denominators of our culture, the digital tools of email, Internet news groups and forums, and user-initiated web sessions enable total customization.

The August 2001 issue of *Business 2.0* ran a feature about the changing patterns of marketing and advertising from mass to targeted communications. Companies like RedEnvelope, an online gift-ordering service, are scaling back their advertising spending on traditional media such as billboards and broadcast advertisements and are instead using targeted direct mail (and email) and online campaigns to bring more business at a lower cost. The company sends out print catalogs of wares ranging from toy fire engines to cigar humidors but closes 70 percent of its sales on its website. RedEnvelope used to spend $70 (US) on average to acquire a new customer using mass marketing but now spends just $30 (US) to land a customer through web ads and email. RedEnvelope's sales increased 75 percent at the same time as its costs plummeted, with the result that the company became profitable for the first time. "If they were still doing outdoor [ads] now, I'd be worried about them," says Jonathan Jackson, senior analyst at the research firm eMarketer, "but they're doing the right things in this [business environment]."[6]

Information technology permits the narrowcasting (instead of broadcasting) of information targeted to interested users, with the benefits of both modern (computerized) automation and old-fashioned, preindustrial one-to-one service.

Individual Paths

The Web is emblematic of the new paradigm of client input and control. Each user follows a unique path of activity with each and every session. In fact, the uniqueness of each path of activity is part of the underlying architecture of the Internet. Every Internet message is broken into packets of data, and each packet has its own identification and destination address. Depending on the data traffic and equipment outages, each packet may take a different route to its destination. The paths cannot be predetermined. Only after reaching their destination are the packets reassembled in their original order, reconstituting the original message.

The new technology accommodates uniqueness and unpredictability, fostering each client's input and control over the transaction.

Such architectural design has been mirrored in the philosophical underpinnings of web browsers and other net applications. Instead of the Industrial Age's control by producer-suppliers and predetermined distribution paths, the new technology accommodates uniqueness and unpredictability, fostering each client's input and control over the transaction.

One-to-One Marketing

Let's look at the twenty-first century's answer to Henry Ford's mass production. In 2003 Mercedes-Benz is bringing out a new car model, the Maybach, that breaks all the molds of Industrial Age automobile manufacturing. The automobile manufacturer will no longer try to guess what each client wants and, instead, will build each car to order. There will be no limited list of available options. Customers can pick and choose whatever strikes their fancy. Do you want a complete business environment in your car with computers and a communications center? OK. Do you want a TV/DVD entertainment system? It's yours. Want to add Dolby surround sound? Why not?

At Maybach ordering and delivery centers, customers will discuss and finalize the specifications for their cars. They will be able to change the dimensions and mechanical components, as well as choose interior and exterior finishes, fabrics, and colors. It's expected that no two automobiles will be the same. Mercedes is betting that by giving clients more input and control over their automobile purchase, they will find a good market for these custom products.

The price of Mercedes's customization starts at about $500,000 per car (for wheels, an engine, and a basic body, all of which can be altered). There is no published retail price since there are no fixed specifications; each car is priced according to the individual order. You get what you pay for in a Maybach.

Will Mercedes find any buyers for these cars? They already have. There were deposits of $50,000 (US) for hundreds of cars more than a year before the first delivery could be made. Mercedes expects to build each car to order in about four weeks, including the time for custom engineering. Customers can even take a trip to the factory in Stuttgart, Germany, and watch the engineers, fabricators, and finishers as they're building the vehicle.

For clients who feel shelling out close to a million bucks for a car is out of their range, how about a Hyundai for less than $20,000? Customers needn't travel to a sales center to design their dream car. Hyundai's website (www.hyundaiusa.com/byo1) trumpets, "Build Your Own Car in Just 6 Easy Steps." Step 1 lets clients select the model and year, step 2 lets them pick an engine and transmission, step 3 allows them to pick the trim and option packages, step 4 is for the paint and trim colors, step 5 prompts clients to enter their email address, and the last step sends them a quote along with the contacts of a dealer in their neighborhood. Although it's not quite the level of choice you would have with a Mercedes-Benz Maybach, the marketers for Hyundai are appealing to the same desire of clients to have more control and choice in their transactions.

Everywhere, companies are empowering clients with choice and control. The Xerox advertising campaign for the 2002 Olympics in Salt Lake City reinforced its new brand identity as a client-focused company of the times. One of the television ads could just as easily have been used by one of the car manufacturers noted above.

Here's the scene: A husband and wife are sitting cuddled up on a couch.

Wife: "We go through this every time."

Husband: "Red"

Wife: "Blue."

Husband: "Leather."

Wife: "Cloth."

Wife pulls out a beautiful picture of a car that looks as if it's from a glossy auto showroom catalog.

Husband (surprised, impressed): "Now that's a car."

Wife: "No … that's *my* car. I built it on the Web and they sent me this the next day, printed and personalized … my color, my interior, where to go … it can be here in a week!"

This example epitomizes the shift from product focus to client focus (and client choice) in the new economy. Without the closing titles of the ad, a viewer would not link the ad to a manufacturer of instant-printing devices that enable a car manufacturer to deliver a custom-printed brochure to each prospective client. The connection is indirect, but the message is clear: If a company wants to service clients in a timely and individual manner, it should do business with Xerox. The point of the ad is that Xerox is a company that helps other companies provide Information Age, client-focused solutions to their customers. The last video frame has the slogan "Xerox One to One Marketing!"

Every marketer knows that mass marketing is giving way to target marketing, enabled by digital databases and the Internet. Giving clients more input and control is just the other side of the target-marketing coin. There is no better way to target, segment, or otherwise select the client group with whom you wish to have a strong bond than to allow them to select your organization, product, and services.

Today marketing is about catering to individual customers.

The new markets are like bazaars, with hundreds of stalls filled with appealing merchandise, all within a client's view, all vying for his business. To be effective, a vendor has to present a potential client with input and control over the transaction—to allow the customer to squeeze the fruit and pick the ripe one, so to speak. Just as in a bazaar, all the fruit will get sold, and yet each client will believe he got the best pick of the crop.

3. Base Pricing on Client Valuation

As competition becomes more intense, setting prices becomes more critical, as well as more difficult. Competition drives margins and prices down, and with greater information being available to clients, it is more difficult to justify prices that are based on a company's costs rather than on the new market. Consequently, companies are forced to adjust their costs of doing business and producing products to fit the new clients' expectations of value.

Supplier-based valuation is easily quantifiable by cost inputs such as labor, materials, and transportation. Client valuation, on the other hand, is based largely on information and experiences online. For example, computer software used to be sold only as a physical product, on media such as CD-ROMs boxed with manuals. Shareware software, on the other hand, became available online, where the savings in production and transportation costs could be passed on to the user. Users' perceptions of value were altered by the availability of cheaper shareware products; thus, most software companies now offer lower-priced versions of their products, differentiated from their boxed products only by their availability online.

What's It Worth?

The *American Heritage Dictionary* provides two definitions for value:

1. An amount of goods, services, or money considered a fair and suitable equivalent for something else;

2. Usefulness, importance, or merit to the possessor; as in the value of an education.

Today, the second definition is gaining importance. The usefulness or importance of a product or service is taking precedence in pricing over the supplier's costs of production, marketing, and distribution. Instead of figuring out how much it costs to produce and deliver a good or service and then marking it up to make a profit, it is more relevant to determine the value of that good or service to your client and then determine if there is a way to produce and deliver it at that price while making a profit.

Businesses that can't do that have to change their cost structure. For example, viral marketing (seeding information that engages a few members of a target market, who then distribute it peer-to-peer over the Web to a large number of potential clients) has become popular as a low-cost alternative to traditional advertising, driven largely by the need to come up with pricing structures that are less influenced by high advertising costs.

A New Currency

As valuation moves from supplier-based costs to client-based expectations, there needs to be a fundamental change in the currency by which the valuation is measured. Pricing in the Information Age needs to be based on a new type of currency that measures non-material experiences, particularly when the product or service is related to content—as with information and entertainment.

People value the *experience* of listening to music rather than the actual CD that contains the music. The value of reading an article, listening to a song, or watching a television show is not as closely coupled to the cost of producing those content items as the value of a refrigerator is coupled to the cost of manufacturing it. Even when the product is a physical item, such as a refrigerator, there are ways to enhance its value to clients.

Paul Cole, global director, CRM Practice, Cap Gemini Ernst & Young LLC, puts it this way: "Since the Industrial Age, we have been building a business model that was designed to help people create, produce, and deliver a product to the market. But that business model wasn't designed to deliver an enhanced customer experience. Until we get marketing, sales, and customer service converging in a way that adds value to the customer, we're going to keep disappointing [the client]."[7]

Since customer experiences exist only in the mind, a company can't add up a series of input costs to arrive at the right output price. Increasingly, the cost of production is becoming less relevant to the price than the value of the experience to the client. And the older valuation model that was based on the scarcity of an item (supply and demand) no longer works when there is an overabundance of everything. When the product is information, for example, customers are willing to pay more for less of it. That's why we have spam filters on e-mail and prefer search engines that return fewer hits.

But just what are a client's value metrics? How can a supplier determine the value of a product or service to a client? Clients are conditioned to value things by the way they spend their money. In the Western world today, consumers' greatest spending, after food and shelter, is for communications and content—Internet, phones, and TV. The value that clients perceive in these media is not in the wired or wireless connections but in the content they experience. On the Internet, it's information, music, video, and text—intellectual property that is so insubstantial it can evaporate instantly after being consumed. And yet these fleeting digital bits of content are being hailed as the new currency.

> As valuation moves from supplier-based costs to client-based expectations, there needs to be a fundamental change in the currency by which the valuation is measured.

Lesley Ellen Harris, noted intellectual property lawyer and author of *Digital Property: Currency of the 21st Century*, notes that "at social gatherings, people tell me about this great idea they have and ask how I can help them make a fortune from it. And when … I speak of the notion of intellectual property, intangible property, and how valuable it's becoming, I can sense that the listener is intrigued but also a little mystified."[8]

The reason people are mystified at valuing intellectual property—information and experiences—is that it was formerly bound to physical products. We speak of the price of a CD or a movie ticket as if the value were in the plastic and the paper. But the values we perceive are derived from their underlying intellectual property.

The price of goods and services may be set lower than the cost of production and distribution if a larger business context can generate a profit as a result of the transaction. For instance, a company may spend a considerable amount of money building and maintaining a popular website that charges no user fees yet earns income from advertising or from linking its viewers to other websites where transactions take place. This strategy is not new to business: Polaroid increased its profit by selling its cameras at a loss, and Gillette frequently sells its razors at a loss. In both cases, the companies make money in their aftermarket businesses, selling film and razor blades.

Making profits is frequently a matter of differentiating a product from those of competitors so that clients cannot compare them based on price alone.

Making profits is frequently a matter of differentiating a product from those of competitors so that clients cannot compare them based on price alone. This strategy allows one supplier to provide additional value to clients over another supplier and to charge more for it. For example, Apple computers has survived in a cut-throat industry that focuses on specifications (such as the speed of microprocessors) by differentiating its products by their superior design and user interface, generating better experiences for users and justifying a price premium and higher margins. Unique products, such as patented drugs, can command the highest profit margins when there is only a single supplier and hence no comparison shopping available.

Products or services that are more or less indistinguishable from each other (commodities) tend to be priced uniformly from one supplier to the next. After all, it doesn't much matter who grew the wheat, who mined the gold, or who pumped the oil. Generally, undifferentiated products do not command high profit margins since competition works in favor of the customer, except when supplies are scarce.

Let's say you own a bookstore (or a chain of bookstores). You base your pricing on the cost of the books, your rent, labor costs, advertising, and so on. You add up your costs and place a profit margin on the subtotal, and voilà, there is your retail price. So far, so good. But competitors who are selling books online are encroaching on your sales. So you decide to start an online book-selling operation to capture that part of your clients' business. Now you need to figure out your pricing scheme for selling books online. So long as customers were in your store, you could deliver unique value in many ways: knowledgeable staff, instant product availability from stock on your shelves, a good rapport with customers, and well-organized and -presented merchandise. Now that your business is online, many of these distinctions are lost to you. The books you sell online have become much like basic commodities, with little differentiation between a book ordered on your website and a book ordered from, say, amazon.com. In addition, online shoppers can easily compare prices by clicking on various websites or using a shopping-agent website that checks prices at a large number of online stores and returns a list of suppliers, with the lowest price at the top.

Your pricing is now determined by how much amazon.com and other online book retailers charge. Unfortunately for you, amazon.com has used a business model that prices its books based on the new model of value to customers, not on suppliers' costs. In this case, it means that amazon.com has been losing money on every book sold. So your challenge is to find a way to profit overall, while losing money on every book transaction.

The pricing of books online has been carefully researched and market tested based on customer valuation. Since a book buyer can buy the same book at a physical store or online, and since there is an additional shipping charge for an online purchase, web retailers have determined that their selling price must be lower than physical store prices in order to make up for the shipping cost.

So, if you want to stay competitive in online book sales, you will lose money on every book you sell. Sound crazy? Welcome to the new economy!

Profit or Loss

If pricing can no longer be set based on internal costs, how can companies hope to make money? This question is being asked in thousands of boardrooms today, frequently without getting any good answers. One result has been the shakeout of the dot.coms that could not figure out how to make money, known as the dot.bomb. The mass failure of dot.coms should not be an excuse to throw the baby out with the bath water, however. Some of the most successful startups in the past decade have been

Some of the most successful startups in the past decade have been based on attracting customers first and figuring out how to make money later.

based on attracting customers first and figuring out how to make money later. The first notable example was Netscape, which gave away its browser product free and raised billions on the stock market, in the hopes that some of its other business ideas would drive income. They have.

Big money can always be made by finding opportunities to deliver high value, as perceived by the client, with low internal costs. So how do you make money?

Using client-based pricing doesn't always result in negative margins. For many products, the cost of distribution for an online sale is much lower than from a physical store, so client-based pricing can deliver a higher margin.

Perhaps the biggest change in the way business is conducted today is that profit and loss are more frequently calculated on a much greater range of business opportunities than just the sale of goods and services. In an online computer store, for example, you might lose money on the sale of each product but make money on advertising that you sell for your website, based on the number of viewers it attracts. In addition, you would likely build a database of online customer inquiries. Whenever someone visits your site you get an email address, and you can ask for more information when a customer completes a transaction. That information is worth money to you and to others, to whom you can sell your lists.

The bottom line? Clients increasingly compare prices online and determine the value of goods and services based on their new and more informed appraisal of the market, which is not necessarily based on a company's cost structures. So you'd better learn to live with this new reality and do your pricing accordingly; otherwise, your sales will drop.

An example of a business that is influencing the new client valuation mind-set is Priceline, one of the dot.com startups that survived the 2001 meltdown. Priceline is an alternative to traditional auctions (online or otherwise) because the buyer posts the price she is willing to pay. Sellers then decide whether they wish to accept the offer and complete the transaction. Priceline already has captured more than $1 billion (US) in transactions annually.[9] This situation flips the traditional seller-set pricing model and puts clients in the driver's seat. Priceline.com now sells everything from plane tickets and car rentals to groceries and gasoline.

Actor William Shatner, well known for his television and film roles as Captain Kirk of the original *Star Trek* series, represents Priceline in the media as its pitchman. That's fitting, since Priceline represents a glimpse into the future of transactions, one in which clients play a decidedly greater role in setting the price of goods and services.

4. Motivate Clients with Emotion

There is no better way to motivate a potential client to close a transaction than pulling an emotional string. Clients research their purchases with their heads but make their purchase decisions with their hearts. Marketers of consumer products know that there are two prime motivators for sales: specs and sex. This oversimplification nonetheless separates those factors that provide functionality from those that bring emotional satisfaction.

There is no better way to motivate a potential client to close a transaction than pulling an emotional string.

A cool-looking sports car, a brochure for a condominium printed on expensive paper, and a box of chocolates all play to client emotional responses that can sway purchase decisions. But what about buying a wholesale contract for natural gas? Are emotive factors at play here? Is there anything a supplier can do to make a commodity product or service more appealing to a customer? Absolutely!

The free-market system fosters innovation and customization for every sales opportunity. Selling real estate is a business in which the cost to the client (the commission) is generally the same from one agent to another, yet agents and companies prosper or fail based on their ability to instill faith in prospective clients. Their business is built on trust—on the clients' sense of security that the job will be done to their satisfaction.

Even if you're wholesaling toilet paper, you can come up with creative marketing, promotion, and other schemes to differentiate your transaction, if not your product, from your competitor's. Now, here's the sexy part: You can be more successful than your competitors if you motivate your potential clients to take action on your products and services.

Motivation

Psychologists define motivation as a desire (or need or want) that activates and energizes goal-oriented behavior.[10] Abraham Maslow first published his theory of human motivation in 1943. It has since become one of the most popular and often cited explanations of the underlying causes of human activities. Maslow suggests a hierarchy of human needs that includes physiological, psychological, internal, and external factors. Others have come up with similar schemes for classifying motivations, including William James, Eugene Mathes, and Clayton Alderfer.[11] I've distilled these theories into a formula for the goal-oriented activity of completing a transaction.

In layman's terms, the motivational factors for transactions, which I call "emotive factors," or EMOs, can be stated as follows:

The Four EMOs
- feeling good
- feeling comfortable/secure
- doing good
- having control/choice

(This is not an exhaustive list—you can add other emotive factors that may apply to your particular clients.)

Consider the following examples of how EMOs affect clients' decisions:

- People spend trillions of dollars on fashion, entertainment, and consumer goods primarily because it makes them *feel good.*
- People choose personal partners, work for large companies, buy homes, and take out life insurance because it makes them *feel more secure.*
- People contribute billions of dollars to charities, in cash and volunteer time, primarily because it *does good.*
- People buy automobiles even though the cost is much higher than taking public transportation because it gives them more *freedom of choice and control* over traffic routes and travel schedules.

Elliot Ettenberg, in his book *The Next Economy,* agrees that client motivations are key in the new business environment.[12] He argues that although companies have used technology to re-engineer all aspects of their operations, from production to finance, very few have managed to satisfy customers better than before. Ettenberg deals with specifics, noting that target marketing is usually done by demographics—age, income, region, and the like. He suggests that it's more appropriate today to use "want segmentation," analyzing customers' values and beliefs in order to reveal not just what they've bought, but why.

EMO charts are helpful in determining the "whys" that motivate purchasing. Businesses may use them to help predict the success of a product launch, a business plan, or even an entire economic system. The following are EMO charts for the two global events that ushered in the Information Age.

Example 1: The Fall of Communism

In the twentieth century, economists were divided on whether the Soviet-style centralized economic model or the free-enterprise economic model was better at allocating a nation's resources. Ultimately, the democratic free-market system prevailed and the Soviet communist system collapsed. Here's how the systems stack up from the perspective of citizen/clients' EMOs:

EMO	Free Enterprise Democratic	Central Control Communist
Feeling Good	High	Low
Feeling Comfortable/Secure	Somewhat	Somewhat
Doing Good	Somewhat	Somewhat
Having Control/Choice	High	Low

Both systems provide a modicum of security for citizens and claim to help the oppressed. But when it comes to citizens being in control, feeling good, and having lots of choice, it's a slam dunk for free enterprise and democracy. The predictive EMO chart has been validated by historical evidence for this case.

Example 2: The Rise of the Internet

The Internet is taking over television's role as the preferred source of information and entertainment. A decade ago, many predicted that television would be the preferred appliance of the information superhighway. Since then, billions of dollars have been lost by industrial stakeholders who bet on the primacy of television. Here's how the systems stack up from the perspective of viewer/clients' EMOs:

EMO	Internet	Television
Feeling Good	High	High
Feeling Comfortable/Secure	High	High
Doing Good	Somewhat	Low
Having Control/Choice	High	Somewhat

This comparison is much closer, but the EMO chart still predicts the victor—the Internet. The chief elements that differentiate the Internet and television are the Internet's provision of greater control and choice and the fact that it hosts many no-cost services and information for disadvantaged groups.

Using EMOs

EMOs are the most important elements after price that affect a new client's purchasing decisions. EMOs can overcome a negative price differential to induce a new client to purchase one product or service over another more costly one. It happens every day. How many times have you heard the following?

EMOs are the most important elements after price that affect a new client's purchasing decisions.

- "The price from supplier A was a few bucks cheaper, but I like dealing with supplier B." That's the "feeling good" EMO.
- "This company has well-thought-out environmental policies. I'd rather deal with them." That's the "doing good" EMO.
- "I was able to customize my deal to suit my needs: the functionality of the product, the terms of payment, the warranty, everything." That's the "having control/choice" EMO.
- "The price at supplier A seemed too good to be true. I went with supplier B." That's the "feeling secure" EMO.

Failure to take EMOs into account can be costly—in fact, it can sink a business. Successful ventures like amazon.com and eBay take EMOs very seriously in trying to re-create the preindustrial personalized service model that leaves a customer feeling good, secure, and unique. Companies that believe they buy technology to satisfy clients' needs are fooling themselves. Computers and spreadsheets do not take off management's shoulders the responsibility of understanding and catering to clients.

EMO tables are an excellent tool for informing and supporting management decisions. EMO tables can be used in spreadsheets by assigning scales of value (such as 0–9) to each EMO when comparing "what if" scenarios. Although EMOs may not be as easily quantifiable as other business factors, they are an important variable for clients and should be evaluated as part of any business planning.

EMOs will appear throughout this book, as litmus tests to determine whether strategies and practices address new client needs. Unlike the complex and sometimes arcane computations of traditional transactional analysis, the new emotive perspective can be evaluated without complicated calculations. That's because the human values and feelings that underpin EMOs are common to all of us—they're part of our DNA.

5. Put Yourself in Your Client's Shoes

It's amazing how much you can learn about your business flaws and strengths by going through the motions and emotions of your clients. Indeed, you may be surprised to uncover some aspects of your business that are appealing to clients. These elements can become centers of focus and promotion.

For example, few executives bother to compare the process of accessing their organization's products and services with that of other organizations. Check out your website carefully. When you think you've got a good grasp of its strengths and weaknesses, go through the steps of a potential client. Type a few keywords into a search engine. Does your company rank near the top of the search results? Check out the websites of competitors whose URLs turn up in the search. Chances are you'll notice several areas in which your products and services are presented less attractively or are more difficult to access.

Putting yourself in your client's shoes can also help you decide how to structure a deal. If you momentarily jettison the party-line sales message and play the role of the client, you might discover that your client does not subscribe to the same assumptions as you do. A simple role-reversal can bring a dead deal to life and make a hard sell a walk in the park. You needn't give away everything to satisfy your client; you just need to understand how to add value to the other side of the deal without breaking the bank. It's easier than you think.

Getting to Know Your Client

The new supplier creates a value proposition that will be a *good deal* for the new client. While this might appear obvious, it goes against the grain of most twentieth-century sales techniques. Earlier sales methods emphasize gaining control over the client in a transaction and restricting the sales pitch to the *supplier's* message, the *supplier's* products, and the *supplier's* services. It is exemplified by the typical offer, "Here's our catalogue. Which of our products (or services) can I sell you today?"

The new supplier creates a value proposition that will be a *good deal* for the new client.

In contrast, a sales agent for the new supplier spends more time understanding the client's circumstances. Yesterday's salespeople must become today's customer representatives. Today's sales pitch sounds more like, "How are things going? How can I be of assistance?" The new transaction takes into account all the elements that are of value to the client—the price, the utility, the service, the novelty, and the EMOs—to produce a sense of satisfaction for both sides, and, best of all, a good prospect for return business.

It's generally more time-consuming, expensive, and difficult to learn about customers than about your own products. That's why client-centered strategies aren't always implemented with the vigor necessary to succeed. But times have changed, and clients have changed too. The door-to-door encyclopedia salesman is gone because customers have information and choices that they lacked yesterday. And those encyclopedias are now available free online, using a business model that delivers eyeballs (website visitors) to advertisers instead of books to stay-at-home moms. *Encyclopedia Britannica,* the stereotypical product sold door-to-door, went online in 1999, changing its business model from selling its information products to making the information available free on the Internet and using advertising and marketing information revenue for income.

Michael Dell parlayed his customer-centric approach into a company that now sells $30 million (US) of computer equipment *daily.* Nearly every bulletin board in every office at Dell Computer has a sign that reads, "The Customer Experience: Own It." Dell believes that the customer experience is the most significant competitive battleground in business. It's the sum total of all interactions that a customer has with a company's products, people, and processes. It starts from the moment a customer sees an ad and continues to the moment when he accepts delivery of a product and beyond. Dell makes sure that its employees put themselves in their clients' shoes by going through every interaction with the company, always asking, "Is this experience more satisfying than if I was doing business with a Dell competitor?"

It's no longer good enough to merely pay lip service to clients, because they frequently have more information about your products and services than you do.

It's no longer good enough to merely pay lip service to clients, because they frequently have more information about your products and services than you do. They also have information about your competitors' products, services, and prices. And chances are, your competitor is wooing your potential client with a new relationship that you need to match or better.

Finding a New Sales Force

"The customer is always right" is a resonating sales pitch coined more than a century ago by H. Gordon Selfridge, founder of the Selfridge department store chain. As it turns out, the customer *is* always right, because her point of view is the one that triggers the transaction.

Many large companies, such as IBM, have already re-engineered their sales structure to accommodate the new reality of customer-centric sales. Louis Gerstner, president of IBM, led the transformation that changed his sales force from product orientation to client orientation. At York University, I witnessed the makeover. There used to be IBM sales reps for each of that company's products and services: large computers, PCs, data processing, and so on. Each sales rep was an expert on IBM offerings in that division but was not very knowledgeable or authorized to do business for other divisions. Doing a deal often entailed many meetings to explain the university's needs several times over to different salespeople and jockey for the best price among different (and frequently competing) IBM vested interests.

Then the company reorganized its sales efforts. Instead of product-specialist sales reps, they now have university-specialist customer reps. The reps learn a university's objectives and operations, then they pinpoint weak areas where it can save money, function more efficiently, or provide better educational services. They suggest solutions that can help the university fulfill its mandate and mission. The client no longer has to be handed off to a number of divisions in order to find a solution that might involve different product components. Instead, the customer rep delivers the solution, stick-handles the internal politics, finds the appropriate information resources within IBM, and sources complementary products and partnerships from other suppliers if necessary. The rep is also empowered to make the final deal with a single price (and discount) that's easy for the client to understand.

This move from product-based to client-based marketing and sales needs to permeate all aspects of an organization's thinking. At IBM, this shift has been evident in its successful marketing and advertising campaigns, which de-emphasize products and services and instead speak of solutions. Viewers immediately identify and empathize with characters in the ads whose tragedies are the consequences of non-IBM solutions: "That's when it hits you. You're so ready for IBM." The EMO almost drips from your pores as you realize the ad is about *you,* not the product.

All organizations need to place stronger emphasis on helping their clients, each and every one of them.

David Siegel, strategic marketing consultant, strongly advocates taking this approach. He says, "Once you know who your customers are, you want to help them in every way that you can. That puts you in the business not of selling products but of solving problems." This client-centered strategy should not be restricted to commercial companies. All organizations need to place stronger emphasis on helping their clients, each and every one of them.[13]

If you restrict your transaction framework to monetary parameters, you run the risk of having your products and services treated as commodities, like soybeans or natural gas. In that event, your profit margins will be thin, your competition will be tough, and you will always run the risk of losing business to a competitor who sells for a penny less than you do.

On the other hand, if you find ways of increasing the value of the transaction to your customer by adding EMOs such as convenience, comfort, an easy-to-understand warranty, or whatever else your client needs, you will differentiate your product or service and win the business.

3

NEW CLIENT
EXPECTATIONS

*Web users are goal-driven and impatient.
They want answers. Now. If those answers
aren't available, all you will see is the long
shadow cast by your potential client as she
walks off into the sunset.... If [clients] can't
find what they're looking for—now—you
may never get a second chance.*[1]

RON JETTE, EDITOR AND PRINCIPAL OF TRISTAN CREATIVE

T he beginning of every successful "new client" strategy is exactly the same and cuts across every type of organization in every type of environment. The first step is to understand your clients' expectations. Once you've done that, you can take action to fulfill those expectations and prosper.

The supermarket is a good example of a business that meets client expectations and makes money at the same time. There, clients have many product choices and no salespeople to pressure them into buying. The prices can't be beat, and there's plenty of information available on package labels, on the shelves (price per pound and per kilo), and sometimes even on computer screens.

However, the gallon of milk and the loaf of bread that customers originally come in to buy are always located at the very back of the store, past the specials on shampoo and potato chips. Shoppers have little choice when it comes to finding their way through the maze of shelves. When they enter the supermarket, they are routed to a path that starts with the fresh produce and then passes the impulse buys, providing first something sensible and then something satisfying. These super marketing strategies allow shoppers to get what they need while encouraging them to buy some extras to satisfy their EMOs. That's why the candy is usually in the same aisle as the cereal.

Supermarket shoppers come back frequently and are in a pretty good mood when they leave the store. If something they've bought is not as expected, they can bring it back for a full refund, no questions asked.

Here's an EMO chart for supermarket shopping.

EMO	Supermarket
Feeling Good	Medium-High
Feeling Comfortable/Secure	High
Doing Good	No
Having Control/Choice	High

Shoppers' expectations are met both functionally and emotionally with the EMOs of feeling good and being in control.

Understanding Clients Online

Replicating the supermarket experience online is not so easy. Shoppers arrive at a website from many different points on the Internet and click along many different paths once they get there. You can't ensure that they enter through the front door because they can bookmark any website in their browser and return there directly, bypassing those high-profit impulse items that you may have placed along your preferred route. If you try to make it tough for a visitor to stray from your navigational plan by hiding some of your pages from general Internet access or by protecting certain pages with a password, your potential customers will be turned off by your attempts to constrain their freedom and will abandon your website, usually for good.

The first step in a successful marketing strategy is to research and understand your clients.

Since it's problematic to force a visitor along a prescribed path, you must turn to less obtrusive methods to entice visitors to stay with your website and become clients, by giving them what they want in the way they want it. First, you need to find out what clients want, then provide a path that allows them to choose it, all the while leading them through the paths that you want them to follow. Remember Hansel and Gretel and the trail of candy? One client's candy may be poison to another, so it's important to research and understand your clients.

It makes sense to learn whatever you can about each and every visitor to your website. You can do this research with software that analyzes server logs, which automatically record information about all the activities on the website. These logs contain detailed information about every visitor, including where they came from, how long they spent on each page, which links they clicked on, what pathways they took through the site, whether they returned for another session, and so on. Increasingly, "netizens" are willing to leave their email address and perhaps their phone number in return for useful information, free demos, and the like. Current browsers automatically input a user's personal information into a website if this feature is enabled, making the process quick and painless. If a visitor does not volunteer her personal information, you can find it by matching the email address to data gathered by others in unrelated transactions. There are dozens of websites that find telephone numbers and addresses based on a person's name or email address.

Statistical analysis services such as WebTrends and HitBox are available to small businesses for as little as $20 (Can) a month. These services boil down the large volumes of weblog data, sort through the minutiae, and present the information as useful patterns of visitor behavior. Larger organizations use sophisticated data-mining services (which find valuable information in the mounds of data slag) or purchase software applications outright, using in-house analysts to track the traffic.

The instant and direct results of measuring website activity are particularly helpful when changes are made to a website. The changes may appear trivial to the site owner, yet they could have a significant impact on clients. Conversely, expensive website renovations may yield only small changes in visitor behavior. The only way to find out what effect the changes will have is to carefully monitor website logs and analyze changes in visitor patterns. Whether you make a cosmetic change, alter the marketing emphasis, or introduce new features (such as chat or email feedback), visitors will react immediately, and their interactions will speak louder than words—sort of.

Interpreting the Data

The problem with data mining and extracting information by analyzing visitor and client patterns is that the numbers don't necessarily tell you what you need to know. It still takes human interpretation and intuition (educated guesswork) to glean the kernels of insight from the data chaff.

For example, www.virtualmuseum.ca is a website that showcases online exhibitions from the hundreds of galleries and museums that are part of the Canadian Heritage Information Network (CHIN). The site is very popular, attracting millions of visitors from around the world and winning awards for its excellent repurposing and repackaging of cultural content online. Lyn Elliot Sherwood, director general of CHIN, notes that one of CHIN's objectives is to develop guidelines for new online exhibitors that will help them make their webpages attractive and compelling to visitors. In order to create these guidelines, CHIN captures an enormous amount of data about the actions and interactions of every visitor to the webpages and uses sophisticated analysis to determine the most frequently visited exhibitions, the ones that visitors linger on the longest, the ones they return to most frequently, and so on. For example, the Butterfly Exhibit has the greatest number of page views, while the Christmas exhibit home page is visited most frequently. The Canada–Germany Migration pages boast the longest average time per visit, and the Highlights of Canadian Collections has the highest engagement rating (average time per visit times the average number of visits). The virtual museum is a government-run site, so the anonymity of each visitor is preserved and no marketing data is kept or sold, although visitors' countries of origin are inferred from their packet addresses, providing useful data about the website's international appeal.

But deducing what makes a successful webpage is still an elusive art. Does the Butterfly Exhibit have the greatest number of page views because the promotion for the site is effective, because the activities it offers are novel and compelling, because many people have a fondness for butterflies, or because the photos are colorful and visually appealing? Finding the answer requires more than just automated analysis of server logs. Questionnaires, focus groups, and other techniques are helpful in shedding light on different aspects of a visitor's experience. In the end, the determination of which factors attract visitors to the Butterfly Exhibit is a judgment call made by experts, based on their experience in the field and their gut instincts.

It is a big leap to believe that you have relationships with your clients simply because you capture information about them.

Activities related to analyzing client experiences with an organization are known as client relationship management (CRM), but, as we will soon see, it is a big leap to believe that you have relationships with your clients simply because you capture information about them.

Client Relationship Management

There is perhaps no greater validation of the growing power of clients than the explosion of CRM as a primary focus for business. This red-hot sector of the IT field has produced thousands of products and services, as well as a large chunk of business mind-share over the past several years, driving home the importance of managing supplier–client relationships.

Managing relationships is more important than ever because businesses today are less concerned about increasing their market share than about retaining their best clients. The numbers that count on a balance sheet are not how many clients you serve but the profit you make. Although this principle may seem obvious, it signifies a major shift from Industrial Age thinking.

It has been only half a dozen years since businesses began to concentrate more on retaining existing clients than on recruiting new ones. The normal process of losing some existing clients and attracting new ones to maintain or expand income is very expensive. Attracting a new client costs, on average, $80 (US) for marketing, advertising, and so forth. Identifying an unhappy client and dissuading him from leaving for a competitor costs about a third as much. That's why if you contact your phone company representatives and tell them you're switching to a competitor's service, they'll offer you considerable incentives to stay.

The volatility and lack of loyalty of today's clients has led businesses to change their strategy for increasing income. Instead of concentrating on their market share, which measures sales but not expenses, they are changing their focus to "customer share," the percentage of their clients' disposable income. It's much less costly (and hence more profitable) to spend a dollar on marketing to a customer whose profile and preferences you already know than to spend a dollar on trying to attract a new customer. For this customer-share strategy, IT applications are very effective. IT tools allow organizations to maximize their client relationships by offering personal transactions tailored to each customer. In this way, the older mass-marketing strategies are giving way to mass customization—using automated technologies to present unique interactions and sales opportunities to each client, based on information gathered in the course of doing business with that client.

Implementing Mass Customization

The secret of mass customization, according to Stanley Brown, leader of Pricewaterhouse-Coopers International Centre of Excellence in Customer Love, is dealing with one customer at a time, but doing this for millions of customers—and quickly.[2] This strategy was not possible a few years ago. Only with the advent of Information Age tools has it been possible to offer clients the same customized care and long-term relationship building that characterized preindustrial trade, while achieving the efficiency and productivity of industrialization.

Customer relationship management, according to customer relations analyst Liz Shahnam, is "a philosophy that puts the customer at the design point."[3] It is more a strategy than a process. First, you build a satisfied customer base, and then you begin to manage the relationship. The technology that allows for these quasi-personalized relationships (they are, after all, machine-mediated and not person-to-person) consists of software programs that track and store personal data about each client and permit an organization to handle each client differently.

CRM is more a strategy than a process. First, you build a satisfied customer base, and then you begin to manage the relationship.

My first encounter with technology-assisted client support was almost twenty years ago on Saltspring Island, off the coast of British Columbia, where David McKerrell had set up an entertainment management service for touring performers. He wanted to live far from the madding crowd and avoid traveling with his artists, while maintaining the kind of client intimacy that is required in his field. So he came up with his own CRM system, more than a decade before the boom in off-the-shelf products. His system, like most good CRM systems, combined computer tools with one-on-one human interactions. Whenever one of his artists played an engagement, the road manager would make small talk with the promoter (the client): "How's the wife?" "Business been up or down lately?" "What acts are hot in your area?" and so on. While flying to the next engagement, the road manager would jot this information down on a piece of paper and give the documents to McKerrell when the tour was over.

Back on Saltspring Island, McKerrell had bought one of the early Macintosh home computers and a database program, into which he entered information about every engagement that his artists played. He could search by client name, territory, date, terms of the contract (advance payments, guarantees, percentages of box office, territorial exclusives), and so on. When the road manager came back from a tour, he added the information from his client contacts into a "personal information" field of the database.

When I visited him, the system had been in place for about a year. He offered to show me how it worked and I quickly agreed. McKerrell called a promoter in Seattle and had the following conversation.

"Hi, it's Dave McKerrell, Valdy's agent.... How's your son doing? I understand he was in the hospital last year and had to miss some school time.... Oh, I'm glad he's back in the stream now.... Valdy's going to be touring in your area next May and I thought you might be interested in one of his dates.... [McKerrell keys the name of the Seattle client into his database and retrieves the information from the last engagement.] As I recall, you did 85 percent business. That was pretty good for a first appearance in your area.... How much is Valdy charging now? Well, last time we went in on a low guarantee of $2,000 and went $1,600 additional into percentage. Now that the new album is out, I think we need a $4K guarantee, but you can probably up the ticket price somewhat because of the national promotion.... [McKerrell types "Northwest" into the territory field.] Let's see, we'll be in Portland on May 15. If you can do a date within four days either side of that I can give you a $400 discount because our travel will be lighter. [McKerrell goes back to the transaction record for this call and types in $400 travel discount offered within four days of April 15.] OK, get back to me next week and, by the way, how is Alice doing with her baking business? [Road manager's notes say that Alice bakes custom desserts for restaurants in the area as a part-time business.] Takes too much time? Well, you give her my best. Maybe I'll see you on the next tour. Bye."

The principles of CRM haven't changed much since then, but the tools are a lot better at capturing the information without a road manager having to jot down notes and someone else entering the data by hand.

The basic tasks for CRM are as follows:

- *profiling:* gathering information about clients and potential clients
- *segmenting:* separating clients according to meaningful demographics

- *researching:* finding out about client needs and concerns
- *personalizing:* using automated tools to solve client problems
- *frequent flying:* providing special treatment for more profitable customers

Information technology allows these tasks to be mostly automated, making it much more cost effective to personalize interactions with each client than in the pre-digital era.

Profiling involves gathering internal and external databases of prospective clients and merging them into a single database. The prospects are then *segmented* into groups according to how well they fit the target-market characteristics generated by the marketing team. Those who fit most closely are most likely to generate business and are given the greatest attention and marketing resources.

Research is an area that still demands hands-on attention because it can involve telephone surveys, questionnaires, focus groups, and other interventions that cannot be totally automated. Even in this area, however, the Internet has made it possible to approximate many of the hands-on approaches using automated online feedback (forms, email) and log analysis. The resulting research should clearly indicate what clients need, as well as what they want. It's the "want" aspect that frequently offers the best opportunities for making profits, since it caters to the EMOs that drive sales.

Personalizing involves taking the information gathered in profiling, segmenting, and research, then constructing personalized communications to the target client. The result is the mass personalization discussed earlier.

Frequent flying, a term used by airlines that segment their best customers (frequent flyers) for special service and free trips, has now entered the marketing vernacular for all businesses. Frequent flyers are those clients who either use your services more frequently or generate more profit on average from their transactions. They are of particular interest to businesses because they contribute disproportionately to the bottom line and because competitors have likely targeted them with their own sleuthing CRM tools and are trying to entice them away from your company. Therefore, you need to make an extra effort to retain them and keep them happy. Companies address these clients in various ways, from "club floors" in hotels to one-on-one contacts with customer service reps.

In 2001, CRM products and services accounted for $13 billion (US) in worldwide sales, growing at 20 percent annually.[4] Of CRM spending, 35 percent goes toward hardware and software, 20 percent toward relationship marketing, 15 percent toward multichannel integration, and the balance (20 percent and increasing quickly) toward eCRM—online Internet tools that gather information, determine pricing, provide product support and help desks, and permit ordering online.

Creating a Transaction Environment

Many organizations jump on the bandwagon of CRM without realizing that they have no client relationships to manage. A transaction is not a relationship, although it can be an excellent point on which to build one. You first have to create a transaction environment that plants the seeds of a real relationship. Then, you have to nurture those seeds with outstanding fulfillment and customer service. Remember, a relationship involves dialogue between the parties, not just a supplier gaining information about a client. Building a relationship takes time (just ask your spouse or partner).

Shoving a tech-heavy CRM application at customers is like demanding sex on the first date: It may push your clients away rather than draw them closer. Hans Peter Brondmo, chairman and founder of Post Communications in San Francisco, puts it this way: "When you think about it, establishing a service relationship online isn't all that different from starting a dating relationship. The problem is that a lot of Internet companies approach their first date with a list of 20 questions: 'Could you please fill out this three-page form about your income, family history, and medical background?' Imagine if that were the first question that a prospective romantic interest asked you! It's absurd to expect people to respond to such questions before you've established a certain level of trust with them." Bryan Eisenberg, CIO of Future Now, notes, "Lots of e-businesses have the software to facilitate CRM.... Nevertheless, most businesses don't have the in-depth customer knowledge they need to use the technology effectively. They wind up getting carried away with trying to manage what they don't actually have."[5]

Companies routinely spend millions on projects to manage relationships and then plow ahead without fully understanding how their clients feel about dealing with them. Until an organization understands and experiences its customer relationships, it can't successfully design an appropriate way to manage those relationships. Angel Martinez, executive VP and chief marketing officer of Reebok International, says, "The problem that I see is that we're so enamored with providing what we need to fulfill the transaction, we forget to provide what we need in **Become a client!** order to build a relationship. Ultimately, customers want a relationship with a brand that reflects their attitudes, whether that brand is Fidelity, because it gives them peace of mind, or Reebok, because it makes them feel cool. Consumers want to invest in that relationship."[6]

The most important step in CRM that businesses most frequently miss is New Business Rule 5: "Put yourself in your client's shoes." Put them on. Wear them.

Become a client! Go through the entire process from transaction to fulfillment to aftermarket support. Buy something from your company. Try to find information about your products or services. Call your company. Place an order. Log on to your website and go through all the links. Try to track the progress of your order. Complain about a problem.

It's likely that you'll quickly find many problem areas and points at which customer relationships fall down. You'll likely learn what early e-commerce website designers learned: The most common reason why clients do not complete transactions (two-thirds do not) and do not return for more business is that companies make it difficult for them to do so. Once you understand the critical path that a client takes and the added values and EMOs that a client may be denied, you are on your way to building good relationships with your customers and managing them to the benefit of both parties.

Identifying Problem Areas

The path to a happy client relationship is strewn with obstacles. The first problems occur at the get-go, when prospective clients are interested in your product or service but have not yet made the emotional commitment to complete a transaction. A client's first attempt at opening a dialogue is crucial because it sets the tone for the subsequent interactions. Philip Say, in an article for *ClickZ,* notes that "breakdowns occur right at the beginning of the relationship cycle, when representatives don't respond quickly enough to prospects. This latency translates into opportunity cost and lost sales."[7]

The next process breakdown can occur when a prospective client requests a quote. In large companies, sales representatives frequently have to go through several nonintegrated procedures to establish pricing and discounts, check inventory, and access account information. Often a client will receive a quote from one sales representative and then get a different quote when going through a different channel at the same organization. Not all sales personnel may be aware of advertised sales or discounts offered to other clients, and there's no worse EMO for clients than feeling that they are about to be swindled.

A third trouble area is at the crux of the order process. All the ducks are lined up, so to speak, but the customer can't pull the trigger because of an incomplete or faulty ordering system. A good example is form-based e-commerce on websites operating internationally that derive their main income from U.S. sales. The address field is sometimes coded to accept only valid U.S. formats, such as five sequential numbers for a zip code. A Canadian customer trying to enter his postal code of six alternating letters and numbers gets an error message and must abandon the attempted transaction; this client will usually decide not to deal with the organization in the future.

Post-sales problems are usually the last item on management's list of priorities, because the payment is already in the company's bank account and any costs incurred will decrease the short-term bottom line. But post-sales interactions have the greatest impact on word-of-mouth marketing and client loyalty. Quality in this area is sometimes difficult to deliver because different departments and employees may be involved in fulfillment, settlement, support, and follow-up activities. Without integration, companies often fail to have a unified view of post-sale customer activity.

Perhaps the best opportunity for an organization to repair ill will and build goodwill in its place is to effectively respond to unhappy clients. Palm Computing is an example of a company that has become a category-killer even though competitive products are available at lower prices. One of Palm's strategies is aftermarket support. This area includes an email newsletter and a website with free downloadable software, information about how other users are taking advantage of its products, tips on hidden features that are not mentioned in the manual, and excellent response to problems.

I bought a Palm organizer a few years ago, and a few months later, the screen became dim and difficult to read. I called the toll-free customer service number and explained my problem. The response was immediate and friendly. Unlike representatives of other companies that try to dissuade a customer from returning an item, the Palm representative immediately offered to replace the unit with a new one. In addition, the company was sensitive to the fact that its customers use Palm products for day-to-day management and are greatly inconvenienced when they are out of service. Palm sent me a new unit immediately, no questions asked. It arrived the next day. There were clear instructions to pack my defective unit in the same shipping box and return it, postage prepaid by Palm. The rep took my credit card number as insurance that I would return the defective unit, but no charges were made to my account.

Choosing CRM Tools

The size of a business and its existing CRM infrastructure will dictate how it should address its CRM needs. Companies with established infrastructures will typically opt for tools that allow existing systems to interoperate. Companies with no CRM infrastructure can choose from many off-the-shelf solutions and avoid high consultation and development costs. Other organizations may choose to outsource CRM, an option frequently used by smaller firms. The time-to-market and cost effectiveness of using a contracted third-party application service provider (ASP) may be the right ticket for newer companies and for companies in which CRM is in disarray.

Integrating Many Communication Channels

Growing demands from clients have quickly been shifting the focus of the CRM industry from sales force–centric applications to customer-centric solutions. Customer-focused technologies, such as email response systems, self-service portals, web collaboration, and chat services, are converging with traditional call-center technologies to provide seamless and efficient customer interaction. Companies that master these technologies can create high-value, lifelong customer relationships.

Nowadays, customers communicate with businesses through a multitude of communication channels, including voice mail, email, fax, and Internet chat.

Understanding your clients requires that you also understand their environments. Nowadays, customers communicate with businesses through a multitude of channels, including voice mail, email, fax, and Internet chat. Therefore, suppliers need to have a CRM system that integrates customer input from different media into a single file, which is easily accessible to all staff, from the bottom to the top of the organization. George Colony, chairman and CEO of Forrester Research, notes, "It's absolute nonsense to think that customers only want to interact through the Web. We have face-to-face contact, the telephone, mail, TV, and then the Internet. Customers want these channels to be woven together. They don't want one instead of all of the others."[8]

For example, a customer may start a transaction on the Internet, receive instructions from an agent using real-time chat, click on a button to have a telephone conversation with that agent to answer a complex question, and then move back to the Internet to complete the transaction. If this customer returns the item or purchases a related service, the transaction information may be kept in different divisions of the organization, making it difficult to piece together the whole customer history. When that customer communicates with the company in the future, her complete background must be retrieved from multiple sources, and there is often no way to match the customer to the service representative most familiar with her interests or background. Organizations need to create complete customer snapshots that are available to multiple channels and match the information to staff expertise, all in real time.

The average large company stores customer data in ten or more different systems. These non-interoperating information stores are a barrier to customer satisfaction. The cost of integrating the databases of customer information can be prohibitively high, leaving organizations in the position of knowing that they cannot deliver expected levels of service and communications.[9] In these instances, it is important to acknowledge the deficiencies while compensating for them with added value such as EMOs.

Just about all of us have run into a snag in making a purchase and then decided to call customer service, only to find the phone line busy. Did the organization put you on hold for fifteen minutes with a message such as, "Your business is very important to us"? Did you get a canned message instructing you to go back to the website? Didn't you just come from there? The new client doesn't want to put up with that sort of nonsense, and he doesn't have to, because there are other suppliers itching for the opportunity to do a better job and make the sale.

The relationship between an organization and its clients is at the core of its business and should be addressed at every level of the company.

The relationship between an organization and its clients is at the core of its business and should be addressed at every level of the company, from the highest levels of management to the receptionists who project the organization's competence and eagerness to please. The bottom line is, the *client*, not the organization, must be at the center of all CRM planning and implementation.

An Example of a Relationship Gone Wrong

While suppliers have concentrated on extracting as much information as possible about their customers, clients also now have access to information about their suppliers, as well as access to the channels of communication to balance the level of power between the two parties.

To emphasize the importance of managing channels of communication, here's an example of how a customer relationship can go wrong and how a client can counter a bad experience.

Tom Farmer and Shane Atchison of Seattle, Washington, were on a business trip to Houston, Texas. They knew that their flight would arrive late, and they confirmed reservations at a well-known hotel chain in advance, using a credit card. When they arrived at their hotel, they went to the front desk and tried to check in. The clerk had the reservation but no rooms available. He told them that because they arrived so late, the room manager had assumed they were not going to make it and had rented their reserved rooms to others. Even though their rooms were supposedly guaranteed for late arrival with a major credit card, Farmer and Atchison were refused accommodation.

The clerk was not apologetic. He was brusque and unwilling to take any blame for the screw-up. According to Farmer and Atchison, the clerk said, "Most of our guests don't arrive at two o'clock in the morning," and "I have nothing to apologize to you for," and he continued to argue that it was the travelers' fault that the hotel could not honor the guaranteed reservation. Worse, when Farmer insisted that the clerk make an alternative arrangement at a different hotel, the clerk refused, offering only a telephone book and suggesting that Farmer make his calls from a payphone.

Furious that he was treated so badly and that his guaranteed reservation had counted for nothing, Farmer decided to take action. His objective was to embarrass the night clerk and the hotel chain so that they would take steps to prevent such shoddy treatment of clients in the future. He made a PowerPoint presentation about his experience. He used the real name of the hotel and the real name of the night clerk, and he included the email addresses of the hotel's head office and Houston locations.

After detailing the experience with added graphics, Farmer closed with the following list:

- Lifetime chances of dying in a bathtub: 1 in 10,455 [National Safety Council];
- Chance of Earth being ejected from the solar system by the gravitational pull of a passing star: 1 in 2,200,000 [University of Michigan];
- Chance of winning the UK Lottery: 1 in 13,983,816 [UK Lottery];
- Chance of us returning to the [name of hotel]: worse than any of those! And what are the chances you'd save rooms for us anyway?"

He sent the presentation to the hotel. He also sent it to a few business associates and to his partner's mother-in-law, asking that they consider supporting his case by contacting the hotel and sharing his outrage.

I received a copy of his presentation about a month later from a lawyer friend of mine in Vancouver. It turns out that Farmer's business associates decided to share the presentation with some of their friends, and, in the same way that viral marketing works online, his case soon became a cause célèbre, with tens of thousands of people receiving the presentation. More than 2,000 of these recipients took the time to write back to Farmer. The deluge of sympathetic replies surprised him. "We never dreamed it would get passed around like this. Trust us. We had NO IDEA. All website postings, including the one at urban legend clearinghouse snopes.com, were done by others without our permission or approval."[10]

When asked how far the PowerPoint file had traveled, Farmer replied, "Now that Cairo and the Maldives Islands have checked in, we've heard from six continents," revealing that the same form of viral marketing that suppliers are so fond of using is now available to clients with a minimum investment of time and at no cost. The symmetrical digital channels of communication give clients a powerful new tool in dealing with their suppliers. Note also that the abused client in this example was able to go to the hotel's website and find the names and email addresses of the night clerk and manager, as well as a link to the corporate parent and its contacts, all within a few minutes. Increased access to information and to communications channels gives the new client much more clout than ever before.

What else is instructive in this example? Well, the hotel chain had doubtless invested millions of dollars in CRM software, hardware, and training, but these products were designed to mine the client information, not to make the client happy.

Increased access to information and to communications channels gives the new client much more clout than ever before.

Using CRM Wisely

Given the rush to implement CRM solutions, how certain is it that investments in CRM will pay off? Not very. If organizations believe they can use off-the-shelf CRM solutions without modifying their corporate culture to make it more client-driven, they are in for an unpleasant surprise. Gartner Inc. interviewed thousands of clients about its planned CRM initiatives and found that more than half of these strategies were destined to fail to meet their objectives.[11] That's a lot of loose change on the floor, considering it costs on average $35,000 (US) to support a salesperson with CRM technology. The costs include purchasing or building the software and hardware, training the salesperson in its use, and integrating the CRM applications with existing company systems.

Don't be a victim of the numbers game. The analysis of data taken from computers and websites will reveal trend lines, graphs, averages, peaks, and valleys. But much of this information can be meaningless. Finding out that interest in your product peaked on a certain day at a certain time may be correlated to an advertising campaign or to the fact that it was a holiday and visitors to your site or call center had more free time.

Don't make snap judgments about what's causing website visitors to exhibit a particular behavior. Many companies note that a majority of potential customers abandon the site when they are in the midst of filling out transaction forms. That's important information provided by site analysis, but it doesn't tell you why they leave. It may be that you are lacking a clearly stated and acceptable security policy. It may be that your shipping prices are too high or that you don't guarantee fast enough delivery. It may be that you request more information than your customers wish to divulge. Or it may be that the navigation of the checkout process is too complex and time consuming. Each of these possibilities (and many more) requires different remedial action. Some problems require redesigning the website, while others require redesigning business practices.

Here's an example of what can go wrong when you rely only on automated systems. A car manufacturer used a CRM system to assist decision-making about which cars to manufacture based on client preferences. The system tracked car models, accessories, and color combinations that were being sold off dealers' car lots. The information indicated that lime green cars were selling like hotcakes, so the automaker began producing lots of them. As the new cars were being painted, someone realized that lime green cars had been the worst-selling color. Conversations with the sales department finally revealed that they had recently created a sales incentive to move these dogs off the dealer lots, and so these sales had been tracked as the positive trend. The automaker lost millions.

Analyzing the Data

Automated CRM tools can inform you about what's happening on your website, but they have no knowledge of what's going on in your visitors' mind. One of the most difficult aspects of finding out what your potential clients want is finding ways to ask them. Focus groups, questionnaires, and personal interviews all provide good information, but there is a less expensive method that can frequently provide much better results because it is unobtrusive. This method involves using a search engine to learn about visitors.

The text that is entered into a website's search engine can provide important insights into visitors' thought processes. For example, the text may reveal that visitors consistently search for a product or service that you don't provide, but perhaps should. Or, you may find that potential customers leave your site after searching for something you do provide, but under a different name. For example, a visitor may type the words "file synchronization" into the search engine and get no matches, even though you offer "disk backup" products that perform the desired task.

Getting to know your clients shouldn't be a marginal activity that you can make excuses to skip. It is central to your business planning.

Analyzing search engine queries is not a job for an outsider. Words that may go unnoticed by an outside expert might trigger associations for a person who is experienced in the field. Remember, getting to know your clients shouldn't be a marginal activity that you can make excuses to skip. It is central to your business planning.

Most small and medium-sized organizations mistakenly believe it is too expensive to do in-person user tests of their call centers and websites. Although it can cost a bundle to hire a professional firm to do a thorough job of testing and the results will probably be worth the cost, you can get very usable results by recruiting a small group of test subjects. Jakob Nielsen, a principal in California-based Nielsen Norman Group, has shown that evaluating even half a dozen target clients while they interact with your company can give you the information you need to cure the major problems. He says, "Sitting with one customer at a time and hearing them think out loud is invaluable. You'll discover certain aspects of your page that appeal to them and certain parts that they don't understand. Watch their body language. Do they hesitate? Look surprised, happy, confused?"[12]

Putting It into Practice

Putting to use what you learn from testing may take more than simple directives, however. The greatest impediments to implementing a new client-focused strategy are the people working in your organization. Traditionally, the departments of marketing, sales, and service have been evaluated separately by managers, who measure performance (and hence job security and bonuses) of individuals and divisions rather than overall company profitability. This separation fosters internal competition and a lack of cooperation, exactly the opposite of what you need to present an integrated face to your client—one that's looking outward, not inward.

Technology is an important component of success today, but it should not drive the corporate train.

André Lebel, CEO of SOCAN, Canada's performing-rights society, believes that it takes up to five years to change an internal corporate culture after management has decided to re-engineer the organization to be more in tune with the times. Staff have a hard time understanding that their responsibility is primarily to the organization's clients, not to the managers.

To make changes, executives must lead by example. They can't expect the rank and file to buy into new strategies unless managers visibly adopt them within the organization. Senior execs can get the message across to staff by taking actions such as linking bonuses and raises to overall profitability and customer satisfaction in addition to individual departmental metrics.

Finally, in order to use CRM wisely, it's necessary to keep those techies in check. Technology is an important component of success today, but it should not drive the corporate train. The goal is to mediate the relationship between the client and supplier as much as possible with cost-effective automated tools, while creating a environment in which clients feel that they have a personal and direct dialogue with a single contact person in your organization. Bryan Eisenberg notes, "Similar to the old-fashioned grocery store, where customers were known by name and by their individual tastes, modern companies must create proactive, non-invasive methods to obtain accurate portraits of their customers as individuals. And they must make all that information available to company representatives dynamically, in real-time."[13]

Security and Privacy

An important EMO for clients is feeling secure. There is nothing more disconcerting than entering into an interaction or transaction for which the ultimate outcome is unknown. Given the increasing competitiveness among suppliers for new clients' business, security is becoming a major differentiator, and it can easily tip the scales of a deal.

Ideally, a company doing a transaction should get the client's credit card information, use it for the single transaction, and then either destroy it or keep it encrypted on a disk that is not network accessible. But this is not always the case. In January 2000, CDUniverse, an online CD retailer, had its security compromised by hackers who took 30,000 credit card numbers, names, addresses—everything. That information lay unprotected in a company database accessible through the Internet. The incident is one in a series of security lapses that has undermined clients' confidence in online commerce. The incident also illustrates the interrelationship between security and privacy for clients and suppliers.

The new clients are very fussy about their privacy.

The new clients are very fussy about their privacy—not just because they want their personal information to remain secret, but also because they realize that others can profit from their information. Privacy is the right to control whether your personal information may be disclosed, and to whom, in what manner, and in what time period.

While the definition of privacy is pretty much agreed on, the definition of what constitutes personal information is not. For example, is an opinion or an email that you send at work personal information or does your employer have the right to examine it? How public is a person's online identity? Should it be available to all once it has been posted on the Internet? However privacy is defined, the days are over when marketers could sit in a room and gloat over the information they had quietly gathered about their clients and sell it to others of their ilk at handsome profits.

Suppliers' concern for security and clients' concern for privacy become intertwined when interactions are online, because both the client and the supplier are part of the same communications system. Organizations originally instituted security because it was necessary to protect their business assets and goodwill. Now they are instituting privacy programs because clients are requiring it as a condition of doing business.

Security issues deal with the technologies of protection that can prevent unauthorized access to information. Secure technology needs to be in place before a business can guarantee privacy to a client. Instituting privacy for a client has the added benefit that the supplier ends up with a secure system for its own business integrity.

The essential aspects of a well-designed online security system have the same acronym as the U.S. central intelligence agency—CIA, which in this case stands for *confidentiality, integrity,* and *availability* of information. A client doesn't want others to have access to his information, doesn't want others to be able to change it, and wants it available to him at any time in order to access it or change it.

The Future of Privacy Issues

Privacy and security are important business differentiators today, but they will soon become absolute requirements for all supplier–client interactions. An increasing number of industry watchers believe that security- and privacy-related software, hardware, and consulting will become as large a market as CRM is today, as clients and suppliers learn about the implications of today's leaky systems.

Analysts predict that access to individuals' personal information online, sometimes known as their digital personas, will become a valuable trading commodity in the coming decades. Some international financial institutions are planning to shift their business roles from custodians of clients' money to custodians of their digital personas, parceling it out according to the customers' instructions and charging companies and others appropriately for its value. The trust clients place in information custodians' security arrangements and the degree of privacy the institutions agree to respect will be key considerations when clients deal online.

Provision of Security

Given the rising prominence of security issues, you'd think that every supplier would make certain they employ the best. There are tradeoffs, however, in implementing tight security, so the decisions are not always easy. For example, the better the security system, the lower the performance efficiency of the communications between supplier and client. Large corporate networking environments try to use as little security as possible because they don't want to burden their users with multiple user names, multiple passwords, tokens, or smartcards to get access to the network. Yet companies must find the balance between the need for security and productivity. They need both in order to remain viable to the clients and profitable for their shareholders.

Companies must find the balance between the need for security and productivity.

The Internet was not designed for security. It is a network of computers designed to communicate in the event of war. Based on its redundancy and protocols, it will allow all connected computers to communicate with each other, even if there are catastrophic failures within its hardware and software. Because it began as a system connecting research universities and military installations on dedicated networks to which outsiders did not have access, security really wasn't a major concern. Today, even though the Internet is available to everyone, the original underlying framework is still in place—the same protocols, the same addressing mechanisms, and so on. Beneath all the wonders of current email, chat, audio, and video lies a design that is inherently flawed from the standpoint of security.

The online attacks on the data integrity of individuals, companies, and government organizations are legion. Anyone who purchases an Internet firewall, available for as little as $100 (US), can monitor the daily attempts to access her computer or network. Whether you use a cable modem, a DSL service, a company LAN, or even a dial-up modem, you are at risk of being invaded by entities that are roaming the Web, looking for computers to hijack for their own ends. Some of them have benign intents, such as logging your webpages (if you have a web server) for use in Internet search engines. Others are commercially focused, and some are definitely malicious. We see viruses, denial of service, sniffing, session hijacking, encryption breaking, and so on because the underlying Internet protocol (IP) was not designed to deny them access. And the world's largest operating-system vendors (yes, even Microsoft) sell programs that cling to the inherently flawed infrastructure, and consequently have massive security holes because they fail to address these underlying network problems.

A study by research firm Ipsos-Reid and web developer Columbus Group found that "one in seven Canadian Internet users report that their privacy was breached online." Nearly 15 percent of Canadian Internet users reported that the personal information they had supplied to websites had been "misused." One in nine said they had been signed up for nonrequested email marketing, while another 40 percent said their data was "sold or transferred to another Web concern." *The Globe and Mail* reported that, "It doesn't matter how engaging the Web site is ... if [users] are afraid to make an online purchase ... then they are simply not going to do it."[14]

Most companies go to some lengths to protect the security of their clients' transactions. At the bottom of home pages, you'll frequently see privacy and security notices. However, after the transaction has been completed, the stored information is vulnerable because of its location on the Internet. It is here that companies fail in providing security. When you hear about an organization losing a database of credit card numbers, that database was not stolen from a Brinks truck in transit, but from insecure databases on their corporate networks or from third parties holding the information. An online transaction with company A may actually funnel the data to a server of company B, a contracted data farm with which the client has no relationship and whose security policies are not necessarily known and verified.

As a result of media exposés, clients are no longer reticent about picking up the phone or sending an email to inquire about the security and privacy policies of suppliers. Is the information destroyed after the transaction? Is it stored? If so, what is the encryption method, what is the lifetime of the data? What security provisions stop others from tampering with the information?

Government Regulations

The right to privacy is fundamental to any democratic society. Part of our freedom is our ability to open a bank account, buy something in a store, or fill out a form without worrying about who will have access to that information. Having control of personal and company information is a key to privacy. If others know the details of our lives and businesses, they have a way to interfere with them.

If others know the details of our lives and businesses, they have a way to interfere with them.

Governments have started to take action to protect the online privacy of citizens. Since January 2001, online suppliers in Canada have had to comply with the *Personal Information Protection and Electronic Documents Act* (PIPEDA), which details how personal user information may be held, disseminated, or exchanged. Additional privacy measures will automatically become law in 2003.

"Personal information" under PIPEDA means information about an identifiable individual, such as name, age, weight, height, medical records, income, purchases, and spending habits. Also included are race, ethnic origin and color, blood type, DNA code, fingerprints, marital status, religion, education, home address, and telephone number. PIPEDA gives individuals control over their personal information by requiring organizations to obtain their consent to collect, use, or disclose information about them. Federally regulated organizations, such as banks, must have a privacy policy in place inside their organizations and must inform their customers about it. When they plan to gather information from their clients, they must first tell them what information they will be taking and what they will be doing with it (or more precisely, what they will not be doing with it).

The Act has some teeth to it. Organizations must destroy, erase, or make anonymous any personal information that it no longer needs in order to fulfill the purpose for which it was collected. Individuals can ask any federally regulated organization what information they have on file about them and how they are using it. If they do not present it in a reasonable amount of time, individuals can take them to court.

Federal Privacy Commissioner George Radwanski blasted Air Canada in 2001 for improperly sharing private information about its Aeroplan frequent-flyer members. Radwanski found that Aeroplan shared personal information about its 6 million customers with corporate partners and agents for direct-mail marketing campaigns. His investigation took a year, and began when an Aeroplan customer complained after discovering that the airline had disclosed his information without first seeking his consent. The airline has since amended its information policies.

In the United States, the *Health Information and Privacy Portability Act* (HIPPA) and the *Graham Leach Blyely Act* (GLBA) for the financial sector provide some privacy requirements, but are not as tough as the Canadian Act. The United States is getting tough, however, on companies that mislead the public on privacy matters. In 2001, the Federal Trade Commission successfully charged an Internet operation that misled consumers about what it did with personal information that consumers provided on a website in exchange for free Internet access. The company sold the information, even though its privacy policy stated unequivocally, "We do not sell or provide ... personal information to outside parties."

In April 2002, the World Wide Web Consortium adopted the Platform for Privacy Preferences (P3P), which consists of answers to a set of questions about what information a site collects and how it uses it. The site's answers are translated into machine-readable code so that users' browser software can filter out sites with policies that do not meet their requirements. The focus is on disclosure. Users can then decide whether they wish to take it or leave it.

Many Internet sites are adopting the Internet's new privacy labeling scheme, which gives visitors a quick sense of how their personal privacy is being honored. The website labels offer consumers a simple alternative to the lengthy privacy policies written in complex legalese on many sites.

Cookies

Cookies are neither a food item nor an acronym: They are mechanisms by which a program running on a web server can retrieve and store information from a user's Internet appliance without the user being aware of the activity. Cookies can be an invasion of privacy and alter the power equation between clients and their online suppliers.

Cookies can be an invasion of privacy and alter the power equation between clients and their online suppliers.

When you request a webpage or an information link, the server sends additional information, the cookie, which is stored on your computer. The cookie can store information gleaned from your interactions with the server, such as your name, address, and email address; the type of computer you use; and the history of interactions you have had with the supplier. In addition, the cookie contains a list of your supplier's website addresses (URLs) for which this information (the "state," in computer speak) is valid. The next time you receive a communication from one of those stored addresses, the cookie information is automatically transmitted back to the server. With the help of these cookies, shopping applications can store information about the items in your shopping basket; applications that require your username and password can store them so you needn't retype them in subsequent sessions; your preferences at the online pizza joint can be saved; and the type of Internet connection you have (modem, DSL, LAN) can be noted. All of this information can help your suppliers serve you better and make your life easier.

Some people, however, see cookies as subversive spying agents, reporting on their activities without their knowledge or consent. In the Industrial Age, suppliers might have gotten away with that type of activity, but in the Digital Age the new clients won't stand for it. Consequently, in the bowels of an Internet browser are preference settings that let you turn off cookies completely, inform you when a server is trying to store one on your machine, or allow them to remain on your disk until you end the Internet session.

Encryption

Consumers are increasingly wary of divulging personal data online. As a result, new companies are emerging to bridge the gap between Internet users and organizations that require information about web traffic patterns, demographics, and purchasing histories. PrivaSeek's Persona and Lumeria's SuperProfile let web users store personal data in encrypted formats. The user chooses when and to whom to reveal this data and can charge a fee for revealing it (a percentage of which goes to these companies).

The technology of scrambling data and messages—encryption—has become a crucial element of computer security for businesses and consumers alike. Law enforcement and intelligence agencies are against the use of strong encryption because it prevents them from cracking messages that contain illegal and dangerous information. When you let the good guys have their privacy, you give it to the bad guys too.

When you let the good guys have their privacy, you give it to the bad guys too.

The ability of encryption to provide private conversations has led the United States to ban the most powerful encryption technology (SSL 128 bit) from use outside its borders and in Canada. The International Treaty and Arms Regulation (ITAR), which regulates the strength of encryption, is under the same rules and regulations as nuclear weapons export.[15] Outside the United States and Canada, SSL encryption is weaker in browsers and can be compromised by a serious hacker or a law enforcement agency.

PGP (Pretty Good Privacy) encryption is not controlled by U.S. laws. Philip R. Zimmerman created PGP to allow human rights groups in totalitarian countries to freely communicate with the outside world without having their messages decoded by their governments. The same free encryption software has been taken up by drug runners and terrorist networks around the world, making it more difficult for law enforcement agencies to track their activities. When asked how he felt about the probable use of his software for planning and carrying out the World Trade Center attacks, Zimmerman said, "After some reflection, my conclusion is still the same. I have no regrets. I did this for human rights ten years ago, and today every human rights group uses it. And I feel very good about that."[16]

Certification of Authenticity

Authorization and authenticity are two issues that are closely related to security and privacy. In order to have control over your information, you must be able to authorize whether others may use it. But how can anyone online know that authorization really comes from you? It is quite easy for a high school–age hacker to falsify email messages as coming from someone else, including you, because the most popular email programs (such as Outlook Express, Eudora, Entourage, and Hotmail) are absolutely not secure. Their messages can be intercepted anywhere along their network route and modified.

Consequently, someone wishing access to any of your information need only intercept one of your messages, forge your Internet address and signature, and send a bogus authorization, giving others access to everything from your digital persona to your bank account. This is not exactly a client-friendly environment.

To counter this problem, a system has been devised that mirrors the certification systems used in the physical world. In fact, it's better than going to a notary public or using a passport to certify that you are who you say you are. The system uses a digital certificate to guarantee that the person who purports to be sending a message is actually that person.

This scheme uses encryption and is fairly complex, but it boils down to this:

1. Someone wishing to be certified is assigned two unique alphanumeric codes, known as "keys." One key is secret—the "private" key—and the other key is "public"—published on the Internet by certification companies such as Verisign.
2. When you send a message that you wish to certify, such as an authorization to use your credit card or bank account, that message is encrypted using both the private and public keys. Remember, only you know the private key. The encryption scheme that uses both of these numbers is so strong that it is almost impossible to break into the message (no encryption is entirely unbreakable).
3. The encrypted message is sent through the Internet, where, if it is intercepted, it will be unreadable and tamper-proof. Any attempt to change the message would render it undecipherable at the recipient's email reader.
4. The message recipient gets the message, accesses your public key on the Internet, and uses it to decrypt the message into regular text. The decryption process requires only the public key. If the recipient can read the message, it is certified as having come from you.

Internet Espionage

Most Internet attacks involve corporate espionage, data mining, spying, or other information poaching that can give a company commercial advantage. These attacks are generally between companies, agencies, schools, universities, research facilities, airlines, and so on. The espionage is launched quietly, first by accessing the publicly available online information and then by sponging out, adhering, and mining all the data that is supposed to be private. Companies have dedicated teams that scan and scour valuable information about their competitors' customer lists, frequent users' clubs, upcoming rate changes, sales projections, hiring/firing policies, and so forth.

The reason we don't usually hear about online information attacks is that the attacked organization wishes to avoid letting its stakeholders or user community know that they are vulnerable. Banks are broken into and lose millions of dollars every day because of cyber-information attacks. But to reveal these security lapses would undermine the confidence of shareholders and clients.

Banks are broken into and lose millions of dollars every day because of cyber-information attacks.

To better understand the issues of privacy and security, I interviewed Mark Fabro, inventor of the first Internet firewall and an internationally recognized security consultant on the faculty of the University of Southern California. Fabro's career closely parallels the emergence of online security and privacy as a dominant issue for the twentieth century.

Fabro started out as a ham radio, CB, and scanner freak. He was fascinated by being able to hear things that weren't intended for his ear—radio transmissions from fire trucks, police cars, and taxis. He moved on to telephone systems, making telephones ring back and making long-distance calls for free.

When he went to high school, he was introduced to computers and networks. By the time he attended university to study experimental physics, he was able to find and read any information on anyone's computer. He started going online in 1987, six years before the Web was invented. His university provided access to the Internet, which connected him with all the computers at other research universities, as well as government and military sites. He found it easy to bypass the network security on those computer systems. He spent most of each day hacking through those systems, sleeping minimally, learning the ins and outs of open-system connectivity and security mechanisms.

By 1991, there was no remote computer that he could not hack. He joined the hacker underground and read zines (online magazines), such as *Phrak* and *2600,* in which hackers exchange information and tricks. There was little interest in what he and his colleagues were doing. He was not being secretive. In fact, he wrote scientific papers and tried to interest authorities in security problems, but they simply did not believe that he could sit at a terminal at the University of Toronto and access the information in a U.S. Navy Institute computer.

Fabro began to predict the escalation of cyber attacks because he knew that others would find the same vulnerabilities he had found. By 1995, he had been recruited to work for the good guy, as a designer of one of the world's first Internet firewalls. From then on, he has continued as a white knight, consulting with and fixing security holes for companies, militaries, and governments.

The following anecdotes are excerpts from my discussions with Fabro in 2001. His comments offer a glimpse into the nether areas of security and privacy, which can translate into opportunities for new commercial products and services.

Tales from the Crypt: Mark Fabro

"If I have your IP address, I can, from my home, get into your computer, open and close your CD tray, read all your files, erase all your files, do anything I feel like. People don't want to hear that because it paints a grim picture.

"I worked with a United States military organization that wanted to test how secure their military installation was, so they agreed to allow my team to try to penetrate their online defenses from outside the U.S.A. Using hacker techniques such as weaving and leap-frogging, we were able to hack into the military installation, bouncing through less than five Internet hops, and compromised military installations in other countries to get into the U.S. command post. As a result, the final target saw our attack as coming from inside the organization. We knew that would cause fewer alarms to go off.

"We were able to weave through their internal network, hop through their web servers, skip over their firewall and read information on a central server buried inside the physical military installation. I was surprised to find that the penetration into the system was so very easy. It cost almost nothing to effect the penetration. The attack was successful in less than an hour. It took another hour to find the vulnerabilities in the internal network and then pull the information out.

"In another instance, we were contracted to evaluate the security infrastructure of a major international financial institution, with offices spread around the world and seats on major stock exchanges. Instead of tackling their computer network, we used our computers to attack their telephone system. We used "war-dialing," the sequential dialing of phone numbers that are allocated to the institution. A large bank of numbers (area code plus a three-digit exchange prefix) is assigned to a large company, which can then internally assign the 10,000 possible variations of the last four digitals.

"We used our computers to phone every one of those 10,000 phone numbers and were able to find out which ranges of phone numbers correspond to their modem banks and computers. It was exactly like the movie *War Games*. You have a computer that dials all these numbers, and if it gets to another computer, it takes a screen shot of the log on screen, and moves on to the next one. So when the dialing is done, out of the 10,000 phone numbers, you

> **"We used 'war-dialing,' the sequential dialing of phone numbers that are allocated to the institution."**
>
> **—Mark Fabro**

might get 150 with relevant screen shots, so you can see what's waiting for you, should you call back.

"A majority of these phone numbers connected us with log-in screens that required no authentication. The financial institution had assumed, because the numbers were unpublished, that they would not be called. One of the lines we compromised was connected directly to the computer that controls trading on the Toronto Stock Exchange. We were able to gain control over the computer and watch real-time information about the trades go through as they happened.

"If a trade took place on the stock exchange for one hundred dollars, we could have modified it, and made it look like it was for one dollar or a one million dollars."

The Benefits of Good Security

Given the vulnerability that companies continue to exhibit, it's no surprise that clients are pushing harder for reassurances about the security and privacy practices of their suppliers. You would think that companies would find it in their interest to make their communications and information leak-proof. The major problem for implementing good security, it turns out, is that there is no easily quantifiable and immediate return on the investment. The benefit of having a good security and privacy policy is that something "doesn't" happen, and that's tough to sell to management. Security and privacy are the only elements of information technology for which the cost benefits cannot be quickly calculated.

But the tide is beginning to turn as clients become more informed and governments enact tougher legislation. The compelling reason for protecting a client's information and refraining from abusing the right to use it is that your competitors are beginning to do so. Now that clients are more powerful, they will migrate their business from those organizations that don't treat their information according to their wishes to those that do. While security will never be 100 percent ensured, it can be brought up to acceptable levels, so that clients' trust will increase, along with your business.

4

THE NEW CLIENTS

Any company that thinks its customers aren't

finding ways to connect with one another is

smoking Web crack. Any company that thinks it

"owns" its customers is not going to be able to

handle the G-forces that are sweeping through

the marketplace. Any company that really

believes that the information on its Web site

corresponds to what customers want is in for a

rude awakening. How many times have you

sent an email to a friend saying, "You've got to

check out this website. The message from the

CEO is awesome"? Zero![1]

DAVID SIEGEL, AUTHOR OF *FUTURIZE YOUR ENTERPRISE:*

BUSINESS STRATEGY IN THE AGE OF THE E-CUSTOMER

The new clients are everywhere and everyone. Consumers, citizens, and students are new clients. Patients, people with disabilities, and seniors are new clients. Organizations are also new clients. Businesses are new clients of other businesses and of governments. And in a reversal of traditional roles, businesses are becoming new clients of their own customers, reflecting the symmetry of the Information Age. Power companies are buying back electricity from customers who have solar or wind power generators on their property. Governments and schools are suppliers of services but are also new clients for products and services that they buy from citizens. Nongovernmental organizations (NGOs), such as trade and consumer associations, lobby groups, unions, arts councils, and museums, are both suppliers and new clients.

Along with the new client–supplier relationship, a new relationship among clients is also emerging, called peer-to-peer (P2P) transactions, in which the traditional give-and-get roles no longer apply. There are money-making opportunities for facilitators of P2P operations (such as Napster and eBay), whose roles are not defined in the older supplier-driven models.

As we examine particular groups of new clients, bear in mind that the same role reversals that help a supplier to better understand its new clients also help it understand its own role as a new client.

A Typical New Client

In September 2001, I created some archetypes of new clients, based on information gathered in marketing studies. Following is my first new client archetype.

> Hadley is a new client. She is seventeen years old and a high-school senior, and she is juggling the hormonal imperatives of finding a mate and starting a family with pressures to continue her education and pursue a career.
>
> She knows what she wants from life: "the everything pass," which gives unrestricted access to the best of the twenty-first century, like an all-day ticket to an amusement park or an all-channel cable TV package. The everything pass would entitle her to emotional and sexual fulfillment without fettering her with a restrictive marriage, to the joys of motherhood without restricting her career path, and to financial security at the end of an exciting, entrepreneurial working life.
>
> She is much more savvy than her forebears when it comes to consumption. She has learned to shop for goods, services, and entertainment by getting informed

through the Internet, which provides instant comparative pricing, reviews by peers, and access to goods and services outside of her neighborhood.

She believes the political system has bypassed her because it has become hostage to large multinational businesses and does not represent her interests. Consequently she has little interest in the political process.

She is carefully weighing her options for education, examining the advantages and costs of universities, colleges, online learning, and on-the-job training. She expects to pay for a substantial portion of her education and is looking for the best overall value.

She wants spiritual nurturing but is not certain whether the religious beliefs and practices of her parents are right for her. She separates her personal faith from organized churches, viewing the latter as nonexclusive distribution channels of faith-based products rather than the source of spirituality.

When she surveys the adult world, she sees overworked, stressed-out people whose goals are not dissimilar to her own. Although they have failed to achieve the happy blend of "everythingness," she believes she will succeed in her quest.

In order to negotiate the terms of her life better than her parents' generation did, she is more self-assertive and better informed. She has grown up with news reports of children suing their parents for lack of adequate financial and emotional support and consumers filing class action suits against Internet providers for excessive downtime, and she has grown accustomed to hearing marketing slogans that inflate her self-worth: "Your call is important to us."

In short, she is a new type of client, a more self-assured, demanding, and informed one. And her suppliers are everyone, everywhere.

Two months later, I was giving the keynote address at a conference in Brandon, Manitoba, an agricultural and ranching community. My topic was the impact of the new global information economy on local economic growth. I decided to test my model of the new client on that small-town audience, so I added it to my presentation and invited comments from attendees. After my talk, Karen Caldwell, an attendee, told me that the description resonated with her. True, she was in her late twenties and married with two children, but her outlook on life and her expectations were congruent with the new client archetype. A few weeks later she followed up our conversation with an email, which I've excerpted here:

I live in Reston, Manitoba, an agricultural community with a population of approx. 500 (Stats Canada says 700, but I think they included cats...). My company, Caldwell Business Solutions, currently does custom database applications and software training. I am going to break into the web development scene shortly, as a project animator, coordinator, and supervisor—speaking with clients about what they want, letting them know what they need, and relaying the job requirements to designers and coders. My customers are most frequently outside Reston, but within driving distance.

I went to college in Medicine Hat and earned a business diploma with a microcomputer major. I was planning on working in the city as a Database Administrator, but Corey (my husband) does not like the city at all, and I knew I couldn't live there forever either. So we moved to Souris, where I got a job in the IT field, setting up a network in a law office, providing a specialized law accounting package and databases and so on. I decided that I would start my own business about the same time I discovered I was pregnant.

Being much like "Hadley'" (your archetype), I didn't see this as a problem— starting a business and a family. Since Corey could support us with his work in an autobody shop, we felt comfortable trading my guaranteed income for the opportunity to start my own business....

I just don't have a need for office space that people come in to, so I didn't bother with the expense. I do computer training at The Learning Company in Brandon or at a company's business site. The meetings I have with database clients also happen either on site or at The Learning Company....

I think that we are a new type of client that takes responsibility as well. I will go home and research what the doctor tells me, I check out everything before I buy and have a price range that needs to be met if I shop locally, or else I will buy online. So, exactly as you say, my suppliers are everyone, everywhere, and I'm not limited by my rural location.

I definitely think that Hadley will have a lot of readers nodding their head.

Karen later told me she intends to bring high-speed Internet to her community because it is a viable and attractive option for those seeking to leave the city but not the office. She has been discussing with the local telco and other infrastructure suppliers the costs of bringing wired or wireless broadband connectivity to her town from the nearest Internet connection, which is fifty kilometers away. She is getting close to making a deal. She is about as far from the old stereotype of an uninformed local yokel as you could imagine. She doesn't let suppliers take her for granted, and she demands that they engage her rather than just sell to her. She is a person in control of her life, her work, and her transactions.

She is a person in control of her life, her work, and her transactions.

Consumers

When I think of the new client, the first thing that comes to mind is a consumer. Consumers are the heart and soul of an economy. They are the engine that drives markets and business. They eat food—commodity foods like milk and manufactured foods like potato chips and TV dinners. They drive cars. They make phone calls. They live in houses, condos, and apartments. They buy CDs, stereos, cameras, computers, and television sets. They subscribe to cable TV and go to sporting events, theater, symphonies, and rock concerts. They buy toys and games for their kids and hobbies for themselves. And they use myriad services, from lawyers to pet groomers to stockbrokers.

Consumers who are getting lots of EMOs make an economy tick. When they stop getting EMOs, they stop investing, stop buying homes, stop buying cars, and, in the end, stop the economy. The new global information economy is being driven by companies that provide lots of EMOs along with their more tangible products and services.

The dot.com boom was the result of early online ventures providing consumers with lots of EMOs, particularly *being in control with lots of choice*. The dot.com bust was the consequence of a glut of startups that were unable to deliver value to the new clients.

According to Paul Sonderegger, a senior analyst at Forrester Research, now that the Internet is becoming ubiquitous, its user base is predominantly nontechnical and uninterested in the latest bells and whistles. Users are no longer early adopters and are less concerned with whether they have the latest version of Java or Flash than they are with getting a good price and aftermarket service.[2] In other words, the Web has gone mainstream.

Consumers around the world use the Web to shop, learn about products and providers, search for jobs, manage their finances, obtain health information, and scan their hometown newspapers. Most of these activities are not yet captured by official output and productivity measures, but they have a positive impact by allowing consumers to become more informed with a minimum of stress and effort.

The new consumers are not loyal to brands, products, or supply chains. Like customers in preindustrial times, they are loyal to those with whom they've established a relationship. Nowadays, that relationship will be mediated by telephone, email, a website, or a chat group, but customers still need to feel they are dealing with real people who care and who have the authority to provide customized and extra-effort service. David Siegel, e-business and Internet author, notes that customers are "loyal to other customers and to company employees with whom they've established relationships."[3]

Shopability

The new consumers have high expectations for transactional relationships. They are looking for "shopability," the sum total of ease of use, positive EMOs, product information, transaction information, shipping information, privacy, and generous return policies, plus the usual price and availability criteria.

Part of shopability is intuitive web design *from the client's point of view*. Intuitive web design means providing consistent buttons for the same actions, the ability to navigate a website without unwanted stops along the way, and uncluttered and clear paths for purchasing that require the fewest clicks. To please today's online shopper, "e-tailers" must provide comprehensive information about a consumer's transaction, including a tracking number, verification that the order has been logged, and continuing information about the status until the order is delivered.

Customer comments are a research tool to constantly adjust and improve the company.

The most common question from customers of e-sites is "Where's my stuff?" The amazon.com site has a box labeled "Where's my stuff?" on every page, starting with the welcome page, because that was the number-one question asked by customers for several years running. And Amazon is an example of a company that doesn't consider customer comments part of the complaint, quality-control, or customer-satisfaction departments. Amazon believes customer comments are a research tool to constantly adjust and improve the company. Customer service is its core business and what it promotes as its corporate differentiator. Consequently, every encounter with a customer, by phone, email, or website interaction, is a source of important information that the company will analyze and use to chart its course.

The new consumers want consistent and timely fulfillment across multiple distribution channels (land, air, sea, download) and support across multiple sales channels (telephone, physical stores, the Internet). After the early online fulfillment nightmares of the late 1990s, shoppers lost their tolerance for delivery problems. But finding the most efficient and rapid delivery method is not enough to satisfy the new client. Suppliers found that they could save time and money by slapping a shipping label on products in their warehouse without wrapping them. It worked for a while, until after Christmas, when there was a flood of customer complaints and returns from people who had ordered gifts for their loved ones and were horrified when the items were delivered in the original packaging, allowing Johnny or Janie to see what Santa was going to bring them.

Companies should constantly monitor key indicators of how well they are serving their customers to ensure that a customer-centric focus permeates every level of the organization. Metrics that successful companies monitor include the average time customers wait to get through to the call center, the percentage of customers who order a second and third time, the number of people using live chat online, and the number of packages that are not delivered on time.

Integrated Sales Channels

Forrester Research advises that "online stores should buttress their Web sites with other sales channels—bricks-and-mortar, catalog, and telephone—to accommodate the full spectrum of consumer needs."[4] The following EMO chart compares the sales experiences of buying online, by telephone, or through stores.

EMO	Buying Online	Buying by Phone	Buying through Stores
Feeling Good	Medium	Medium	Medium
Feeling Comfortable/Secure	Medium	Medium	High
Doing Good	No	No	No
Having Control/Choice	High	Low	Medium

From an emotional perspective, physical stores offer the greatest comfort and feelings of security, while online shopping offers the greatest choice and control. Telephone shopping on its own is the weakest, but it can be used effectively as a complementary channel to the Internet, offering person-to-person voice communication that the Web is not yet able to duplicate.

Retailers such as Kmart have learned that they cannot keep their online divisions separated from their in-store sales. The new reality is that retailing and e-tailing are seen as complementary parts of a whole. Stores must now integrate their traditional selling with online activities. BlueLight.com provides kiosks in Kmart stores that mir-

The new reality is that retailing and e-tailing are seen as complementary parts of a whole.

ror the Kmart website. In-store customers can browse the catalog online, and off-site customers can buy on the Internet and return their merchandise to a Kmart store if necessary.

Lands' End, a retailer that has sixteen outlet stores in four states but is known mostly for its catalog, also encourages customers to return goods bought online to its bricks-and-mortar stores.

Newgistics developed a client-friendly return system for the Spiegel Group, which includes Eddie Bauer, Spiegel, and Newport catalogs. Customers can drop off returns at a nearby postal outlet without having to fill out forms, repackage the goods, or spend hours waiting to talk to customer service agents. In many instances customers can receive instant credit card refunds and shopping credits. The process is said to take less than five minutes.

Even Amazon acknowledges the benefits of bricks and mortar. Amazon.com customers who buy certain electronic products online can pick them up from their closest Circuit City store and return them there if they have a problem.

The integration of physical products and digital products is becoming more popular. Until recently, physical books and e-books have been sold through separate marketing, sales, and fulfillment channels. SmartEcon Publishing changed that in July 2000 when it published Soon-Yong Choi and Andrew B. Whinston's *The Internet Economy: Technology and Practice* as both an e-book and a print book. SmartEcon marketed the two products as a single unit. Buy the book and you get free access to the password-protected online version; buy the e-book and you're sent a free print version. The products are more complementary than overlapping. The tables and charts in the book are constantly updated in the online version, while the paper product is available for those who prefer a printed book.

The SmartEcon.com website has the complete text of the book's chapters. The online content also provides hypertext links and other resources that are not part of the print title. The online book is considered the primary version and the print version secondary. The website notes, "[The] print version contains all necessary texts to stand alone without using its online version. But we do encourage you to access the online version and use, download, print it as you need."

At Staples, the sales equation is $1 + 1 + 1 = 5$. With more than a thousand retail stores, a catalog business, kiosks, and a website, Staples can easily measure the impact of cross-channel buying. The company finds that when a customer moves from shopping through a single channel to shopping through two channels, that person typically spends two-and-a-half times as much as a single-channel shopper. When a customer shops through three or more channels, he spends four-and-a-half times as much. A shopper in a retail Staples store has a choice of almost 10,000 products. If a product is out of stock, the customer can go to a kiosk in the store and place an order for the item, then have it delivered the next day.

Online Car Shopping

You can't test-drive a car or truck online, but 65 percent of new vehicle buyers and 43 percent of used car buyers use the Internet for automotive information before they purchase.[5] They do their homework online and then approach dealers with a wealth of information that can strengthen their bargaining position and reduce some of the stress that comes with buying a car. The average buyer visits seven sites before making a choice, many more than the number of dealers she might have visited before the advent of online shopping.[6]

The biggest change, though, is that consumers are beginning to use the Internet for *buying* cars, not just getting information about them. The conventional wisdom that big-ticket items like automobiles are unsuitable for online shopping is proving to be just another Industrial Age myth.

My son and daughter-in law bought a car online in 2002. First, they checked out www.edmunds.com, a website that offers staff and consumer reviews as well as recent selling prices for all auto makes and models. Then they went to the www.vehix.com website to make head-to-head comparisons of cars they were interested in and to use the financing calculator, which explained the purchasing and leasing options. It informed them (after they entered how much down payment and monthly payments they could afford) what price car they could afford to buy. They then checked out www.autobytel.com, which had similar information and some unique features such as comparisons between rebates and other incentives. They narrowed their choice to a single make and model, the Hyundai Elantra, which had the best customer reviews in its price range, and then decided to use the www.drivechicago.com website to find local dealers (they live near Chicago). After keying in their zip code, the webpage returned a list of a dozen dealers within a forty-mile radius of their home, along with exact locations, distances, and contact information.

They visited the closest dealer and test-drove an Elantra, which validated their choice. Then the fun began. They committed to buying the car online and entered

The conventional wisdom that big-ticket items like automobiles are unsuitable for online shopping is proving to be just another Industrial Age myth.

their personal information into the website. Within a few hours, they had been contacted online by six nearby dealers, who began bidding for their business. They watched as quote after quote passed through their computer screen, each one lower than the previous. An hour later, they made their purchase … for almost $2,000 less than the average price paid for the same car in the local autodealers' showrooms.

How can dealers sell for less online? Easy. They get qualified leads for zero effort, and they don't have to pay a salesperson for the time it takes to qualify the customer, lead him to the sales trough, and then close the deal. They save sales commissions altogether. The dealers get to their lowest quote quickly because they know that the customer has seen their actual cost and knows how much profit they are making on the deal.

Let's look at the EMO chart for buying a car online:

EMO	Buying a Car Online
Feeling Good	High
Feeling Comfortable/Secure	Medium-High
Doing Good	No
Having Control/Choice	Very High

My daughter-in-law felt great about the online purchase process. She had been dreading going into a car dealership to buy the car because she hates haggling about price and knows that the salesperson will present only positive information to close the sale and earn a commission. She is the type of person who would be upset if she found out that she had not paid the lowest price. Online, she felt totally in control of all aspects of the process and enjoyed the bevy of dealers that were vying for her business. This was certainly a client-centric transaction.

It's unclear what the future holds for the dealers who maintain customer-friendly showrooms and provide vehicles for test-drives. The more they spend on customer care in the sales process, the less they can afford to compete on price for the final buy. Some analysts believe that test-drives will become a paid-for service, with a full rebate to the customer if she decides to buy the car from the dealer who provides the service.

After purchasing a vehicle, consumers continue to use the Web to find authorized repair shops, read warranty information, find out about recalls, and chat with other owners of the same types of vehicles for tips and troubleshooting information.

Since price has become more important online, as a result of automated and easy product-to-product comparisons, how can a company differentiate its products and add value to the client to overcome a competitor's price advantage? The answer is EMOs, which build brand loyalty and figure strongly in consumers' purchasing decisions. In the auto industry, companies are coming up with novel strategies to deliver on EMOs.

Toyota's home page, at www.toyota.com, has career advice, fitness articles, chat areas, and other lifestyle features that appeal directly to its target market. Toyota has found that building a lifestyle-oriented brand affinity has a strong influence on its target clients once they decide to purchase a car, even if that decision is months or years down the road. This website builds relationships with potential customers by being relevant to their lifestyles and interests and pressing lots of EMO buttons. Here's the EMO chart for the Toyota website:

Building a lifestyle-oriented brand affinity has a strong influence on its target clients once they decide to purchase, even if that decision is months or years down the road.

EMO	www.toyota.com
Feeling Good	High
Feeling Comfortable/Secure	High
Doing Good	Medium
Having Control/Choice	Medium

The strengths of the website are that it makes people in the targeted market feel good and makes them feel comfortable. There are elements of doing good (fitness, good diet), and there are plenty of choices of website paths, with no pressure to purchase a product.

The second EMO of feeling comfortable and secure provides a way for car dealers, for example, to maintain their place in the automotive sales chain. The experience a customer has with a dealer (positive or negative) in pre- and after-sales interactions greatly influences that customer's desire to purchase a vehicle from the same dealer. Many sales are determined more by a desire to work with a dealer than by the actual automobile model, because buyers sometimes see cars in similar categories and price ranges as more or less equivalent.

Lastly, if a dealer or a salesperson can establish a positive relationship with a customer, there is a much better chance that the customer will return for repeat business. "Relationship" is, in fact, the first of the new four Rs of marketing (see below).

Forget Your Ps, Remember Your Rs

Veteran ad executive Elliot Ettenberg believes that the four Ps at the foundation of traditional consumer marketing—Product, Price, Place, and Promotion—no longer hold much relevance. Products can now be quickly duplicated; price is less consequential now that "guaranteed low price" is a standard offering; place is no longer critical now that the Internet sales channel reaches global markets; and traditional promotion, while still important, can be supplanted or replaced by viral and other new marketing approaches that don't require large resources.[7]

Ettenberg suggests that businesses apply the four Rs— Relationships, Rewards, Relevance, and Retrenchment.

In their stead, Ettenberg suggests that businesses apply the four Rs—Relationships, Rewards, Relevance, and Retrenchment. Relationships are the building blocks for sales to new clients; rewards are the special treatments given to frequent flyers (see "Client Relationship Management" in Chapter 3); relevance is the personalized target marketing for each customer; and retrenchment describes the new clients' immunity to traditional marketing and the need to reach them through targeted campaigns that use direct mail and the Internet. Note the strong resonance between the new four Rs of marketing and the new business rules, particularly the fourth rule: Motivate clients with emotion.

Today, business is not so much about selling as it is about providing an environment that encourages customers to choose a particular product. Some very successful websites are devoid of product information but provide strong EMOs, relationships, rewards, relevance, and retrenchment.

Making Money from New Client Opportunities

Entrepreneurs who wish to take advantage of new consumer opportunities can do so by following these steps:

1. Put yourself in a new client frame of mind.
2. Go through typical work, play, and family cycles and make a list of the things that bug you or that would make your life easier/happier.
3. Come up with a product or service that satisfies an item on your list.
4. Develop and market it.
5. Ask your close friends to help you carry your profits to the bank.

Here's an example. Martin Charlwood used to go ballistic when one of his flights was canceled and he was already at the airport. Like everyone else who was booked on that flight, he would go to the airline's customer service counter and wait in a line of perhaps 150 people, most of whom were freaking out because they were about to miss their flight and the business or family commitments at the destination. Frequently, he would end up stranded, sometimes in a foreign city like Tokyo, trying to contact his U.S. travel agent to change his reservation when it was 3 a.m. back in the States. He went through steps 1 and 2 outlined above and decided to come up with a service that would solve this problem.

So he founded Uniglobe.com in 1997, along with his brother, Chris Charlwood, and his father, U. Gary Charlwood. Uniglobe is a travel service that provides its clients with a toll-free 800-number for a 24/7 rescue line. Instead of fuming in line at the airport, you call the number and an agent brings up your file and says, "Oh, there's a flight on another airline. It leaves from Terminal 3 in forty-five minutes. Why don't you run over and catch it?" The agent automatically prepares your new electronic ticket and lets your hotel know that you may arrive later than expected. And if you still miss your connection and get stuck in the wrong city, the agent will make sure that your car reservation is held until the following day. The company also has a policy of responding to every customer email within 20 minutes.

Uniglobe's EMO chart looks like this:

EMO	Uniglobe Travel
Feeling Good	High
Feeling Comfortable/Secure	High
Doing Good	No
Having Control/Choice	High

Uniglobe Travel gets high EMO scores for giving clients more comfort and security for their traveling. The service makes clients feel very good and puts them back in control of their travel planning, instead of making them feel they are part of a nameless lineup.

Here's another example that will resonate with everyone who has a telephone. Bob Bensman is president and founder of Ver-a-fast, a telemarketing firm in Ohio. Because he knows telemarketing, he is well aware of how intrusive it is and how negatively some people react to it. So, he put himself in those clients' frame of mind and decided to make their lives easier and happier. He came up with a product that defeats telemarketers.

Bob Bensman is president of a telemarketing firm. He came up with a product that defeats telemarketers.

Telemarketing is a huge business. Companies spend about $100 billion (US) on telemarketing annually, according to the Direct Marketing Association. That's almost 40 percent of direct-marketing expenditures. There are hundreds of telemarketing call centers in North America, and more than 80 percent of them use software known as predictive autodialers, which can call several numbers simultaneously and make as many as 500,000 calls between 8 a.m. and 9 p.m. When you answer your phone, the computer connects you to a live telemarketer who tries to sell you something.

If you are not home or if the computer gets your answering machine, your number is put back in the database to be called again later. But if the number dialed is not in service, the autodialer hangs up and takes the number out of the queue. It is never dialed again and is removed from that database.

That information gave Bensman the ammunition he needed to build an autodialer killer. He calls it TeleZapper. TeleZapper turns the automatic-dialing technology against itself. Before your phone rings, the device sends out a short beep that indicates to the autodialer that your phone has been disconnected. It sounds like the beep of an answering machine, but it is actually the first tone of the three-tone tune that the phone company sends out when someone calls a disconnected number. The autodialer hears the beep, records your number as disconnected, and hangs up, but all other incoming calls get through without interruption. Bingo, no more bothersome telemarketer calls!

In June 2000, Bensman pitched his concept to Royal Appliance, who market Dirt Devil vacuum cleaners. Royal embraced his idea and paid Bensman more than $1 million (US) for rights to the product. Bensman went directly to Step 5, above: Carry the money to the bank. Here's the EMO chart.

EMO	TeleZapper
Feeling Good	High
Feeling Comfortable/Secure	High
Doing Good	No
Having Control/Choice	High

In these cases, a high EMO score is an excellent predictor of a successful entrepreneurial venture, one that can be more accurate than traditional spreadsheets and pro forma budgets.

Companies

Business-to-business (B2B) trade between companies has moved online, big time. Online B2B transactions, estimated at $2.5 trillion (US) for 2003, dwarf e-commerce with consumers (B2C) by a ratio of about ten to one. It is no longer necessary to stand on a soapbox and proclaim that this is the future of business—the future has already arrived.

Online B2B transactions may be more prevalent than B2C for now, but companies as clients are not unlike consumers. They shop around for the best deals, demand that their suppliers pay attention to them, and have more supply sources and information today than ever before. While some might argue that EMOs play a lesser role in B2B transactions, the desire for stable, secure suppliers (the second EMO) and the need for freedom to choose among many suppliers (the fourth EMO) are perhaps stronger in intercompany transactions than in B2C. Corporate commerce brings some notable differences, however, such as the importance of secure and private communication channels and the need for new networks of supply and distribution to replace the older supply chains and single distribution channels.

One of the most fundamental changes in business strategy today, however, is the redirection of company objectives from delivering products (internal focus) to delivering client satisfaction (external focus). It is still a big leap for many executives to understand the difference between the two, but that difference is crucial to profitability.

Companies are awarding more contracts to outside suppliers for more money than ever before as a result of decentralization, disintermediation, and digital connectivity. In most ways, business is booming, even if profits are not always doing so.

It's the client's experience and perception of value that drive sales.

The new economy values intangibles such as engaging people's attention, building relationships, exchanging information, and delivering EMOs—things that are best measured in a client's mind. While the price and functionality of physical goods continue to have important value, it is the client's experience and perception of value that drive sales. Angel Martinez, chairman and CEO of Forrester Research, says, "I'd say move away from purely transactional thinking to the experiential. Emphasize imagery to support your brand, build customer participation into your brand, and make the relationship one that's based on experiences."[8]

The New Company: Both Supplier and Client

Most companies engage in three fundamental activities:

- They are clients for staff, raw materials, and/or products.
- They add value by providing processing or services such as manufacturing, marketing, and promotion.
- They are suppliers, selling the resulting goods or services.

Businesses are thus both suppliers and clients, fitting well within the new symmetrical framework of the Information Age. Digital media, such as the Internet, are designed differently from their Industrial Age, mass-media predecessors, which use few-to-many distribution structures. Consider newspapers, radio, and television, which provide almost all of their information bandwidth downstream (from supplier to client), leaving only letters to the editor and phone-in comments as a tiny upstream channel from clients back to their information suppliers. On the other hand, the Internet and intranets (private networks that use Internet protocols) are based on P2P (peer to peer) architectures in which any user/client can also be a supplier and has access to similar information bandwidth upstream as downstream.

This new infrastructure permeates every aspect of communications and has a major impact on the way we perceive other interactions as well, facilitating and encouraging the power shifts embodied in new client thinking. Dial-up modems use a symmetrical bandwidth of 56 kilobits per second upstream and downstream. Higher-speed cable modems and DSL modems are typically configured to deliver about 75 percent of their bandwidth downstream (to the client) and 25 percent upstream (back to the supplier). This configuration is based on bandwidth utilization patterns in which video and audio, which contain lots of data, are sent primarily from websites (suppliers) to individual users (clients).

Unlike the older media, the upstream and downstream bandwidth allocation can be adjusted as new usage patterns emerge. For example, P2P distribution of music using Napster-like software architecture would require such reconfiguration if it were to become the norm. For this type of use, a fifty-fifty allocation of upstream and downstream bandwidth would be more efficient.

The symmetry of B2B online transactions, in which companies are both clients and suppliers, provides a good fit for twenty-first-century commerce. The Internet enables this symmetry, providing a motor for change and a lubricant for e-commerce. In fact, the resurgence of North American productivity and prosperity in the 1990s coincided exactly with growing use of the Internet, even though many of the key industries that flourished were old-economy businesses such as manufacturing and housing construction.

General Electric provides a good example of a company that has applied new-economy business models to old-economy business. Jack Welch, longtime CEO of GE, was considered the king of the old economy, reigning over a fiefdom of manufactured products ranging from refrigerators to jet engines. Today, he says, "You have to be in e-commerce in every element of your business … in all of your supply chain, in all of your information flow, in all of your communications, in all of your customer interactions. This is not some activity outside the business; it *is* the business. It's like breathing when you come to work! You have to breathe all day to stay at your desk, don't you?"[9]

"[E-commerce] is not some activity outside the business; it *is* the business."

—Jack Welch

For a company like GE, e-commerce takes many forms. GE executives use it to source components more quickly and inexpensively than before. They use it to tender contracts to outside suppliers and to monitor their progress. They use it to sell GE components and products. And they use the basic tools of e-commerce to integrate their internal activities among divisions and with their suppliers.

Erick Schonfeld, writing in *Business 2.0,* says, "The Web's infiltration into every pore of the economy is proceeding with the force of pure logic. No company can resist it. None can afford to. With the Internet rewiring the world—connecting companies and people in ways they've never been connected, giving them information they've never seen—adaptation is everything. Those who learn the language of the new order will survive, even flourish. Those who fail could lose their heads."[10]

Companies as New Clients

Companies have quickly learned how to become new clients, and they now demand much more from their suppliers in every way: quicker response times for quotes, just-in-time deliveries, lower margins, and greater control over all aspects of the transaction. It is ironic that many companies that have difficulty satisfying their own new clients have no trouble acting like new clients in their dealings with their suppliers.

For example, most companies become fussy new clients when it comes to outsourcing components, sub-manufacturing, and services, demanding more from their suppliers than ever before. They require that their suppliers acquire or modify their internal computer systems, network connections, and work processes to conform to their own, so that they can manage the external products and services as easily as if they were in-house, driving and controlling these transactions with a new power based on digital information technology and networks.

Much of the outsourced work involves computer software and websites. Veterans of the dot.com boom and bust manage the work from inside the company. Some of these employees were briefly dot.com millionaires whose paper fortunes evaporated when measures of profit and loss were reintroduced into the stock market. In their current positions, these tech-savvy employees manage the outsourcing of work that is familiar to them from their previous positions. Formerly suppliers, they are now clients for products and services that can be delivered more cost-effectively outside rather than inside their companies (reflecting the first new business rule: Shift from internal to external focus). They are knowledgeable clients: They know how to specify the deliverables of a software contract with the same detail and acumen that an automobile manufacturer provides to its parts suppliers, penalizing contractors who deliver late or incomplete work. With myriad suppliers bidding for work, outsourcing corporate clients are in the driver's seat.

B2B Networks

The Internet provides inexpensive bandwidth, but the Internet is public and has therefore been unsuitable for B2B communications and transactions. Private digital networks, on the other hand, have become the norm for business because they can be configured for the security and reliability that companies such as financial institutions require. Online B2B transactions over private nets were big business long before the Web was invented. Companies that required mission-critical information or transaction communications built their own secure communications infrastructure (laying cables, and so forth) or rented cable lines from a phone company, public utility, or private company. These networks, along with their associated hardware and software, are known as Electronic Data Interchange (EDI). EDI is used to communicate purchase orders, invoices, inquiries, planning, acknowledgements, pricing, order status, scheduling, test results, shipping and receiving, payments, and financial reporting.

The EDI industry is made up of telecommunications suppliers, software and hardware providers, and consultants who custom design and maintain systems that meet individual needs. For example, SOCAN is a company that tracks the use of music by Canadian broadcasters, bars, and the like. It collects royalties that it distributes to its members, who own copyright for the music. It maintains a database of Canadian musical works but must exchange that information with other societies, such as BMI and ASCAP in the United States, which maintain similar information about their U.S. members' copyrights. These companies require a digital connection to exchange their data, and the connection must be secure and private. Otherwise, a copyright holder could hack into the data stream and increase the number representing the use of his music in order to receive a higher payment. The implications for financial institutions are obvious.

The EDI approach has some negative consequences, however. The first is that it is very expensive, which precludes use by small and moderate-sized businesses. The second drawback is its closed architecture, which encourages the development of proprietary and non-interoperable software, hardware, and protocols. As a result, typically each business solution has been more or less custom crafted for a particular client or class of clients, inflating the cost.

There are important implications for business clients who wish to use this approach. The most important one is that unless a company has enough resources to allocate for implementing and maintaining the EDI system, it cannot play with the "big boys" and must resort to less efficient and more manually intensive processing of the external data, converting it into the company's internal formats for processing and then reconverting it to the EDI formats when shipping it out.

Virtual Private Networks

The telecommunications industry began to address the cost issue by introducing virtual private networks (VPNs). VPNs make public networks operate like private networks. They allow telecom clients to custom configure their network connections so that these appear to be private (with full security, firewalls, and such) but allow the communications traffic to travel over

VPNs make public networks operate like private networks.

the standard infrastructure of a shared telephone network. The cost savings are significant.

The older EDI solutions required building or leasing network capacity based on accommodating the highest anticipated data throughout. That's a problem for most companies whose communications needs vary from project to project, from season to season, from weekdays to weekends, and at different times of the day. This type of traffic is called "bursty"—it is sometimes high, sometimes low. Imagine paying an electricity bill based on the moment of highest usage, a hot summer evening with the lights and TV on while the air conditioning is blasting, or a water bill based on the moment that you're taking a shower while your spouse is watering the lawn.

The newer VPN services let each client, not the telecommunications supplier, configure its company's network capacity as needed. With VPNs, clients can set their own network bandwidth on demand, paying telcos only for the bandwidth they need at a particular time. Scott Martin, network manager for Canada Life Assurance, notes, "Bell's IP VPN Enterprise service lets us expand and contract our bandwidth according to the amount of traffic on our network—which is a very useful feature during our peak periods—and we are only billed for what we use."[11]

The new tools translate each company's information into common languages and protocols so that each party to a B2B communication can speak with and understand the other online.

VPNs set the stage for the biggest change in B2B communications—moving business communications traffic to the Internet, where the costs are dramatically lower and standard off-the-shelf products can be quickly adapted for custom needs.

To accommodate the needs of business, new technologies have been introduced to the Internet, such as XML, web services, and SOAP, that allow for the functionality of EDI while using the Internet's almost cost-free infrastructure with standard software tools. The new technologies translate each company's information into common languages and protocols, so that each party to a B2B communication can speak with and understand the other online. It's like an IT version of the Babble fish in Douglas Adams's novel *The Hitchhiker's Guide to the Galaxy*.

XML

A key to making the new systems interoperate is XML (extensible markup language), the information language based on the Internet's html (hypertext markup language) that can be understood by diverse corporate systems. XML was developed by the World

Wide Web Consortium (W3C) and is spreading like wildfire throughout businesses around the world.[12] XML is not fixed in its structure of data and fields but rather is extensible to any required data structure, so it can embrace the wide variety of structured information that is in place throughout any business. Structured information includes things like databases, spreadsheets, address books, financial transactions, configuration parameters, and technical drawings. XML is platform-independent (it can be used with Unix, Windows, Macintosh, Java, and so on), and it supports internationalization and localizations.

The attribute that makes XML data different from traditional computer data is its use of text rather than binary computer formats, so that the data may be examined and used without requiring the program that produced it. XML text can be viewed in the simplest text editor, making it much less costly to create and administer. It allows different programs running in different computer environments at different companies (suppliers and clients) to easily share information and interoperate.

The Internet's XML is now being introduced into business systems with big savings in costs and time. One of the results is that smaller companies that could not have afforded EDI can now have the same benefits. Since XML is adaptable to any use, it can be modified to contain any type of data. There are already thousands of different applications, each aimed at a different industry or niche application—everything from invoicing to gene sequencing.

The revolutionary potential of XML is so great that even Microsoft, known for its proprietary and non-interoperating software, is rewriting its key software (including its operating systems) so that they can communicate using XML.

With XML, many aspects of a company's operations can be integrated for the first time, linking diverse computer platforms and software internally and with the company's suppliers and clients. The specification of parts, for example, can now include input from internal designers and external component suppliers. A needed part might work equally well if constructed from any one of several different materials, some of which may be much less expensive than others. By putting the supplier and client teams in direct communication during the design process, the best specification can be generated at the best price.

Web Services

One of the technologies that makes use of XML is the web service. A web service allows a remote application to use programs running on a web-based server. From the network's perspective, a web service resembles ordinary Web traffic and thus is platform-independent—it doesn't matter what brand of computer and type of operating system are used. Like an Internet browser and the html language of webpages, XML doesn't care what hardware and software are at the other end of the network connection, only that they speak the language of XML. But instead of creating html webpages intended for human readers, web services contain XML data designed to be read by computers.

Web services are fast becoming the programmatic backbone for electronic commerce. For example, one company's computer will call another's web service to send a purchase order directly via an Internet connection, or a web service might calculate the cost of shipping a package of a certain size or weight via a specific carrier. What makes these examples different than before is that the services need not be created for the particular use, but can be common to thousands of client companies that might need to calculate shipping costs, say. The consequence for clients is that products and services are cheaper and quicker to market, both hallmarks of new clients' expectations.

Following is an EMO chart comparing the older EDI technology with the newer B2B technologies enabled by the Internet, including virtual private networks, the XML language, and web services.

EMO	EDI	Internet Technologies
Feeling Good	Medium	High
Feeling Comfortable/Secure	High	Medium-High
Doing Good	No	Some
Having Control/Choice	Low	High

Few things bring such good feelings to business managers as reduced operating costs. Consequently, the newer Internet technologies have an edge in making customers feel good, because they are much cheaper. When it comes to feeling secure, the older EDI networks have a slight edge because they are private and more difficult to hack into than the Internet. Internet B2B technologies do some good because they shift infrastructure spending into the public network, where economies of scale ultimately lower prices for all users. But the biggest tip of the scale for Internet technologies is that they provide more control and choice. With EDI, a company has limited choices of computer platform, operating system, and software because these need to be compatible with those on the other end of the EDI. The Internet-enabled technologies, on the other hand, are cross-platform and have open standards, providing much greater choice. On the whole, the newer Internet approaches win.

Supply Networks

The introduction of standard Internet-compliant technologies for business has enabled the complete re-engineering of how companies order component goods and services. Think of the customer at the end of a long chain of companies, each of which provides the client-process-supplier activity detailed earlier. This supply chain, as it is called, has been the fundamental architecture for Industrial Age business. Today, the serial chain of command is being superseded by the supply network, in which all companies involved in a product or service are simultaneously interconnected. Businesses today are moving to online supply networks, participating in online marketplaces, and expanding their use of networked systems to improve a host of business processes. New products and services are being created as a direct consequence of the networked world.

New products and services are being created as a direct consequence of the networked world.

It is no longer newsworthy to report that a large company has moved its purchasing operations online, but some new twists are worth mentioning. DaimlerChrysler, General Motors, and Ford Motor announced in 2000 that they would jointly develop the world's largest online marketplace to handle their purchasing of a quarter-trillion dollars' worth of parts annually. They expect that the increased competition among a larger pool of bidding suppliers will reduce costs by 10 percent, a significant savings. Since half the cost of a low- or mid-priced vehicle is parts, a $20,000 car could cost $1,000 less.[13]

Alcan, Inco, Noranda, and Barrick Gold are a few members of an international consortium that paid up to $10 million (US) each to join Quadrem, an online procurement market. Quadrem will help cut costs for explosives, chemicals, bulldozers, tires, computers, and other items by automating the buying process. For example, an online catalog would allow members to order products from thousands of suppliers from around the world.

Most B2B e-commerce technologies focus on automating ordering and fulfillment. But there is a largely untapped application that uses the Internet for what it does best: passing information among users. And new business clients want to be more collaborative with suppliers than just purchasing from them.

The new collaborative model of e-commerce integrates every aspect of product specification, design, production, marketing, and sales into a single workflow. For business collaborations, this interaction entails overcoming differences in computer languages and security systems among the participants. The process can be a lot of work and costly, particularly if integration with sourcing and channel management is required, but the results are well worth the effort and cost. As described above, XML and web services are greatly reducing the cost and the time needed for conversion.

The change from supply chains to supply networks transforms each participating company from a separate commercial entity into a larger virtual organization that has benefits for both clients and suppliers. John Cisco, CEO of Cisco Systems, notes, "In a virtual network organization you (a company or a government agency) do only what adds sustainable value. You outsource what others are better at, tying together applications to create the killer application which is the virtual network."[14]

Online Business Marketplaces

In just about every industry, the race is on to create Web marketplaces. Almost 1,000 online marketplaces have cropped up worldwide.[15] Some are aimed at consumers, but a greater number are for B2B transactions.

Almost 1,000 online marketplaces have cropped up worldwide.

Web marketplaces fall into three broad categories: online catalogs, auctions, and exchanges. The first aggregates and integrates the catalogs of all the suppliers in a given industry and puts the resulting meta-catalog online. For a catalog of marketplaces, B2BExchanges.com profiles an extensive database of Web marketplaces and exchanges.

The second marketplace category—the auction—provides mechanisms for negotiating prices. Sometimes these are conventional auctions set up to help the seller get the best price. Frequently they are reverse (Dutch) auctions, in which suppliers compete for contracts by bidding down the price.

Tradeout.com is an auction site that sells only surplus goods.[16] More than 10,000 companies have posted, sold, or bought goods on the Tradeout site. Dovebid, an auctioneer of used capital assets, has an online site with more than 200,000 items for sale. United Technologies Corporation, which makes Carrier air conditioners, Sikorsky helicopters, Pratt & Whitney engines, and other products, uses an independent auction site, Freemarkets.com, to save almost a billion dollars a year by consolidating its buying of items like cast-iron gears, electric motors, and molded plastics at the Internet auction site. United Technologies has received discounts of between 6 and 30 percent by moving its transactional processes online. Even consumer-to-consumer (C2C) auction markets such as eBay have expanded their activities to include B2C and B2B transactions because they are so numerous and popular.

The third category of marketplaces—the commodity exchange—deals in products or perishables such as energy (Altra Energy Technologies) or livestock (eMerge and CattleinfoNet).

Merrill Lynch estimates that total worldwide B2B e-commerce sales in 2003 will be $2.5 trillion (US), and about 20 percent of that ($500 billion) will be captured by Web marketplaces. That industry should generate earnings close to $25 billion a year.

The generality of Web marketplaces makes it easy to replicate this type of business for almost any imaginable product or service. There are now online markets for everything from surplus medical equipment sitting in hospital basements to excess electrical or water capacity at utility companies and unused patents sitting on a drug company's shelf.

Online Markets and the New Business Rules

Online marketplaces conform well to the new business rules. The first rule is "shift to an external focus." The new virtual organizations accomplish that in spades. They are composed of companies, each with its own agenda and business model, linked together for the purpose of fulfilling the needs of their clients. Clients deal with a single entity that can respond quickly to changing environments, re-forming itself as needed without the fixed and cumbersome infrastructure of older integrated company models.

The second rule is "give the client more input and control," and online marketplaces certainly provide this. In fact, the proliferation of online marketplaces has been driven by the new client's desire to control specifications more closely and participate in all stages of the transaction, including pre- and after-sale.

The third rule is "use client valuation for pricing." In this case, auctions are the optimal mechanism, since they replace the supplier-controlled business models such as list or catalog pricing and make products and services available at use-set competitive prices. Online auctions provide pricing that is totally client based.

The fourth rule is "motivate with EMOs." Here is an EMO chart of online business marketplaces:

EMO	Online Market	Traditional Market
Feeling Good	N/A	N/A
Feeling Comfortable/Secure	Medium	Medium
Doing Good	N/A	Some
Having Control/Choice	Very High	Medium

Feeling good is less of a factor for business markets than for consumer transactions. And the security and comfort level for online marketplaces is not particularly better than for traditional markets. As for doing good, there is some general benefit since moving the bulk of business to the Internet helps pay the cost of constructing and maintaining that infrastructure, which makes it more affordable to ordinary users throughout the world.

Online marketplaces provide the greatest pool of suppliers ever assembled.

The biggest EMO differential for B2B transactions is providing greater control and choice. Online marketplaces provide the greatest pool of suppliers ever assembled. In many cases, companies find themselves with a significant choice of suppliers for the first time, as they are no longer limited by geographic or territorial boundaries.

The fifth rule is "put yourself in your client's shoes." For most businesses, this happens as a consequence of using online marketplaces, since businesses tend to buy and sell in these markets, using their roles as both clients and suppliers as required.

Not-for-Profits and NGOs

Not all companies are incorporated for making profit. A large part of the economy is driven by not-for-profit and nongovernmental organizations (NGOs). These range from credit unions and pension funds, some of which manage billions of dollars of assets, to arts councils, trade associations, unions, and special-interest groups. The fundamental difference between these organizations and for-profit companies is that the former don't have shareholders and consequently can't distribute profits.

Aside from the fact that NGOs can't retain earnings (according to their charters and bylaws they must spend them), they succumb to the same forces as the for-profit sector. Whether a university or a hospital, all these organizations fit the three-tiered corporate model of acquiring resources as a client, performing a process, and providing goods and/or services as a supplier. All of them are more responsible and reactive to their clients than ever before.

Take trade unions, for example. The days when union bosses, like Jimmy Hoffa of the Teamsters Union, could operate their organizations like fiefdoms, using workers' union dues to feather their personal nests and agendas, are over. Union members now expect their executives to give them value for their union dues and to account for where the money goes. And union members can no longer be counted on to ratify agreements negotiated by their elected executives. They, like everyone else, have become new clients with new expectations.

Trade associations are another example of a not-for-profit organization. Some, like the Motion Picture Association of America (MPAA), are enormously powerful, influencing legislation and elections in order to get their members' agendas heard and acted upon. The MPAA's board, for example, includes the presidents of the Walt Disney Company, Sony Pictures, Metro-Goldwyn-Mayer, Paramount Pictures, Twentieth Century Fox, Universal Studios, and Warner Bros. Although MPAA is a not-for-profit association, each of its members is a formidable economic force, and together they exert enormous commercial power.

For many NGOs, members are also clients.

For many NGOs, members are also clients, an interesting twist because the company's clients also elect the board of directors. In this way, NGOs are the ultimate client-focused organizations because the clients directly control company policies and activities.

In all cases, not-for-profits can benefit from the same new business rules as other companies. For example, putting yourself in your client's shoes is a process that works well for NGOs. Patricia Seybold, a marketing consultant, suggests using "customer scenario mapping," a process by which an organization picks three to six scenarios for each area in which clients are experiencing problems and then designs solutions. She notes, "It's very simple, it's very tactical, and you can start doing it on Monday."[17]

Citizens

Citizens are clients of governments, the largest sector of suppliers. As suppliers, governments have a more complex role than companies do because a government's clients belong to several groups that are also stakeholders in the organization. Government includes both elected officials—the politicians—and government bureaucrats, called the public service in Canada and the civil service in the United States. Whereas politicians are mostly responsive to voting blocs, the bureaucracy must serve all citizens, businesses, and also politicians, whose demands sometimes conflict.

Citizens are demanding more accountability, more transparency, more information, more say, and quicker results. As Jason Bater, a U.K. taxpayer, says, "The federal government is my employee because I pay for its operation and existence; therefore, I would like to be included in more than a sixty-day campaign blitz.... Inform me, include me; let me know when you make a mistake; tell me why and what is being done about it; we (the government and the people) have a symbiotic relationship; we need each other to exist, so let us start working together."[18]

It is no longer acceptable for governments to provide faceless services in a "we know what's best for you so don't bother us about the details" manner. Citizens want to hold elected officials and individuals in the public services responsible for their activities, and they want to be informed of and involved in many aspects of policy implementation.

Government has a different role than business does because its stakeholders and clients are everyone. Consequently, in order for government to serve its clients, it must operate for the common good, concentrating on the third EMO—doing good—and in the process deliver the second EMO—making people feel secure.

Despite the insistence by social democrats that government has no business operating as a business, most citizens today believe that government bureaucracy should indeed operate in a businesslike manner, with the same sort of efficiency, outcome metrics, and responsibility to stakeholders that we observe in the private sector.

Elected officials are like a board of directors, to be removed and replaced when shareholder value is insufficiently realized.

The parallel is fairly straightforward. Elected officials are like a board of directors, to be removed and replaced when shareholder value is insufficiently realized. Since the shareholders (citizens) in this instance are also the clients, it is much more difficult to satisfy all of them, particularly when the deliverables are as diverse as security (armies, police), international trade relations, education, health care, and assistance to the disadvantaged. Nonetheless, democratic governments have shown tremendous flexibility in reacting to the changing times, re-engineering their operations to meet the demands of their citizen new clients almost as quickly as the business community does.

Moving Government Online

Like businesses, governments have moved their operations online. And their operations are big business. In the United States, federal procurement totals over $200 billion annually, dealing with 300,000 separate suppliers. Federal benefits programs transfer $50 billion annually through Electronic Benefit Transfer (EBT) to 50 million beneficiaries.

Since government does big business, it is natural to apply the tools and measurements of business to government. An example is measuring client satisfaction.

Politicians are increasingly using business methods, such as focus groups, question-naires, and data mining, to measure the level of voter satisfaction with the government's performance.

Portland, Oregon, is a city in which the elected officials treat their residents like new clients. Vera Katz, mayor since 1993, says,

> The best way to find out how well we're serving our customers—the citizens of Portland—is to ask them. ... we've mailed a survey to almost 10,000 citizens, asking them ... the following questions: Do you feel safe walking at night in your neighborhood, in your parks, in your downtown? Are the streets clean enough? What do you think of the city's speed limits? ... We benchmark those results against those of six other cities. And if we're not doing as well as those cities, we try to find out what they're doing that we're not.[19]

Not everyone believes that government serves its client citizens best by operating like a business. Elaine Bernard, executive director of the Harvard Trade Union Program, notes, "In this age of reinventing government there is a tendency to ... substitute markets and market competition for democratic decision-making. In a democracy, it's 'one person, one vote'.... But in the marketplace, it's 'one dollar, one vote.'"[20]

Not everyone believes that government serves its client citizens best by operating like a business.

It doesn't matter whether your political leanings are to the right (biased toward business) or the left (biased toward social programs). All citizens agree that government must be more responsive to its clients than ever before.

Changing Politics

Political affiliation used to be part of a family's culture and was loyally passed from generation to generation. The working classes voted for labor parties and the wealthy voted conservative. As the twentieth century created more mobile and less class-conscious populations in the industrialized democratic world, that loyalty and certainty of party affiliation waned. Most important, as transactions have increasingly become part of everyday life, political parties have turned to the supplier–client model.

In the new model, voters shop for the best deal: the party and candidate that can deliver the best value proposition, including the EMOs. The new citizen-as-client is well informed and has many expectations that need to be fulfilled, including

- *value for tax dollars:* efficient government that delivers a credible value proposition
- *transparent operation:* easy public access to all documents related to government programs and operations
- *two-way communication:* direct communication between citizens and those who set and implement policies
- *performance evaluations:* citizen input into officials' metrics for performance and governmental accountability
- *less bureaucracy and more online automation:* more convenient, online procedures for citizen–government transactions such as business matters, motor licensing, tax returns, and payment for government services
- *more personalized service:* one-to-one interaction for matters that are not routine, such as dealing with complaints
- *instant response:* Internet-like time frames, not traditional snail's pace government response
- *single-point service:* service provided by one appropriate, accountable department, rather than officials passing the buck from department to department

These expectations can be captured by a single thought: Government systems should be there for the citizens, not the other way around. Evidence of this new client attitude is cropping up throughout all levels of government today. The U.S. Office of Electronic Government is charged with using technology to enhance access to and delivery of information and services to citizens, business partners, employees, agencies, and government entities. The office states its objectives as

- deliver customer-centric services rather than agency-centric processes
- interoperate across government and with industry partners
- provide access to government services and information via government-wide portals organized around the needs of communities of customers
- build strong privacy protection, confidentiality, and trust
- adopt commercial products, practices, and standards
- foster strong inter-agency, inter-organization, and cross-sector leadership to promote the sharing of information and leading practices[21]

Comparing the EMOs of traditional versus online government yields the following chart.

EMO	Traditional Government	Online Government
Feeling Good	Medium-Low	Medium-High
Feeling Comfortable/Secure	Medium-High	Medium-High
Doing Good	High	High
Having Control/Choice	Low	High

The second and third EMOs—feeling comfortable and doing good—are more or less even for both types of government. The first—feeling good—is more prevalent with online access because many more citizens have the relatively pleasant experience of communicating with their government and getting a reply. The fourth EMO is the biggest differentiator, because users have more choice in where they can access government (at any computer) and when (any time), and they are much more knowledgeable about their options as a result of accessing government websites.

Still, the largest factors for government are that the online services are less expensive and more citizen-focused, a double bonus that satisfies the new business rules of focusing externally on the client. Governments, like businesses, are making strides to redefine and then re-engineer the way they operate. Those governments that are not doing so are finding that they pay the price at election time.

The governments of Alberta and Ontario were defeated in the 1990s by opposition parties (led by Ralph Klein and Mike Harris, respectively) whose platforms were based on empowering ordinary citizens and re-engineering government by adopting commercial practices and standards. Like the private sector, these governments cut staff and spending. They implemented e-government services and paid more attention to citizen polls than to the advice of their bureaucrats. Both governments were elected for successive terms.

Just as the Web has made competitive information available about suppliers and services, it has also made it much easier for citizens to evaluate how their governments perform in comparison with other municipalities, counties, provinces, states, countries, and trading blocs.

Because voters have come to discount election promises, EMOs figure even more prominently in elections than they do in transactions. How comfortable do you feel with the candidates? How closely will they heed your advice (client control)? How much good will they do? And how good do they make you feel? The four

EMOs figure even more prominently in elections than they do in transactions.

EMOs are all at work here. Candidates who satisfy the EMOs attract votes, even from those who might normally vote for another party.

In the November 2000 Canadian federal election, the Canadian Alliance party lost in key sections of the country because voters did not trust its leader, Stockwell Day. Voters were concerned that his religious and ideological beliefs would override the will of the people once he was elected. The incumbent, Jean Chrétien, won in a landslide, largely because he was seen as a populist who could take the temperature of the public and express it in public policy.

Citizen-to-Citizen Communication

One of the recent revelations for government has been that citizen-to-citizen (C2C—a form of P2P) communications can be more effective, more trusted, and less costly than communications from the government to its citizens. Steven Clift, chairman of the Minnesota e-democracy forum, notes, "Many people look at the crisis in government as a disconnect between government and citizens. The [larger] problem is that citizens are disconnected from one another.... How often do government web sites encourage you to interact with others interested in the same issue?"[22]

In 1999, I presented a report on connected communities to the Gorbachev Foundation's Conference on Technology and Democracy at Northeastern University in Boston. Graham Allan, then the whip for Tony Blair's government in the U.K., was among the world leaders who participated. He spoke about the tensions in Northern Ireland and the difficulty of crafting a peaceful solution between the antagonists, who have been living side by side but within two solitudes for so long. Catholics and Protestants each have their own radio, television, and newspaper media that cater to their different political perspectives. What was missing was a forum in which citizens from both sides might share their perspectives and experiences.

A breakthrough came when one of the local radio stations decided to do a series of phone-in talk shows on the subject of bereaved mothers who had lost children to the conflict. The station advertised in both Protestant and Catholic communities, and the programs took calls from people on both sides of the conflict. The programs attracted a broad audience, and so the government ran focus groups to determine whether public opinion was affected by the broadcasts. They found that the radio programs had a large and positive influence on listeners' tolerance for the other side's positions, that they lowered tensions, and that they provided a better environment for a peaceful solution.

In this example, government recognized that technology could promote good government by enabling C2C rather than G2C (government-to-citizen) communications. One of the results was the government's support for online citizen discussion groups.

Direct Democracy

Direct democracy allows each citizen to vote directly on issues of importance. As the Internet has gained penetration, offering a new tool for easy and inexpensive voter input, direct democracy has gained favor. Direct democracy provides a new, nontraditional alternative to the representative government we grew up with. It gives citizens the ability to directly comment on and influence legislation, greatly empowering the electorate at the expense of elected officials. It exemplifies the new client influence on voters.

For example, the nonprofit OpenDemocracy online forum promotes discourse by presenting a variety of ideologically clashing voices. Their "city and country" thread is co-edited by Roger Scruton, associated with the intellectual right, and Ken Worpole, a left-wing urban thinker. Paul Hilder, senior editor, believes the site provides a "fair space in an unfair world."[23] The Open Democracy Forum on Globalization has become a must-read in Britain. Many in the news media believe that its coverage of September 11 was the best and most informed discussion of the issues, in the tradition of the debates in Paris following July 14, 1789.

Websites that present multiple points of view have become very popular, as illustrated by the proliferation of public diaries, or "blogs," a contraction for the word *weblogs*. The name also refers to the technology available at www.blogger.com, which offers "push-button publishing for the people." Blogs are not-for-profit websites, maintained by concerned and committed individuals who believe the public deserves objective and balanced opinions. Statistics are hard to come by, but some estimate that as many as a million active bloggers are ranting and fuming on issues that range from the local to the global.

Some estimate that as many as a million active bloggers are ranting and fuming on issues that range from the local to the global.

In many states, voters can cast their ballots for individual pieces of legislation. This tactic allows politicians to avoid taking the heat on such contentious issues as the legalization of marijuana, raising taxes, and rights to life, since the only recorded votes are by citizens, not their representatives. On the negative side, many are concerned about complex issues being decided by ordinary people without the benefit of expert and unbiased (bureaucratic) advice and without the financial or time resources necessary for in-depth analysis. Those concerns may become less serious as voters become more informed by more up-to-date and in-depth information about complex issues.

The EMOs for direct government stack up strongly in its favor when compared with the representative government we have today. Enabling voters to control the outcome of individual pieces of legislation and government policies makes them feel much better about their role in government and certainly empowers them with more choice and control.

EMO	Representative Government	Direct Government
Feeling Good	Medium-Low	High
Feeling Comfortable/Secure	Medium-High	Medium-High
Doing Good	High	High
Having Control/Choice	Low	High

In 2000, the U.S. National Science Foundation sponsored the Internet Policy Institute e-Voting Workshop, with representatives from the United Nations, Switzerland, Denmark, Canada, and the United States (see www.netvoting.org). The workshop sought to identify the critical issues related to online voting. Not surprisingly, most bureaucrats and elected officials were against direct democracy, since it would decrease their powers. A 2001 U.S. survey indicates that senior civil servants and members of Congress doubt that Americans know enough about important issues to form intelligent opinions.[24]

E-Democracy

While direct democracy has its critics, so-called e-democracy is almost universally supported. E-democracy is simply the use of online technology and channels to make government more efficient, responsive, and transparent. Most governments have been moving their information stores, communications, application forms, financial transactions, and other activities online. The results dramatically support the claimed advantages. When governments move online, the volume of communication from companies and citizens increases about tenfold (email versus telephone and letters), while the cost of providing the communication decreases.

Here are some examples of government services moving online:

- The United States Patent and Trademark Office online search system, available at www.uspto.gov, enables anyone with an Internet browser to search and retrieve more than 2.6 million pending, registered, abandoned, canceled, or expired trademark records. This is the same database and search system used by the Patent and Trademark Office's examining attorneys.
- Government portals in Canada (www.canada.gc.ca), the U.K. (ukonline.gov.uk), and the United States (FirstGov.gov) provide single entry points to millions of pages of government information, services, and communications.
- The Canadian government business portal (www.businessgateway.ca) helps businesses move to e-commerce. The U.S. *E-Government Act* of 2001 establishes a federal chief information officer to promote e-government and implement government-wide information policy, improve on the centralized online portal, establish an online national library, and require federal courts to post opinions online. In the U.K., the Small Business Service website (www.sbs.gov.uk) delivers information and support to the country's 4 million entrepreneurs.

Citizens are beginning to take control of their governments from bureaucrats and politicians.

- Provincial, state, and local websites let individuals and businesses find information on a wide variety of topics, such as registration (voter, business, property, pets), parks, and trash removal. Local property taxes and parking tickets can be paid on websites such as www.govworks.com or www.ezgov.com.

With overwhelmingly positive feedback from citizens–clients, e-government is here to stay. Access to government information and services is much quicker and easier, and, perhaps most significantly, citizens are beginning to take control of their governments from bureaucrats and politicians.

Taxation

One of the most serious ramifications of the Information Age infrastructure affects taxation, the lubricant without which government could not operate. An essential requirement for taxation is territorial exclusivity, since municipal, provincial (or state), and federal governments can tax only those in their jurisdiction. But the Information Age networks are pan-national, making it difficult or impossible for governments to collect taxes when servers are outside their jurisdiction. When you go to a movie, your ticket price includes provincial (or state) and federal taxes, as well as a content fee levied by a national music copyright collective (SOCAN in Canada). When you watch a movie that has been streamed to your computer online, there is not yet a mechanism for collecting these taxes. The result is a growing fear within governments that their ability to levy duties, sales taxes, and income taxes is fundamentally at risk.

They have reason to be concerned. The methods governments use to monitor and police tax evasion are all based on being able to identify and verify taxpayers and their transactions. They do this by tracking the transport and points of sale of physical products at borders, truck and train depots, warehouses, and retail stores. With online sales, many of these checkpoints are bypassed, particularly when goods and services can be delivered online.

When information, entertainment, or computer software is the product, it is difficult or impossible to capture a transaction in order to apply local taxes because the product can be delivered through a website or as an email attachment. Short of monitoring everyone's email and website activity, which would be a gross invasion of privacy, governments have no way of knowing that a transaction has taken place. And if the territory of the supplier is outside the jurisdiction of the government levying the tax, the supplier may not be doing anything illegal by failing to charge the tax.

For example, a business supply network may include programmers in India or the Soviet Union, whose work is delivered online as computer files. It is unclear how the tax would be captured and by which governments, if any.

An internal document titled "Impact of E-Commerce on the Canadian Tax Base" was obtained through access-to-information rules by Ottawa researcher Ken Rubin. The report notes that "these requirements are increasingly difficult to implement given the nature of the Internet."[25]

The Digital Age is fundamentally changing the nature of governing.

One of the biggest challenges for the international community of nations is to come up with a new method for capturing the value of online transactions as a substitute for the older territorial model, taking into account the pan-nationality of online transactions while ensuring that tax is charged and paid in appropriate jurisdictions. In the interim, there is likely to be chaos as governments realize that their treasured income sources are eroding.

The Digital Age is fundamentally changing the nature of governing, strongly supporting the greater involvement and informing of citizens. Many believe it will prove to be the magic bullet that puts an end to the trend of citizens' apathy and lack of trust in elected officials that has accompanied the Industrial Age in Western democracies.

Students

Education is the second-largest sector of the economy, even larger than the automotive or communications sectors. It is about to undergo an upheaval that will have far-reaching consequences in every aspect of our lives.

In postsecondary education, the following changes are taking place:

- Student fees are rising steadily as public subsidies are falling.
- Online courses and degrees are giving students new options for accreditation.
- Campuses are increasingly accepting advertising and corporate sponsorships to help make ends meet.
- Universal education is diminishing the cachet of postsecondary education.
- Students' desire for knowledge is becoming less important to their desire for employment.

As a result, students are increasingly viewing educational institutions as commercial service suppliers, asking, "What value am I getting for my money?" These changes are bringing a client–supplier context to education that is different from the historical academic context.

Until the nineteenth century, education was considered a luxury. It was not expected that ordinary people would be able to read and write. As democracies began to flourish and a middle class of businesspeople expanded, the idea of universal, publicly funded education took hold. Universal education meant that schools began to serve society as a whole, increasing per capita productivity and gross national products. Thus the client of education was no longer the student; instead, it was the general public, as represented by government, who was footing the bill.

But governments do not agree on what constitutes good value for educational dollars. Left-of-center governments measure success by the increased attendance by underrepresented groups—racial and ethnic minorities, women, and people with physical challenges. Right-of-center governments focus on how well graduates' skills match the needs of industry. Governments in the political center believe that education should prepare graduates to become informed and contributing members of society. This last outcome is the most difficult to measure.

Work and Study

Today, the new client is taking control of the educational system from government. Students' desire for greater choice and control—the fourth EMO—has become a driving force in education. And the path students are increasingly choosing in high-school and postsecondary education is work-study. These programs are now entrenched at all levels of education, allowing high-school students to get a sense of what it's like to work in a particular field and giving postsecondary students on-the-job experience while allowing their industrial sponsors to evaluate them as prospective employees.

Work-study programs are moving from the workplace back into traditional school settings as well. Companies are becoming directly involved in training students in public schools. For example, Cisco Systems, a large manufacturer of computer and Internet networking equipment, has 5,000 Cisco Network academies throughout the United States, with 150,000 students enrolled. Most of the courses are part of high-school and college curricula.

Companies are becoming directly involved in training students in public schools.

In 1997, Cisco was finding it difficult to make sales of its products to schools that had neither the in-house expertise to maintain them nor the cash to hire professionals. So Cisco developed training programs for teachers, staff, and eventually students, an excellent example of client-focused business management.

At Eastern Regional High School in Voorhees, Pennsylvania, about a dozen students enroll for the two-year course. They learn how to set up a network of computers and get it up and running on the Internet. They learn what equipment they need, how to interface it with the phone company, and how to program network switches and routers.

The Cisco curriculum includes traditional instruction, an interactive website with movies, graphics, and sound, and experience in a computer lab. Teachers agree that these courses connect with some students who are difficult to reach with traditional classroom-only techniques.

There are many benefits to this program. The industry gets trained employees, of which there is a shortage; the students are likely to use Cisco products because they know them; and these inner-city kids will be able to earn salaries of $30,000 to $50,000 (US) after passing a rigorous certification test. A benefit for schools is that these students help to operate the schools' computers and networks. They are usually paid minimum wages for this work, saving the schools a bundle and earning the students extra pocket cash. The program was started because schools lacked trained computer and network technicians.

The EMOs are positive for work-study programs compared with traditional schooling. Students generally feel better about themselves because they can be functional and productive in society, a benefit that is generally absent from traditional schooling. They feel much more secure because their employment prospects are greatly improved and this is, for most, the driving motivation for getting an education. Although their choices for industrial placement are limited, they still have more choice over their educational path than in the traditional system.

EMO	Traditional Schools	Work–Study Programs
Feeling Good	Medium	Medium-High
Feeling Comfortable/Secure	Medium-Low	High
Doing Good	Medium-High	Medium-High
Having Control/Choice	Low	Medium

There are some concerns about this approach, however, not the least of which is bringing captive marketing into a publicly funded school environment. Another worry is that these kids may not go to university. Some of them can earn up to $60,000 (US) within a few years of certification, so why would they move on to postsecondary education? Young network techies with skills such as website programming and network maintenance are in demand, even after the dot.com meltdown. The result is that many teenagers do skip college or at least defer it.

There is no simple answer to these concerns, and much depends on the individual students and their circumstances. One perspective is that university may not be the best option for some of these students, at least for the time being. Other students may not wish to have their earnings capped, however, so they move on to higher education and a much greater depth of knowledge beyond their certification.

Students might argue that Michael Dell, the most successful computer manufacturer, and Bill Gates, the most successful businessman of the century, don't have university degrees. In fact, a significant number of successful startup companies are

Michael Dell, the most successful computer manufacturer, and Bill Gates, the most successful businessman of the century, don't have university degrees.

founded by entrepreneurs who enroll in college or university, get enough exposure to the terrain to come up with an idea for a missing product or service, and then quit to pursue their business ambition.

Schools without Campuses

Another avenue of learning is correspondence courses and their modern equivalents. The first correspondence courses were by mail. Then came radio courses, and after that educational television. Audio and videotape materials followed, and then online courses, which add the crucial element of interactivity. Online learning materials are very client focused because they allow students to

- access learning at convenient places (at home, at a library, at work)
- access learning at convenient times, often before and after traditional school hours
- repeat sections that cause them difficulty as often as needed, without the stigma of falling behind the rest of the class
- skip quickly through material that comes easily to them
- test themselves frequently so they can get a sense of their strengths and weaknesses

The growing popularity of non-campus-based institutions is a testament to many students' need to learn wherever and whenever they are available. Enrollment in distance-education courses was growing at a remarkable rate in the late 1990s, doubling every twenty-four months or so.

The Open University, Britain's largest postsecondary institute, is an example of a correspondence- and television-based university migrating online. Spread over thirty landscaped acres in a prefabricated city forty-five minutes from London, the university is home to 1,000 faculty members who do research and prepare course materials for more than 100,000 students. BBC staff members produce accompanying television programs, videos, and CD-ROMs, which are divided into thick packets and then mailed to students. As the courses move online, interactivity is incorporated. The hope is that online mediation will compensate for a lack of direct student-to-mentor contact by offering greater access to tutors through video conferencing, chat, and email than a student would typically have on a campus.

There are no classrooms and no students on this campus. Yet the Open University has, since 1971, provided off-site education to more than 2 million students. In

Britain, an off-campus student is likely to be someone who, because of social or economic circumstances, is not well served by the British university system.

Athabaska University calls itself Canada's Open University. Established in 1970 as a virtual university for distance education, it has 17,000 students. Athabaska offers both undergraduate and graduate degrees, and its MBA program is rated third in the country, close on the heels of Queen's University and the Richard Ivey School of Business at the University of Western Ontario. Athabaska delivers course materials through hard-copy and electronic course kits, CD-ROMs, televised lectures, Internet materials, email, chat rooms, and electronically connected team assignments with fellow students located across the country. Athabaska University is located in Canada's sparsely populated North and is a magnet for those who do not live near a large university campus.

Satellite Programs

Many traditional universities and colleges are opening satellite campuses in the heart of urban business areas so that students who work can be easily served. York University has the Miles S. Nadal Centre near the Toronto Stock Exchange, and Simon Fraser University has the Harbour Centre campus in downtown Vancouver. These campuses cater to clients who are part of the booming adult student market.

The shift to the new economy requires higher levels of education and is sending adults back to school in record numbers. By holding night and weekend classes and offering accelerated degree programs with credit for "life experience," the institutions sell convenience to adults trying to juggle work, family, and learning responsibilities. Adult programs are typically money-makers for schools because they cost less to run than undergraduate programs. They don't require dormitory living accommodations, athletic facilities, counseling departments, or other services. And unlike fresh-from-high-school students, adults usually pay full tuition, with their employers frequently picking up most or all of the tab. Scholarship funds are generally untapped by this market, making more funds available for young students in need.

Trade unions have long been involved in upgrading the skills of their members. Now, they are moving into more general fields of learning. For workers who belong to a union, the motivations and resources are different, but their impact on the educational system is the same: They cause educational institutions to redesign their curricula and delivery systems. For example, seventeen universities and colleges are participating in the United Auto Workers–Ford University Online program that allows UAW members to work full time while earning a certificate or post-graduate

As tuition rises, students are becoming more discriminating about where they buy their education and what they get for their money.

degree or just taking a course or two. The distance education is provided through a variety of delivery channels, including online and CD-ROM technology (see www.uawford.com).

As tuition rises, students are becoming more discriminating about where they buy their education and what they get for their money. The new student-as-consumer is beginning to compare value from a larger number of educational choices.

Kindergarten to Grade 12

For primary and secondary schools, the institutional structure is quite different but the trend is the same. The suppliers of education—schools, teachers, administrators, and school boards—are losing power to clients of the educational system. Even in these lower grades, clients want more control (the fourth EMO), but in this case the clients are students' parents. K–12 educational systems are also becoming more accountable. Many jurisdictions have introduced mandatory professional development for teachers, with periodic recertification, teacher evaluations by parents, and standard teacher testing.

Parents want to see evidence that student achievement is improving, particularly in literacy and numeracy. They want more comprehensible report cards with frank rankings of under- and overachievement, a more rigorous curriculum, and standardized testing to give them feedback about how their children are progressing and where they need to improve.

Private and Charter Schools

Governments are moving toward more diversity and privatization of K–12 schools. The result will be a much less uniform educational system, one that is more tailored to the students' individual needs and capabilities.

Private schools tend to differentiate themselves to serve niche markets. Some are known for helping students who are having a tough time qualifying for university, some are focused on the arts, and some stress military-style discipline. They generally offer students more course variety, bringing greater opportunities for teachers who have qualifications outside the core curricula, such as special skills in the arts and sports.

Charter schools are a good example of the new client focus in education. These operate with freedom from many of the regulations that apply to traditional public schools. The "charter" establishing each such school is a performance contract with its clients, detailing the school's mission, program, goals, student body, and methods of assessment. The length of time for which charters are granted varies, but most are for three to five years. At the end of the term, the entity granting the charter decides whether to renew the school's contract.

The term "charter" is said to have originated in the 1970s when New England educator Ray Budde suggested that small groups of teachers be given contracts or "charters" by their local school boards to explore new approaches. Albert Shanker, former president of the American Federation of Teachers, then publicized the idea, suggesting that local boards could charter an entire school with union and teacher approval. In the late 1980s Philadelphia started a number of schools-within-schools and called them charters.

Charter schools operate independently from school boards and often focus on alternative philosophies of teaching and specialization, such as academic achievement, the arts, business, sports, or greater discipline. They differ from "alternative schools" in that their mandate is quantified in a contract that obligates them to produce measurable outcomes. They are accountable to their chartering entity—usually a state, province, district, or school board—only when their charter is up for renewal. In return for this accountability, they receive greater autonomy.

For example, High Tech High, a San Diego charter school, receives public education funds but does not have to comply with many of the regulations normally attached to such funding. Its impetus came from high-tech business executives who were looking for a way to solve their labor shortage. The school opened in September 2000 with 200 ninth- and tenth-grade students selected through a lottery from a pool of 1,000 applicants.

High Tech High students divide their day into halves, one half focusing on independent work, another stressing group work. There are no traditional classes. Students have their own workstations, similar to those in the workplace. The school has also recruited local engineers to work with students in the school and has provided students with digital portfolios so they can display their work online or on a CD-ROM.

The school provides a broad-based education and uses technology to tie it together. Students work independently and in groups on projects based on a theme set at the beginning of the school year. Over one summer, all students were required to read the book *Guns, Germs and Steel* by Jared Diamond, which explores why some civilizations developed at different rates than

Students have their own workstations, similar to those in the workplace.

others. The students then used Diamond's thesis as a framework for studying the year's theme of the history and power of human communication.

Charter schools, originally a U.S. phenomenon, have been viewed with caution in Canada, a country where citizens jealously guard their universal access to health and education. Yet attitudes in Canada are changing as well. A *National Post* survey of more than 500 parents found that 71 percent of Canadian parents want to have the choice of sending their children to charter schools.[26]

New Solutions

As parents' frustration with the lack of accountability for educational spending has peaked, new clients have become empowered and institutions have become disintermediated. Consequently, alternative modes of delivering education are becoming popular, and learners, the clients, are taking control of both the delivery and evaluation of their education.

As learners become the focus of education, we are witnessing the birth of a much more diverse educational system that will satisfy more varied interests than any single institution could represent. And all the new educational options, from self-paced interactive study to charter schools, satisfy the EMO of providing students with more choice and control.

Accountability to clients of the educational system—students and their parents—is now the number-one issue for boards of K–12 schools, colleges, and universities.

Accountability to clients of the educational system—students and their parents—is now the number-one issue for boards of K–12 schools, colleges, and universities. Government funders are putting pressure on teachers and administrators to allow students and parents greater influence over curricular and extra-curricular activities.

The educational systems of the twenty-first century are likely to offer more choices in institutional, home, and on-the-job education than the systems in place today. In fact, many of these options are available now in selected areas, generally with good outcomes, although the massive traditional educational infrastructure has yet to come to terms with them. The changes are inevitable because they are driven by the most important part of the educational system—the clients.

Patients

The cost of health care in the developed world has spiraled out of control over the past decade. It doesn't matter if you live in Canada, where the universal public health care system has become too costly, the United States, where the private sector has proven to be even more costly, or the United Kingdom, where the parallel private and public systems together fail to provide adequate service. Health care costs too much and delivers too little. Most alarming, there appears to be no end in sight for the escalation as technologies such as MRI and patented drugs raise the bar for what patients expect—unlimited access to the best that modern medicine has to offer. It is difficult to find anyone who is satisfied with health care. Professionals (nurses, radiologists, doctors), hospitals, private and government plans, and patients are all under siege.

Patient-Controlled Care

Some basic aspects of modern medicine need to be examined and understood if better solutions are to be found. First of all, health care has been focused on and controlled by those who supply it (hospitals, health professionals, health plans) instead of those who receive it (patients). Consequently, when something goes wrong with us or with a loved one, we feel particularly helpless and left out at the very time when we are most motivated to be of assistance.

It is time that patients take control of the health care system and start looking out for themselves. Doing so will encourage them to spend their own time and resources to maintain and improve their health, saving the cost to the health care system; to be more satisfied with care; and to be less likely to overuse or abuse the system, since they will be part of it.

Consider that when you check into a hospital, even in the emergency room, the procedures have been designed to accommodate the institution and the health care professionals. Hospital administrators design procedures to be cost effective and to minimize their legal liability. Doctors design procedures to fit into their rotational shifts and to train student interns. Nurses design them to keep a patient's pesky friends and relatives from interfering with the health care team, and so on.

Let's take a look at the EMOs for health care:

EMO	Health Care
Feeling Good	Low
Feeling Comfortable/Secure	Low
Doing Good	Medium-High
Having Control/Choice	Medium-Low

Generally, the EMOs for a patient in the current system are low. Patients don't generally feel good about the level of service they receive; they don't feel in control; and they don't feel comfortable. Overall, the health care systems do good, improving average lifespans and treating many illnesses that were not formerly treatable. That's one out of four, a failing grade. Interactions with the health care system generally leave a patient in a bad frame of mind. And we know that one of the largest determiners of successful treatment is the patient's attitude and frame of mind.

Like companies, institutions in the health care system need to approach their patients as new clients. Once a month, say, top-level health care administrators should test a different aspect of their organization by posing as a patient, implementing the fifth new business rule: Put yourself in your client's shoes. They should test their organization's performance on a weekend and at peak hours. Chances are they will be reminded of the other meaning of patient!

Patients are upset with doctors and clinics that book appointments, only to make the patients wait for hours in a germ-filled room with a lot of sick people.

Speaking of low EMOs, many patients are upset with doctors and clinics that book appointments, only to make the patients wait for hours in a germ-filled room with a lot of sick people. What's the point of having an appointment? Is the doctor overbooking to make certain that every available minute of her time is billable? What about the patient's time?

Fortunately, as in every other sector of the economy, things are changing in health care. As patients become more demanding, alternatives are cropping up that bode better for the future. The transitions will be as tough as in other industries, but the outcome will be a system that is much improved and more responsive to patients.

Some of the biggest changes in health care are being enabled by the Internet (surprise!). This channel of information and assistance is now available to most patients. With patients and suppliers connected online, the benefits are enormous. For example, in selected areas where health care suppliers are online, patients can

- book appointments with doctors and preregister at hospitals online
- store their health records
- track their personal health histories
- get advice on how to maximize their genetic legacy
- decide whether or not they need to visit a doctor or facility and, if so, which one
- be reminded to take their medication on time

- keep track of all the interactions among their medications
- communicate directly with health care professionals from home
- communicate with others who share their health condition and find out how others cope[27]
- receive medical information and, in some cases, medical assistance at their home or workplace

The Internet encourages patients' active participation in matters related to their own health. It offers at least 17,000 health care sites, which more than 40 million adults access today. In fact, almost half of all online consumers access the Internet for health information.[28]

Informed Patients

One result of greater Internet usage is that patients today are much more informed about general health matters and about their own conditions. It is not uncommon for patients to arrive at their doctors' offices carrying possible diagnoses downloaded from websites such as Healtheon/WebMD or the AOL Health Web Channel. In addition, people with Internet access can obtain information about their health care plans, find doctors, and in some cases submit claims for fee reimbursements. Doctors, too, are increasing their use of the Internet as a source of information on the latest in medical research.

Doctors, too, are increasing their use of the Internet as a source of information on the latest in medical research.

Having access to your personal health records is one of the most important means of taking control of your health care. It seems absurd that the confidentiality of health records allows all sorts of medical professionals to have access to patients' personal information, while the patients themselves are generally kept in the dark and allowed only brief glimpses of information by health care gatekeepers.

Almost everyone has had blood and urine tests as part of a physical exam. The results are usually available within a day or two to doctors and clinics, but patients have to wait weeks or sometimes months for an appointment with their health care professional to find out and discuss the results. While it's true that patients don't always have the knowledge and experience to interpret this information, many of them do, and others want to become more informed about the details of their body's functioning. Common indicators such as levels of blood sugar and cholesterol (high and low density) are easy to track and can be adjusted by changing diet and lifestyle.

Most patients could monitor these levels to make appropriate adjustments before arranging for follow-up visits to their physicians.

But whether or not you think patients should take health care into their own hands, surely they should have access to their own records. Patients who want to change doctors or clinics have to arrange for their records to be forwarded, and they are never informed when they are sent or when they are received.

All this is about to change as patients begin take control over their own health. One option is a website called PersonalMD.com. It features medical record management and enables members to store and retrieve personal medical information, including paper-based records such as EKGs, lab results, and X-ray reports, in a safe and secure manner. All patient records are stored in a single confidential file that can be accessed via the Internet or faxed anywhere in the world. Users of the service authorize physicians, clinics, and hospitals to access their medical records, and patients carry a card that provides access to the data in an emergency. All patient records, from information about allergies and doctor visits to actual EKGs, can be entered in this confidential file. Emergency room physicians welcome the centralized information file and agree that this feature can save lives.

Sites like PersonalMD.com use current privacy standards, such as the Health on the Net (HON) Code of Ethical Guidelines, which guarantee confidentiality. Patient information is encrypted online and requires an authorized password for access.

Family Participation

Sometimes the clients of the health system are not just patients but also their families. When a close relative becomes incapacitated by a stroke, coma, mental illness, or other affliction that makes it impossible for the patient to make a rational decision about care, relatives are called upon to make decisions on their behalf. These decisions are the most agonizing that we ever face, because we have not been trained in the ethics of life and death, particularly when they affect those with whom we have strong emotional ties.

I recall vividly when my mother-in-law had a stroke. She was rushed to the hospital, and my wife and I waited nervously for the diagnosis. A doctor finally told us that the damage to her brain was severe, that she would be at least partially paralyzed, and that she had been placed on life support. Then he asked us a question for which we were totally unprepared: "Given the probable quality of her life after this and her age and her condition, we question whether life support should be maintained. What are your wishes?"

We were given a few minutes to think before deciding whether she should live or die. Her sister arrived just then and we included her in the deliberation. Brenda's mom was in her eighties but had led a very independent and full life before the stroke. On the other hand, her sister reminded us that their father had been incapacitated by a stroke, and, at the time, Sally had said she would rather be dead than require constant care.

It was agonizing because there was no clear right or wrong decision to be made and the consequence of our decision would be a person's life. We decided to keep her alive, and we bought a large house with room for her and a caregiver to live with us. Now, three years later, she has regained most of her former mental capability and has begun to paint beautiful pictures. Although the left side of her body is paralyzed, she speaks well and has enjoyed hundreds of hours playing with her great-grandchildren.

Millions of others have to make the same types of decisions every year. A client-focused health system should provide more assistance to them. "The minute I put my signature on the document to put my father on life support, I was questioning it," said Marilyn Schwilm, a bartender in Pittsburgh. "Was it the right decision? Was it what Dad would want? We weren't equipped to make those decisions, and the doctors, as good as they were, didn't help us make them."[29]

Schwilm and others are turning to nontraditional sources for help at times like these, including their computers. Schwilm used a computer program called LifePath, which walks users through decision-making processes similar to those that business executives use, except the issues to be decided are life and death. LifePath helps users rank factors that are most important to them with respect to their own deaths or the deaths of family members. The program helped Schwilm and her sister verbalize the complex issues that were running through their minds. The family finally decided to remove life support. There are other resources available for help in making these decisions, including a CD-ROM called *Completing a Life* and a website (www.completingalife.msu.edu) created by a Michigan university and a hospital.

Dr. Ira Byock, former president of the American Academy of Hospice and Palliative Medicine and author of *Dying Well: The Prospect for Growth at the End of Life,* says, "It's a highly personalized and inherently relevant way for people to learn about end-of-life decisions because computers and CD-ROM's allow them to go where they are interested, and they can be used in the privacy of the home." But computer programs alone are not enough, Dr. Byock notes, adding, "It is a tool to be used with other tools, like discussions between doctor and patient and written material."[30]

When you or someone close to you becomes ill, there's a feeling of helplessness.

The search for cures to intractable illnesses has been the bailiwick of medical and biochemical researchers and scientists. Consequently, when you or someone close to you becomes ill, there's a feeling of helplessness as you realize there's not much you can do to help find a cure for cancer, HIV, or a stroke. But this situation is changing now that computer scientists have designed software that lets nonprofessionals contribute the computing power of their home or office computer when it's not in use to search for cures. The technology, called grid computing, is an offshoot of supercomputing, which harnesses the power of thousands of PCs to build a virtual supercomputer that can solve difficult research problems.

For example, Internet users can help in the search for cancer-fighting drugs by downloading a software application and letting it run when their computers are idle (see http://members.ud.com/projects/cancer/index.htm). Sponsored by computer-chip maker Intel, the program allows millions of volunteered computer cycles to help process molecular research being conducted by Oxford University in England and the National Foundation for Cancer Research in the United States. The University of Oxford has identified 3.5 billion molecules that could potentially be used to help cure leukemia and other forms of cancer. The software is testing each of these molecules against known cancer-inhibiting proteins, one at a time, using the processing power of PCs around the world.

The EMOs for greater involvement of patients and their relatives in health care—in prevention, treatment, aftercare, and research—are very positive. Following is an EMO chart comparing the traditional health care system with the newer approaches. The EMOs for the newer approaches are four out of four—100 percent—in favor of involving patients and their families in health care decisions.

EMO	Traditional Health Care	Patient Involvement
Feeling Good	Low	High
Feeling Comfortable/Secure	Low	High
Doing Good	Medium-High	High
Having Control/Choice	Medium-Low	High

Doctors and Nurses Online

From 1996 to 1999 I directed a connected-community trial, Intercom Ontario, that delivered online applications to 100 residents in Newmarket, Ontario, through video telephone and other appliances. One of the applications was a nurse-on-demand service, through which residents could contact a health worker from their homes and sometimes avoid a trip to a hospital or other health facility. This is the type of service that most people ask for, especially since doctors rarely make house calls nowadays.

Another medical service that is moving online is psychological counseling. Traditionally, therapists get their patients to relax and talk openly about their problems by having them lie down on a couch in their office. Today, a virtual couch is beginning to take the place of fabric and cushions.

Today, a virtual couch is beginning to take the place of fabric and cushions.

There are more than 200 websites providing mental health services online. Some services provide counseling through email, some require you to schedule an appointment, and some have counselors on standby, so you can get immediate counseling. Here2listen.com is one such site, offering online therapy and real-time chat with a counselor. Karen Pereyra, a California resident, is an online client who used the service. She says, "You can talk to someone at any time. It's almost like having someone come to your home."[31]

These services don't take the place of face-to-face meetings, because they can't reveal the body language and eye contact that therapists find useful. Although such additional cues will be available with speedier video-capable network connections, the current text-based systems are still useful. They fill a gap for people who don't live near a therapist, for those who need to communicate with someone right away, and for those who feel awkward going to a counselor's office, perhaps because they fear that someone they know will see them there.

Most of the counselors place their credentials and experience online, perhaps more visibly than those who practice in bricks-and-mortar offices. In Pereyra's case, the counselor advised her to read a particular book about surviving broken relationships. She says she is doing much better now and would use the service again.

One of the more controversial trends is the online marketing of doctors' services and, in some cases, bargaining for them. *Wired News* followed Dawn Buchanan as she used the Internet to find a surgeon who would fix the bags beneath her eyes. She logged on to "Bid for Surgery" at Medicine Online, and within seventy-two hours had five surgeons bidding to perform her lower-lid lift. "I can't believe how simplified it made my selection," Buchanan noted.[32]

Other websites, such as HealthAllies.com and WebHealthy, market similar medical services. These sites facilitate matches between patients and doctors. Primarily, they assist patients who are seeking elective surgery not covered by insurance, such as breast enlargement, laser eye surgery, and teeth whitening.

Doctors divulge their license number and whether or not they have had any malpractice suits or pending litigation against them when they sign up for the site.

Patients are free to look over their records. Buchanan examined the doctors' bids, which ranged from $1,500 to $3,000 (US), did some further online research on the procedure, and then visited her family physician, who agreed with her choice of surgeon. She visited the surgeon, had a consultation, and then went through with the surgery.

Websites such as CounterBuy bring a market approach to health care. If a patient likes a doctor but cannot afford the doctor's rates for a particular service, he can make a lower offer for the service. The doctor has seventy-two hours to accept the patient's counter-buy. The site has over 5,000 doctors registered, and so far it has focused on markets in Georgia and Florida.

Online Drugs: Bypassing Regulations

Individuals are buying more than just professional services online: They are also buying drugs. Every sort of drug imaginable, from over-the-counter alternative medicines to illegal and potentially dangerous drugs, can be easily purchased on the Internet and easily imported into any country with virtual impunity.[33] There are an estimated 15,000 online pharmacies worldwide, all of them vying for a piece of the $200 billion (US) annual online pharmaceutical sales. In 2001, about the same number of people who bought books online bought drugs online.

Reporters for Canada's *Globe and Mail* newspaper and CTV network were able to buy a vast array of powerful drugs online using credit cards but no prescriptions. They bought human growth hormone, steroids, narcotic painkillers, sleeping pills, antidepressants, antibiotics, weight-loss pills, cancer treatments, birth control pills, and Viagra. The drugs were shipped from such diverse locations as Fiji, the Channel Islands, Thailand, and Florida. When the drugs arrived by mail, most had been labeled as dietary supplements or gifts, and thus had slipped easily through customs. It is so easy to circumvent the traditional purchase of drugs in a pharmacy that online drug traffic in North America has quickly grown to an estimated 2 million shipments of prescription drugs annually. While the purchase of prescription drugs is highly regulated in most countries, with prison penalties for abuse, there are no restrictions for buying drugs online from offshore suppliers.

The trend is part of a much larger societal change of empowering individuals to be more proactive and autonomous about their own health care. Although many see this change as inevitable and urge health care professionals and regulators to adapt to it, officials warn that a client-oriented health care system that allows individuals to self-medicate is dangerous and should be avoided.

The Response of Health Care Institutions

Health care institutions are not taking these changes sitting still. Many are responding positively to the challenges of new patient/clients, and the health care system is improving as a result. The Texas Children's Hospital in Houston, for example, is helping sick children recover more quickly while relieving stress on their families. Providing positive EMOs such as making patients and families feel good, in control, and more comfortable about the hospital experience goes far beyond providing better service: It also assists in the children's recovery. It makes sense that if children can feel the same level of nurturing and security that they feel at home, they will recover much faster. Mark Wallace, the hospital's president and CEO, puts it this way:

It makes sense that if children can feel the same level of nurturing and security that they feel at home, they will recover much faster.

> Sick children need the opportunity to play and be distracted from their illness, and they need easy access to their parents. We take kids to our playground, which has swings and sandboxes that are accessible to wheelchairs and gurneys. And we operate Radio Lollipop, a hospital radio station that receives volunteer support from local disc jockeys.... Often the children are so sick that their families don't want to leave the hospital … so we've created sleeping areas at the hospital where families can stay free of charge.[34]

In most ways, though, the health care industry can be indicted for being among the most backward when it comes to adopting new business tools that have been proven in other businesses. B2B health care marketplaces, such as Medibuy.com and Neoforma, have websites for doctors and hospitals, but instead of using EDI or new Internet-based automated systems, the orders are processed manually and relayed by fax. It is not so surprising, then, that health care costs have spiraled out of control while most other businesses have reaped the cost-saving benefits of supply networks. MedChannel got into the health industry to supply outsourced IT networks, then found that it took them eight months to get all of the industry's disparate computer systems to interconnect. MedChannel believes the medical supply industry can cut its inventory levels by 50 percent and whack as much as $11 billion (US) in inefficiencies out of the system by bringing their supply systems into the twenty-first century, as other industries have done.

As the health care system moves toward allowing greater involvement of patients, it will increasingly tailor services to use the available funds in the way each patient wishes. Some patients may want blanket coverage at a minimum level, and others may opt to spend their health dollars on premium coverage that is not inclusive, topping up the costs as needed. But the greatest savings in a client-focused health system will be in the area of prevention. If the general population were less overweight, smoked less, and exercised more, hospitals would empty, the need for drugs would decrease, and the costs for health care would plummet. As we gain control over our health care, perhaps we will become more responsible for it as well.

Long-Term Disabilities

All of us have disabilities that challenge our access to the rich environment we live in. Some challenges, such as poor eyesight or hearing, can be corrected with appliances (glasses, hearing aids) or corrective surgery. Other challenges, such as mental disabilities, are not yet reversible. If we are fortunate enough not to have any disabilities today, we are certain to have them as we age, as eyesight and hearing dim and memory fades.

So, when we speak about those who are challenged, we must include a large segment of the population, some of whom have serious disabilities and others who can function in everyday situations, albeit with some difficulty. And as the baby boomers age, a larger fraction of the population will face challenges of reduced dexterity, vision, hearing, and mental acumen. Consequently, developing technologies that allow for increased human functioning presents opportunities for growth. Providing these technologies would respond to client needs and would be the right thing to do (fulfilling the third EMO, doing good).

Those who are challenged are increasingly becoming new clients, as they are coming out of the shadows of society and expecting the same opportunities in all aspects of life that others have. *Faces of AT in Illinois* is a book and a website created by people with disabilities about people with disabilities. One of the contributors, eight-year-old Auggie Gimenez, writes:

> I'm a second grader at Chatham Elementary.... I was born blind.... In school, a CCTV helps me read, print, write, and sometimes, I use it to follow the teacher's directions on paper. I also work with computers.... When I write in Braille, the printer does my work in print, so my teacher ... can read my work.... Do you want to know about the Mad Minute? In school we get a page full of additions or subtractions ... 15 per row! We only have a minute to do as many as we can. I am one of the best in my class.[35]

People with disabilities face plenty of obstacles. They have the lowest levels of income, home ownership, education—the lowest levels of everything except unemployment. And as with other disadvantaged client groups (such as visible minorities and women), a greater integration of the disabled into the workplace would have a positive effect on the economy, allowing them to contribute to productivity and be more self-sufficient economically. For people with disabilities, technology can be the key enabler.

For people with disabilities, technology can be the key enabler.

Assistive Technologies

Assistive technologies cannot remove all the difficulties faced by people with disabilities, but they do go a long way toward leveling the playing field. As new clients, people with disabilities are driving legislation that requires the provision of assistive technologies ranging from special-needs access ramps and washrooms to high-tech appliances and websites designed for people with various challenges.

The Internet is an excellent tool for many people because it is readily available, easily configurable, and relatively inexpensive. "Providing access to the Internet will help people with disabilities advance economically, as well as provide them the technical skills to compete professionally in today's digital economy," says UN Secretary General Kofi Annan.[36] The UN estimates that as many as 500 million people with disabilities do not have Web access.

People with visual impairment or reading difficulties can use text-to-speech converters, Braille displays, and screen-magnification software that makes type and images larger and easier to see. In many cases, a keyboard instead of a mouse can be used to navigate webpages. People who can't use a keyboard can rely either on voice recognition for spoken commands or on devices controlled by head, mouth, or eye movements.

The Internet has been a major boon to deaf and hearing-impaired people, who now can use instant messaging and email in lieu of the telephone. In the Intercom Ontario trial described above, we provided the residents of a Toronto suburb with video telephones. The neighborhood included a deaf child and a special-needs teacher who knew sign language. They had regular conversations online, the first "phone" conversations that the child was ever able to participate in.

Websites could be much improved for the hearing disabled if guidelines were adopted, such as the text captioning of streaming videos. Netizens with visual impairments benefit from the use of highly contrasting colors between text, links, and backgrounds and the use of large, easy-to-read typefaces and font sizes. Small fonts, when necessary, may be used provided they are scalable (can be made larger) by reading machines and operating systems. In this regard, the Web has some built-in advantages over normal print, because font sizes and styles can be controlled in the browser's "Preferences" menu, provided the text is not embedded as part of a graphic image.

Many people with disabilities have screen readers, which allow them to navigate their operating system and software using speech or Braille input and output. This feature lets them use most mainstream applications. For quadriplegics who can't use a keyboard, voice-recognition software has become sophisticated enough to allow them to browse websites using speech commands.

Raymond Kurzweil is a brilliant scientist who has dedicated much of his innovations to assisting people with disabilities. In the process, he has pushed the boundaries of computer input and output devices and revolutionized the industry for ordinary users. He invented the first CCD flatbed scanner in 1975, and a year later he invented the first multifont text-to-speech converter. In 1987 he invented the first large vocabulary speech-recognition system, completing the circle for voice communications with computers.

One of his inventions, the Kurzweil 3000, reads electronic or scanned text aloud with a remarkably human-sounding synthetic voice. It also takes the extra step of highlighting each word on the computer screen as the program speaks it. This feature makes the program an effective tool for teaching people with learning disabilities to read better. Some believe that every school and employer should provide the program. Assistive technologies like the Kurzweil reader can make a big difference in the progress and productivity of people with disabilities at school and at work.

Ann Adams, a Florida-based educator who specializes in home teaching for the blind, uses Home Page Reader, an IBM program that allows her to surf the Web on her own, either through verbal instructions or by typing on her Braille keyboard. It reads text in a clear and easy-to-understand voice and describes frames, image and text links, and image maps. Using the program's special table-navigation features, Adams says she can understand even the most complex tables, such as television listings. Guided by the program's commentary, she knows where she is on the Web at all times.

Assistive technologies score improvements in every EMO. The following chart illustrates that people with disabilities feel better when they increase their interaction with their communities using assistive technologies. They are more secure because they can better communicate their problems and access solutions. Thus, assistive technologies are good for both the users and for society as a whole.

EMO	Assistive Technologies
Feeling Good	High
Feeling Comfortable/Secure	High
Doing Good	High
Having Control/Choice	High

Changes to Regulations

People with disabilities as new clients have been influencing corporate policies and government laws to make public buildings and workplaces more accessible, friendlier, and assistive to those who find them challenging. An important success story in this regard is the U.S. landmark legislation known as Section 508 of *The Rehabilitation Act*. It makes goods and services accessible to those with disabilities and helps bring them into the mainstream of commerce and everyday activities. It is a far-reaching law that is beginning to have a ripple effect throughout the public and private sectors. According to the Equal Employment Opportunity Commission, the Act requires that the 167,000 U.S. federal employees with disabilities have the same access to information technology as all other federal employees. It also requires that all people seeking information or services from a federal agency have comparable access.[37]

Section 508 of *The Rehabilitation Act* is a far-reaching law that is beginning to have a ripple effect throughout the public and private sectors.

From June 2001 onwards, contractors selling computer hardware and software and telecommunications equipment to the U.S. federal government had to ensure that federal employees with disabilities could use their products. Over time, websites hosted by U.S. government agencies (about 30 million pages) will be accessible to all people with disabilities. The regulations raise awareness of the need for all people with disabilities who work for government agencies and in the private sector to have the widest possible access to assistive technology.

At stake for vendors is $40 billion (US) in annual federal spending on IT. Billions more are expected to flow from state governments that have either passed similar legislation or are considering doing so. More than 50,000 vendors have registered as suppliers under the legislation, including Microsoft, IBM, Hewlett-Packard, Adobe,

Compaq, and National Cash Register. All must provide assistive-technology products and training programs.

Assistive technology will open the doors for millions of people with disabilities who want to work. The benefits work both ways, since the law creates employment opportunities for those with disabilities and helps address the shortage of qualified workers for hundreds of thousands of openings in the IT field. In the United States alone, there are an estimated 8.5 million unemployed people with disabilities who want to work and can become qualified to do so.

Businesses hoping to expand their markets can now look to those with disabilities, who are using their new client power to bootstrap themselves into the new economy.

Seniors

The baby boom generation was born in the two decades spanning 1946 to 1966, in the euphoria following World War II. The first of them became seniors—at least fifty years old—in 1996. The bulk of them will be seniors during the first decade of the twenty-first century. Fully one-third of Canada's population is in this cohort, with similar fractions in the United States and Europe.[38] In fact, throughout the world, the elderly are increasing by an unprecedented 800,000 people a month.[39] The phenomenon of a global aging population will continue well into the twenty-first century, with the numbers and proportions of older people continuing to rise in both the developed and developing worlds.

The phenomenon of a global aging population will continue well into the twenty-first century.

David Foot, demographer and author of the best-selling book *Boom, Bust and Echo: How to Profit from the Coming Demographic Shift*, notes that seniors are the wealthiest group and should be courted as clients by a wide variety of suppliers. He says, "[Seniors] are part of the reason the cruise ship industry is expanding at a furious rate. Quality and service are the only way to sell to these people. They don't need much, but they can afford what they need. That's the good news for retailers. The bad news is that when seniors have to replace refrigerators or cars, they are very tough customers because they have had plenty of experience buying refrigerators and cars."[40]

Seniors are powerful new clients who need to be viewed from a different perspective than other client groups. Although they have many needs that have yet to be addressed, seniors have had earlier success at flexing their new client muscles than other groups because they are a potent electoral force. This is a large group with a high percentage of the vote. Seniors have large financial resources, experience in organizing and lobbying, and lots of volunteer time. Perhaps most important, they are in charge of most businesses and governments. Consequently, this client group, which frequently uses the "gray power" moniker, has been successful in moving its transactional, political, and social agendas forward and is a good model for other new client groups.

The advantages that seniors as clients achieved include discounts for local (bus, subway) and long-distance (air, sea) travel, discounts for entertainment and leisure activities (movies, theater, fairs), guaranteed government pension payments, reduced automobile insurance premiums, subsidized drug and medical costs, early retirement benefits, and waiving of entry requirements for university and college programs.

These advantages kick in from the age of fifty to sixty-five, depending on the government or private-sector program. There is a great deal of variability in the age of retirement as well, which used to be the determinant for being a senior. But retirement is no longer coupled with a specific age. For example, the downsizing of companies, governments, and other organizations over the past two decades has encouraged (and sometimes forced) millions of workers to take retirement sooner than they had planned and frequently with generous financial packages. Some of these seniors stay out of the workforce, others go on to second careers, and still others do part-time work to earn additional income and keep busy.

Many seniors start their own businesses, consulting or contracting work that they had previously done inside a company. In addition, there are large numbers of government, military, and unionized workers (teachers, police, and so forth) whose collective agreements bring them to retirement at the low end of the senior age range. They too follow diverse work patterns after they leave their primary life's employment.

The general diversification of occupational lifestyles means that seniors can no longer be taken as a homogenous group of retired people. What they have in common, compared with other cohorts, is an accumulation of information, wisdom, culture, assets, and connections with colleagues in positions of power.

Perhaps the defining aspect of seniors is that they no longer have to look after their children.

Perhaps the defining aspect of seniors is that they no longer have to look after their children. They may still be supporting them in university, college, or business, but the kids are out and on their own, giving seniors something that no other client group has: discretionary time and discretionary income. So, although seniors are focused on stretching their assets through their retirement years, they have a combination of greater savings and much lower expenses: the house is paid for, and the kids don't need two sets of clothes a year and five meals a day.

It is not surprising, then, that these new clients are not only demanding but also getting the attention of their suppliers. Stockbrokers, insurance salespeople, politicians, colleges, and every type of goods or service supplier have their eyes on this group. Although seniors are a tough sell, they make up for it by having low rates of defaulting on payments and the wherewithal to close a deal.

Seniors' EMOs

When it comes to EMOs, seniors want the whole lot of them: feeling good, doing good, feeling secure, and being in control. As a group, however, they are more focused on the third EMO—doing good—than most other client groups. Because they have more available time and income, seniors are the most visible segment of volunteers. They volunteer for the arts. They volunteer to help the less fortunate. They raise money for hospitals, colleges, and the United Way. And they donate their expertise to developing companies and countries trying to move up the economic ladder.

Businesses that wish to capitalize on senior clients need to focus on their hot-button EMOs. Here are some suggestions:

- *EMO 1: Feeling good.* Seniors go to the theater, travel, go on cruises, and enjoy all sorts of entertainment. At their stage in life, they are more motivated by saving money than by making it, so discounts are a proven attractor. Because they don't have to synchronize their vacations with school breaks or work breaks, they can take their holidays during the off season for travel. It's the same for entertainment. These are the folks who go to Tuesday matinees, when the price is right. The bottom line is they still like to have a good time and can afford to, but they will always go for a bargain.

- *EMO 2: Feeling comfortable/secure.* As a rule, seniors are not big risk-takers. When they gamble at a casino, it's a form of entertainment with a fixed limit on losses. Otherwise, suppliers should play to their need for comfort and security.

- *EMO 3: Doing good.* This group reacts very positively to projects that help the disadvantaged, the sick, the poor, and even the environment. Using a portion of transaction proceeds to do some good is a positive inducement.

- *EMO 4: Having control/choice.* Interestingly, this EMO, which has been paramount for most of the other client groups in this book, is less important for seniors. They are more likely to be happy traveling in a group, with a fixed itinerary, and so on. The other EMOs override the desire for choice at this age.

EMO	Senior Hot-Buttons
Feeling Good	High
Feeling Comfortable/Secure	Very High
Doing Good	High
Having Control/Choice	Medium

Seniors and the Internet

In the 1990s, analysts were convinced that computers were too complicated for seniors to use and that they would much prefer to access the Web from their television sets. Companies such as Sony and Microsoft poured huge sums into creating services like WebTV, which deliver the Internet through TVs with a simplified user interface. The problem with Internet through a television is that, in simplifying the interface, the services can deliver only a subset of a computer's website functionality. In other words, you don't get everything that computer users get.

The facts speak for themselves. In a SeniorNet survey, 94 percent of seniors said they used a computer to access the Web, and the remaining 6 percent did so through a TV.[41] Journalist H.L. Mencken may have been correct in 1927 when he penned the oft-quoted aphorism "No one in this world ... has ever lost money by underestimating the intelligence of the great masses of the plain people," but today you can go wrong underestimating the intelligence of your target market, particularly if they are as savvy and experienced a group as seniors.

Seniors who are online use the Internet about twenty hours a week.

The same survey indicates that seniors who are online use the Internet about twenty hours a week, which is a big chunk of their time. Their top activities, in descending order, are staying in touch with friends and relatives, staying current with news and events, researching various topics, checking stocks and investments, making purchases, and playing games.

Another myth about seniors is that older women are greater technophobes than men. But, like younger women, female seniors show no particular aversion to the Web and, once online, spend more time at it than their male counterparts, perhaps because of the social aspects of online communications.

There are thousands of websites devoted to seniors. The general-interest portals have links to fitness, health and medicine, nutrition, lawyers, politics and government, finance and stocks, leisure and travel, homes and gardens, genealogy, shopping, and pets, all with a spin toward seniors. In addition, there are senior-specific topics such as gerontology, medical equipment and supplies, aging, grandparenting, death and dying, reverse mortgages, retirement, medical plans (public and private), Alzheimer's, and elder care. Each of these areas provides opportunities for entrepreneurs who wish to provide for the physical and EMO needs of seniors.

Seniors have taken the bull by the horns and twisted it in their direction. They are organized. They maintain a constant public relations presence. They know how to bargain for the best deal and when to close it. They take advantage of personal as well as computer networks. In short, they've figured out how to be effective new clients.

THE ANTI-CLIENTS

New York's Times Square ... trumpets globalism with its giant, flashing, electronic billboard—an instantaneous, real-time score-card of the world's winners and losers. Like the city it serves, its ticker never sleeps, as it tracks globalization's inexorable sweep, from Beijing to Bombay, Moscow to Montreal, Manhattan to Tokyo to London and back again, 24 hours a day, seven days a week—a market-driven global casino of commodities, currencies, indices and exchanges.... Behind the apparent progress looms a force that is as threatening in its power as it is promising in its potential.[1]

GLOBALIZATION AND HUMAN RIGHTS, *PBS TELEVISION SPECIAL*

C hanging from a supplier- to a client-based culture is difficult for most organizations. This difficulty is to be expected, since, in the process, organizations must cede some power and control to outsiders. Yet the idea of satisfying clients is congruent with most organizational objectives and the process of change is being successfully undertaken every day.

For some organizations, however, the new way of doing business is antithetical to their objectives and threatens their very raison d'être. These anti-client organizations find new client concepts unacceptable, in some cases because their organizational objectives are based on preventing clients from having input, choice, or control. Some of these organizations are among the largest and most powerful, since the Industrial Age emphasized such organizational objectives as controlling distribution channels— objectives that no longer contribute to success in the Information Age. Such organizations are out of sync with the times and must either change fundamentally or suffer a diminution of their power, as alternatives to their goods and services crop up that are more relevant to our times.

This chapter looks at four areas where anti-client forces are at work:

- *globalization,* a legacy of industrialization that focuses on suppliers
- *mega-mergers,* which give extra control over the market to organizations, taking away choice from clients
- *information pipelines,* which aim to control supply and distribution channels
- *business training,* which has not yet incorporated client-centered approaches

Globalization

Globalization describes a world in which markets are the driving forces and national borders are erased as big business homogenizes culture. From the perspective of the new client, globalization presents the Industrial Age supplier-centered framework. Instead of embracing the new localism, the proponents of globalization hang on to the twentieth-century model of supplier-dominated business and world economies. Globalization is a logical consequence of industrialization, which is being superseded by a new era of decentralization and localism, brought about by the introduction of digital networks and computerization.

Globalization is a logical consequence of industrialization, which is being superseded by a new era of decentralization and localism.

The modern corporation is a creature of industrialization. Until 1844, incorporation was available only in England, parsimoniously granted under special circumstances by the king or by Parliament. But as the steam engine revolutionized travel and the distribution of goods, there was not enough capital available to build the enormous railroad infrastructure necessary to move raw materials to the new factories and finished goods from the factories to population centers. In order to raise the large investments required for acquiring rights of way, building tracks, and buying rolling stock, a financial structure was needed that offered shared and limited risk. Therefore, federal, state, and provincial governments began chartering corporations, which provided shared profits (as in a partnership) but also limited liability (in case the venture failed). Corporations could raise money publicly or privately and quickly became the major engine of capitalism and industrial growth.

Corporations successfully withstood a century and a half of growth and change while making few fundamental changes to their structure. But as industrialization flourished and created branch plants and global business opportunities, large multinational corporations came into being, and their functions and objectives were different from those of ordinary corporations. Instead of being subservient to governments, the new multinational corporations have become so large and powerful that governments are subservient to them. In fact, of the hundred largest economies in the world, more than half aren't countries—they're corporations.

Of the hundred largest economies in the world, fifty-two aren't countries— they're corporations.

Globalization is the logical extension of the power large companies have to transcend governments, with responsibility consequently shifting from citizens to shareholders. This outcome may be good or bad, depending on your perspective. Robert Hormats, vice chairman of Goldman Sachs, says, "The great beauty of globalization is that it is not controlled by any individual, any government, any institution. It provides people with the ability to communicate across borders, trade across borders, raise capital across borders." George Soros, billionaire investor, speculator, and philanthropist, and chairman of Soros Fund Management, has a different perspective: "The capitalist system is very powerful," he says, "and due to its success it penetrates into areas of life—of society—where it doesn't really belong. There are needs in society that cannot be fulfilled by the market and those needs are neglected. The system is currently stacked in favor of the lenders to the detriment of the debtors."[2]

Underlying globalization is the idea that countries and regions of the world are suppliers and clients, like businesses. As in business-to-business (B2B) transactions, countries enter into contracts for raw materials, parts, and labor. And as in B2B transactions, other countries may offer the finished goods and services for sale. For example, the assembly of toys, electronics, and clothing has generally moved to regions of cheap labor: to Japan at the end of World War II, to Taiwan and Korea after Japanese labor became too expensive, and now to China. The manufactured goods are mostly sold in areas of greater prosperity: first the United States, then Europe and Japan, and now also Taiwan and Korea.

But unlike B2B transactions within the developed world, transactions between developed and less-developed countries have not yet exhibited the characteristics of new client empowerment. Instead, the less-developed world remains in a much less powerful position, whether it is a client or a supplier of raw materials, labor, finished goods, or services. This inequality results primarily because access to capital has determined the position of power. Within the industrial world, clients and suppliers both have power, but in transactions between developed and developing countries, only one side has it. This continuing asymmetry is at the root of the malaise that has fed the forces of anti-globalization.

Anti-Globalization

Anti-globalization has become the rallying issue for a wide variety of causes focusing on general anti-capitalist sentiment. The sub-issues, such as environmental sustainability, poverty, labor exploitation, human rights, and cultural imperialism, are each very complex, but they fit under the same umbrella thesis: Capitalism places all human activities in transactional frameworks in which values can be calculated using equations and spreadsheets, but this is an improper perspective of human activities because it neglects important issues such as culture, long-term sustainability, and human rights.

A more appropriate framework would include these factors, which are important but less easily quantified. Here's one way to do that. Let's add the EMOs into the equation: feeling good, feeling secure, doing good, and being in control/having choices. With the addition of these factors, many of the issues that appear outside the framework of business can be incorporated.

Here's how a few hot-button anti-globalization issues stack up in EMO charts:

Issue A: *Preserving the environment and promoting sustainable energy systems* would make us feel good, make us more secure, do good, and give us greater control of our future.

Issue B: *Decreasing poverty and protecting human rights* would make us feel good, make us more secure (as there would be less chance of uprisings, etc.), and do good.

EMO	Issue A	Issue B
Feeling Good	High	High
Feeling Comfortable/Secure	High	High
Doing Good	High	High
Having Control/Choice	High	Medium

The Three Agents of Globalization

The current framework for globalization was set more than half a century ago when the world was reeling from the aftershock of World War II, which was arguably the consequence of an outmoded industrial economic framework. In 1944, twenty-three nations at a Bretton Woods, New Hampshire, conference decided on a structure for world trade that would foster orderly and peaceful transactions. The new organizations were the International Monetary Fund (IMF); the International Bank for Reconstruction and Development (IBRD), now known as the World Bank; and the General Agreement for Tariffs and Trade (GATT), now known as the World Trade Organization (WTO).[3]

These three organizations continue to dominate world trade today. The primary aim of the World Bank is to help the poorest people and the poorest countries. It is the world's largest source of development assistance, providing more than $17 billion (US) in loans to its client countries in 2001. The IMF, with 183 member countries and headquarters in Washington, D.C., promotes global currency stability and supplies member states with funds to help them overcome short-term balance-of-payment difficulties, provided that the recipient country agrees to economic policy reforms and structural adjustment programs (SAPs). IMF policies have been used as an instrument for deregulating national economic systems and opening markets to foreign investment.

IMF policies have been used as an instrument for deregulating national economic systems and opening markets to foreign investment.

The third major organization that promotes globalization is the WTO, created in 1995 as a successor to GATT. The WTO administers international trade agreements, monitors national trade policies, and handles trade disputes. Its 142 member countries maintain a staff of 500 in Geneva, Switzerland.

When GATT was signed in 1947, it was meant to be an interim arrangement pending the ratification of the Havana Charter of the International Trade Organization (ITO), which would incorporate GATT and then supersede it. The ITO had a much broader scope than GATT and recognized the role of governments in maintaining high levels of employment, regulating foreign investment, correcting market failures in commodities, and preventing restrictive business practices. It incorporated a much more symmetrical approach in terms of the obligations of its members.[4]

But the ITO was not to be. U.S. President Harry S. Truman decided not to submit the ITO to Congress for approval in 1950, and only GATT survived. When the

WTO was created to supersede GATT in 1995, its agenda was moved further from the original interests of nations and closer to the interests of large corporations, which by then had become the dominant forces in world trade, vying with and sometimes eclipsing the role of nations. The more corporate-oriented WTO now targets "non-tariff barriers to trade," such as national programs that provide local incentives, if these are judged as prejudicial to foreign corporations.

Anti-globalization critics argue that the World Bank, the IMF, and the WTO, contrary to their stated objectives, have in fact exacerbated poverty in most countries where they have been active, contributed to the suffering of millions and caused widespread environmental degradation. They charge that IMF structural adjustment programs (SAPs) have resulted in a net outflow of wealth from the developing world, which has paid out much more capital to the industrialized countries than it has received—estimates range from two to five times as much.

Critics note that the WTO and the IMF are dominated by wealthy northern industrialized nations that dictate the agendas of these institutions with little input from and no notice of the desires of the less developed countries. The organizations' economists use orthodox neoclassical economic theories, which hold sacred the efficiency of free markets and private producers and the benefits of international trade and competition. There are good arguments for running the organizations in this manner. Unfortunately, those arguments are trumped by the failures of these policies to achieve the agreed-upon objectives.

Why Globalization Is Not Working

In the early 1980s, the world experienced a debt crisis, owing to a collapse in the prices of commodities exported by developing countries (such as coffee and cocoa) and to rising oil prices and interest rates. This combination of events forced many developing countries to default on their loan payments to the World Bank. Because there is no bankruptcy protection for a country, the world monetary system grinds to a halt in such circumstances—exactly the type of situation the World Bank and the IMF were created to prevent. The financial meltdown called into question the efficacy of these organizations.

The poor financial health of developing nations ensures that they have no bargaining power when negotiating with the World Bank and the IMF.

Since the 1980s the debt situation of the developing world has steadily worsened. Third world debt currently equals one-half its combined Gross National Products and nearly twice its combined annual export earnings. The poor financial health of developing nations ensures that they have no bargaining power when negotiating with the World Bank and the IMF and must accept any conditions and structural adjustment programs imposed on them.

But these bankers to the world have not been prudent in their business practices. In 1992, an internal World Bank review found that more than one-third of all its loans did not meet the institution's own lending criteria and warned that the Bank had been overtaken by a dangerous "culture of approval." Bank officials, in other words, feel heavy pressure to push through new loans even when presented with overwhelming evidence that the project in question is ill advised.[5]

Interviewed on Brazilian television in 2001, British Prime Minister Tony Blair said, "Everything is going global. Communication is global, culture is global, and the role of government is to equip people for this. It would be a disaster for the economy of the world to retreat into protectionism.... It is more vital than ever that countries such as Brazil and Argentina be able to trade freely and sell their products across the world."[6] Six months later, the Argentine economy, which had been built on the economic principles of the World Bank, IMF, and WTO, was in ruins.

Argentina suffered a monetary collapse and defaulted on payments of hundreds of billions of dollars of international loans. Critics argue that if the economic infrastructure of a country like Argentina can fail after closely following the policies of the IMF, WTO, and World Bank (Argentina was the poster child of these organizations), then their policies must be fundamentally flawed.

The Basic Flaw: A Built-In Supplier Bias

The main flaw of the IMF, WTO, and World Bank is that they operate almost without regard for the perspective of their clients. The level of each member nation's financial contribution to these organizations determines its voting power, and thus client nations essentially have no say. The United States has almost 20 percent of the vote, with the seven largest industrialized countries (the G-7) holding a total of 45 percent. The controlling (wealthy) countries have a great self-interest in approving international loans because for each dollar they contribute, on average, the large donor countries receive two dollars of contracts to supply infrastructure, goods, and services to the debtor nations.

Given this self-interest, the World Bank tends to finance very large, expensive projects that require materials and technical expertise from industrially sophisticated contractors, while passing up smaller-scale and arguably more appropriate local alternatives. Consequently, critics argue, the mission to alleviate poverty has been perverted and the intent is now to provide business opportunities for industrialized nations and corporate contractors.

**From the perspective of the new
client, the World Bank and the
IMF are asymmetric suppliers
that dictate transactional terms
and conditions to client states.**

From the perspective of the new client, the World Bank and the IMF are asymmetric suppliers that dictate transactional terms and conditions to client states that are powerless to refuse them. Their clients are part of the world's new economy and have the same aspirations as other new clients, but they have not benefited from the general empowerment of clients elsewhere. Hence, the less-developed world has come to resent the entire transactional framework under which Western-style capitalist trade is conducted.

Is it really so incomprehensible that large populations in poor countries like Afghanistan and Pakistan hate the industrialized West? Why should it be so difficult for us to put ourselves in our clients' shoes? Where are the EMOs for these clients in their international transactions? There are none!

Here's the EMO chart for clients of the World Bank and IMF.

EMO	Client Rating
Feeling Good	Very Low
Feeling Comfortable/Secure	Very Low
Doing Good	Some
Having Control/Choice	None

The populations of client countries of the World Bank, IMF, and ITO generally don't feel good about the assistance that has been provided to them (the first EMO). Their attitude toward the United States and other powerhouse nations that use these organizations as their globalization proxies is worse today than before the assistance was offered. There has been, in fact, growing resentment of the North–South (developed–less developed) prosperity gap, which has not closed as promised by these instruments of global trade.

Client countries do not feel secure or comfortable (the second EMO), with good reason. The repeated collapse of monetary systems and entire regional economies has left client countries uneasy about their futures, as they wait to see which country or region will be next to experience the sort of catastrophic financial demise that these organizations were supposed to avoid.

There is not much agreement about how much good these organizations have done over the long haul. There are many benefits and successes that can be pointed to, as well as the failures highlighted above. In fairness, since it is difficult to compare the outcome with hypothetical alternatives, we'll give the third EMO—doing good—a passing grade, as some good has certainly come of these efforts.

The lowest score is for the fourth EMO—being in control. There is a feeling of helplessness in less-developed countries because the conditions for support are so rigid that they are left with little room to innovate in response to local conditions. In other words, they have no bargaining power, no control, and no choice.

Anti-globalization groups accuse the WTO of being a dictatorial tool of the rich and powerful that destroys jobs and ignores concerns about health, the environment, and local development. Moreover, WTO policies frequently destroy local cultures, preventing governments from fostering or sustaining them if to do so would restrict the access of global businesses to their markets.

You don't even have to look to developing countries to see these forces at work. Countries such as Canada and France have had success in developing local film and television production industries by using government support. These governments, like most others around the world, see their national book, film, television, and theater productions as expressions of their culture. The U.S. government, on the other hand, under strong lobbying pressure from Hollywood, does not recognize a cultural component to these industries but instead treats them as entertainment, using the global trade organizations as justification for attacking the support of local culture. If wealthy countries such as Canada and France find it difficult to maintain their cultural expression against the tide of international trade organizations, what chance do poorer countries have to avoid the cultural imperialism of globalization? It is now clear to most observers that the economic mechanisms left over from the twentieth century are not working well and need to be amended if they are to survive in the Information Age.

Perhaps the scariest aspect of globalization is that it is invoked as the logical consequence of capitalism and free markets, while, in reality, it has come to repress these ideals rather than represent them. The ideas of free markets, free trade, deregulation, and competitive capitalism resonate well in the twenty-first century. But many of the organizations that claim to be striving toward those ends have instead effectively shut down competition and raised prices for consumers. For example, the deregulation of the energy and airline industries in the United States has not spawned the greater competition and lower prices that were advertised but instead have led to the rationalization of those industries into fewer, larger suppliers that have increased costs to clients.

It is time to re-examine the underpinning agencies and policies of globalization now that the results have not met the objectives. It is just not necessary to exclude local client perspectives in order for companies to make money. There is ample evidence that large multinational companies (IBM, for example) can include cultural sensitivity, recognition of human rights, environmental sustainability, and localized solutions in their international dealings while making a tidy profit.

> **It is time to re-examine the underpinning agencies and policies of globalization now that the results have not met the objectives.**

The concept of globalization needs to be expanded, in any case, because it posits only two exclusive levels of commerce: global or national. But there are many levels of economic, political, and cultural associations that are important today, such as trading regions and regions within countries that operate on neither national nor global scales.

Mounting Protests

Anti-globalization protesters began making noise at the 1996 Singapore ministerial WTO meeting, gained significant momentum at the 1998 Geneva meeting, and were successful at shutting down the 1999 meeting in Seattle.

In March 2002, there were mass demonstrations in Barcelona, Spain, against the gathering of the advanced democracies of the European Union. More than 8,000 police were needed to contain the crowds of protesters who rallied against the globalization policies of the EU. That same month, the University of Toronto's Munk Centre for International Studies and York University's Robarts Centre for Canadian Studies brought together leading world thinkers and bureaucrats for a conference on world trading systems and international governance. The consensus was that the framework for global trade is not working and that the public in North America and Europe has become hostile to corporate-driven trade liberalization.[7]

There is ample evidence to support this view. The previous month, the streets of New York were filled with angry demonstrators denouncing the agenda of the World Economic Forum meeting there. The WEF is the annual gathering of the top 1,000 corporations, world leaders, and opinion makers. The WEF used to be a club for the rich elite who were utterly unapologetic about their wealth and uninterested in the concerns of the rest of the inhabitants of the planet. But over the course of only three years, as a result of the public protests and demonstrations, the WEF has been transformed into an annual parade of public shaming. Attendees nowadays discuss the nonsustainability of their greed.

In order to move from negative criticism to positive action, the dissenting groups have formed an alternative to the World Economic Forum, called the World Social Forum (WSF). This umbrella organization represented 800 groups at the Genoa, Italy, G-8 conference in July 2001, where it urged world leaders to reduce or remove huge debts and damaging high levels of interest for the world's poorest nations. It also endorsed the Kyoto global climate treaty and other environmental protections. In 2001, British Prime Minister Tony Blair acknowledged that the WEF had helped move free trade and globalization to the top of the world's political agenda.

WSF meetings are now held concurrently with WEF meetings, as a political antidote and to siphon media coverage from the WEF. In 2002, the World Social Forum attracted 60,000 participants to Porto Algegre, Brazil, including a European prime minister, World Bank directors, and corporate executives who skipped the New York WEF meeting to attend.

In fact, support is building in the corridors of many businesses for a global framework of commerce that values client-friendly social and environmental issues, and EMOs ahead of push economics. Naomi Klein, in an article for the *Globe and Mail,* notes that "young people have concluded that it is not individual policies or politicians that are the problem, but the system of centralized power."[8]

The alternative to globalization is, not surprisingly, localism.

The alternative to globalization is, not surprisingly, localism. There is a growing sense that we need to find mechanisms that can incorporate local and territorial solutions within global frameworks.

The Rise of Localization

In theory, with a global economy, a company can sell the same products anywhere in the world, effecting economies of scale, but this is often not the case. Local tastes, local cultures, and historical brand loyalties all continue to play important roles in product sales, frequently overriding price as the purchase trigger. This tendency is consistent with the EMOs we have been discussing and helps explain why large multinational companies are frequently unsuccessful in marketing products in different parts of the world. The products may look competitive on a spreadsheet, but the spreadsheet misses key sales factors based on EMOs.

Alan Rugman and Karl Moore note that countries in each trading triad—NAFTA, the EU, and Japan—sell most of their products and services within their own trading group.[9] About 90 percent of automobiles sold in North America are built in North America; more than 90 percent of the cars sold in Japan are made there; and more than 90 percent of all steel, industrial equipment, and paint is manufactured and used regionally. The service industry, which is driving the economies of North America, Europe, and Japan, also operates with a mostly local and regional focus.

EMOs have major effects on purchasing decisions and vary from culture to culture. The Toyota Camry automobile, for example, is a consistent bestseller in North America yet sells poorly in its home country of Japan. On the other hand, the Volkswagen Golf was the best-selling car in its native Europe but was a dud in North America. And regionally produced home appliances, such as refrigerators, air conditioners, and washing machines, are preferred throughout the world over North American appliances, even though the latter are usually lower priced.

EMOs must be evaluated on a case-by-case basis for each of the culturally diverse regions of the world. Sometimes the same EMOs can weigh in on different sides of the sales equation. For example, comfort, security, and doing good for the local economy are usually highest when local products are purchased, but there may be a prestige factor (feeling good) for buying foreign products. The rule of thumb here is not to take for granted that EMOs in one region will be the same in another region. Comfort factors may not always be obvious, such as the use of metric-system parts for products manufactured in most regions of the world except the United States. U.S. manufacturers either have to accept a discomfort factor with their parts and services or manufacture different models for Europe and Asia, which negates the economy-of-scale argument for mass production.

Even the notion that multinational companies remove decision-making from regional offices is no longer true. In fact, the recent trend in multinational subsidiaries has been the opposite, particularly in Europe, where subsidiaries now report to pan-European rather than global headquarters.[10] Therefore, globalization is actually quite different from how it is portrayed by the mainstream business establishment.

Here's an example. McDonald's hamburger chain is a company that strongly embodies the global ethos of homogenized culture, uniform branding, and standardization of ingredients and products. Its global identity has been focused on the icon of Ronald McDonald, the clown. But in France, McDonald's has succumbed to local pressures and adopted a different local identity: a cartoon of the Gallic hero Asterix, known for beating up the Roman legionnaires who occupied France more than 2,000 years ago.

The move to a French icon with television commercials, posters, and a series of "ancient Gallic" burgers has generated a good deal of controversy in France, where hostility to American fast food is widespread. The localization of McDonald's in France is seen as a major victory by anti-globalization forces, who have used the hamburger chain as a favorite target of their grievances. In 2001, French farmer José Bové led a gang that tore apart a McDonald's restaurant under construction in Paris, to a surprising large echo of support throughout the country.

The localization of McDonald's in France is seen as a major victory by anti-globalization forces.

In fact, McDonald's has allowed substantial changes in local formats over the past decades, giving lie to the image of globalization as an effective tool for large corporations. The localization has not been restricted to France, either. I remember walking into a McDonald's restaurant in Mexico a few years ago and noticing the first item on the menu: the Chorizo (hot Mexican sausage) McMuffin. This is an about-face from the strict codes of food preparation and standardized menus and decor of earlier years. It is, in fact, evidence of the capitulation of global business to local forces.

Localization as a Consequence of the Information Age

The global outlook of the twentieth century is gradually being supplanted by a more local focus. The new localism, like the Information Age itself, is just beginning to emerge. David Morris, vice president of the Institute for Local Self-Reliance (ILSR), notes, "For the last 100 years the direction we've moved in and the rules that we've devised have encouraged globalization, long distribution routes, and absentee ownership and they have discouraged strong, productive and self-reliant geographic communities…. In brief, we have built a society in which we have separated those who make the decisions from those who feel the impact of those decisions. This is not only undemocratic. It is also inefficient."[11]

Industrialization moved people from small rural communities to large industrial centers, where they worked in factories that mass-produced goods. The industrial centers were located at stops along water routes and train routes, and later along auto routes and air routes. These centers grew into large urban population magnets, drawing people in to find work and to buy the material goods that were the evidence of progress and new wealth.

Although industrialization brought great material benefits, longer lifespans, and better education to most of the population, it had disastrous side effects for families and local communities. When families left their local communities, they also left behind the social support structures that are intrinsic to small towns and rural life. In hard times locals might buy on credit at the local grocer, but not at the supermarket in the big city. Friends and relatives would no longer be neighbors; instead, migrants to the city moved next door to unknown people who spoke different languages and had different traditions.

As the Industrial Age progressed, it spawned the globalization that we have today. The availability of transportation routes gave rise to national companies with branch offices. Now bosses, not just workers, were being transferred from city to city, ripping their kids out of schools and severing friendships that they had begun to establish in the cities. Faceless government programs gradually replaced the safety nets that had been provided by relatives and churches. Families became weaker and local communities faltered.

When families left their local communities, they also left behind the social support structures that are intrinsic to small towns and rural life.

Whereas industrialization moved people to wherever the products, services, and production were, digitization moves products, services, and work to wherever people are, fundamentally reversing the social dysfunction of the past few centuries. Consider buying a book today. If you order it online, it will arrive in a few days no matter where you live. You no longer have to live in New York, London, or Montreal to get the best selection. In fact, if you shop at a physical bookstore in any of these cities, you will not find as good a selection of, or information about, books as an online shopper in the smallest burg.

As for work, more than half of the population now works at least part of the time at home, whether for a large company or increasingly for their own home business, connecting to today's digital routes through wired and wireless networks.

Changes Afoot

The results of localization are fundamental and absolutely disruptive to industrial and global frameworks. The mass production that is the hallmark of the Industrial Age produces high-quality and inexpensive goods that are, however, uniform. Consumers today, on the other hand, want personalized products. Your cell phone can be customized with different-colored cases, and your computer may have a different screensaver and accessories than that of your friends and co-workers. You can buy a custom-made suit that will be tailored largely by robots to your exact dimensions and fabric choice within a few days. The mass marketing that still dominates mass media, such as magazines and network television, is quickly being replaced by targeted marketing, in which the most valuable aspect of your transaction may not be your purchase but your personal information.

The same mass media that carry mass-market ads are being encroached on by digital media, such as CD-ROM, DVD, and the Internet. These new media allow for localization of services because every customer can have a direct channel of communication with the producer of the goods and services. And the general decline of Big Brother governments that oversaw the social, education, and health service needs of citizens is now matched by the ascent of individual empowerment and a much greater freedom of choice over more aspects of our lives.

Best of all, the proliferation of information that caused Alvin and Heidi Toffler to write *Future Shock* is slowly being replaced by an assortment of technology filters that will bring us much less information, tailored to meet our immediate needs (just-in-time information).

Putting these changes together draws a clear picture of a return to a much more local focus in the Digital Age, one that ironically is similar to social interactions in preindustrial times.

Table 5.1 provides some comparisons between Industrial Age and Digital Age frameworks, illustrating essential differences that support a return to a more local focus.

TABLE 5.1 INDUSTRIAL AND DIGITAL FRAMEWORKS

Industrial Age	Digital Age
People to products and services	Products and services to people
Mass production	Mass customization
Mass marketing	Targeted marketing
Asymmetric (mass) media	Symmetric (new) media
Big Brother governments	Personal empowerment
Information proliferation	Just-in-time information
Supplier focus	Client focus
Ascent of global focus	Return to local focus

The harsh truth for those who believe that our future lies in a global village with harmonized goods, services, and culture is that such a global village is a myth. Marshall McLuhan, who coined the term "global village," was a colleague and friend of mine in the 1970s.[12] He was a brilliant visionary and predicted many of the impacts of increased global communications. But he did not intend for the term "global village" to imply that the world would become homogenized with a single culture.

The reason that global economics will not result in a single global culture is twofold: First, humans are genetically coded to trust only about 20 people (extended family size) and to keep track of a maximum of about 150 relationships (the size of a tribe or local village). That's why the vast majority of people in the Western world are not moved by slaughters and famines in Africa or Afghanistan, until their own cultural representatives (troops or aid workers) intervene. Second, the Digital Age is bringing back a preindustrial emphasis on person-to-person relationships and local communities.

People want to retain their cultural heritage and can do so more comfortably in the Information Age.

Immigration has turned most industrialized countries into multicultural polyglots. Some, like Canada, celebrate the diversity, while others try to eradicate any notion of hyphenated nationals (African-Americans, Chinese-Canadians, Indo-Brits). No matter. People want to retain their cultural heritage and can do so more comfortably in the Information Age.

The New Localization

A growing trend is taking power from provincial and national governments and giving it back to municipalities and cities. John Manley, Canada's finance minister, suggests that the top priority in federal budgeting should be reallocating more money for cities. In Brazil, a growing political movement known as the Workers Party (PT) is now in power in 200 municipalities, and is systematically delegating power to municipalities, rather than hoarding it at national and international levels.

Many PT cities have participatory budgeting, which allows citizens to directly participate in allocating scarce city resources. Residents vote on neighborhood issues that affect them directly, such as which roads to pave and which hospitals to build. In most of these cities, resource allocations are opposite to those of central and global governments. For instance, rather than scaling back on public services for the poor, these cities increase the services substantially. And rather than voter apathy and nonparticipation, PT cities experience an increase in citizen participation in the democratic process every year.

I directed a wired community research trial from 1995 to 1999 in a Toronto, Ontario, suburb. My colleagues and I connected 100 homes with a broadband network that enabled each home to have private text, audio, and video communication. The residents agreed to share their email addresses with their neighbors, provided outsiders could not gain access, an important consideration. We set up a community bulletin board through a listserv, which forwarded a message to everyone in the neighborhood when any resident posted one.

The subscribers to listservs on the Internet do not cohabit a physical neighborhood, so they have no opportunity to meet with their colleagues and share a coffee. In our trial, they could, because the *physical* community was the same as the *virtual* community. As a result, the communications were very different from those found on the Internet. Within a few weeks, a family posted this message: "Barbecue at our house Friday night. Everyone invited. We'll provide the hot dogs. You bring the drinks." The result was a get-to-know-your-neighbors party where almost everyone in the community met face-to-face.

This anecdote contradicts trend-spotter Faith Popcorn's cocooning metaphor, which suggests that residents will increasingly remain indoors, glued to their television and computer screens at the expense of face-to-face social interaction. The experience in our neighborhood and in other connected community trials is that digitally connected neighbors are more social and meet face-to-face more frequently, not less.

Barry Wellman, professor in the Department of Sociology and the Centre for Urban and Community Studies at the University of Toronto, and Keith Hampton, assistant professor of Technology, Urban and Community Sociology at MIT, studied social changes within our community and found that connected residents invited neighbors to their homes one-and-a-half times more frequently and socialized with their neighbors twice as often as unconnected residents in the neighborhood. Wellman notes, "The Internet facilitates local as well as global connectivity. Nearly three-fifths of people's daily email contact with friends is to those living within 50 kilometers, as is more than two-fifths of their email contact with kin. Indeed, the volume of daily users' email contact is highest with nearby friends (118 days per year), followed by distant friends (85 days per year), distant kin (72 days per year), and the less numerous nearby kin (52 days per year)."[13]

The Digital Age may well enable us to celebrate our diversity while sharing the common bonds of territorial and political association.

Imagine an apartment building or a condo in which residents actually get to know each other. These buildings are roughly analogous in size to villages, communities in which residents have much in common. Frequently, residents share common economic and cultural backgrounds. Yet despite the most egalitarian aspirations of planners, members of cultural and ethnic groups tend to congregate only with members of the same group. While some believe this multicultural fabric is divisive, it is part of human nature. People who follow a religion will always prefer to live in a neighborhood that has a church of their denomination.

Whereas the Industrial Age fostered a global environment in which we tried to hide our unique cultures, the Digital Age may well enable us to celebrate our diversity while sharing the common bonds of territorial and political association.

The new supplier understands the trend toward localization and takes advantage of new tools to tailor and target services and products to the new local clients.

A New Globalization

Illuminated in the light of localization, the globalization of the twentieth century and its agents are seen as out-of-date and certainly anti-client in the fight to maintain control of transactional power using surrogate supplier companies and countries. If free enterprise and capitalism are to continue as the dominant frameworks for trade in the twenty-first century, it will be necessary to abandon Industrial Age notions of globalization.

As mass customization continues to replace mass production, globalization will have to be reactive to the new localization. The new economic model will look a lot like other disintermediated systems of the Information Age. Territorial boundaries will be slowly replaced by cultural boundaries, a natural consequence of localization. What is needed is a mixed approach that links the best of localization with the best of globalization to create a more client-friendly environment.

Recognizing the role of the new client is an excellent way to begin that evolution, since rebalancing the supplier–client relationship will automatically rebalance global and local interests. The result will be a new way forward that promises to reconcile the need to live in a globally connected world with the need to live in local communities; the need to invest capital in less-developed regions with the need to respect local cultural differences; and the need to earn profits with the need to preserve the earth's ecosystems.

Content Mega-Mergers

In the twentieth century, the counterbalancing forces of corporations and trade unions grew alongside each other. The former became known as big business for its insatiable appetite for merging with and acquiring competitive businesses, and the latter became big unions, which grew proportionally to protect workers' interests.

Union Power

Workers were needed to perform repetitive jobs for the mass production of agricultural, natural resource, and manufactured products. These workers were natural fodder for union organizers, who viewed business as being fundamentally anti-labor. Unions greatly improved the working conditions and wages of industrial and agricultural workers and helped fulfill the democratic dream that anyone willing to work could partake of the prosperity brought by the Industrial Age. In the 1950s, fully 35 percent of all American workers belonged to a trade union. But as the century wound down, so did the Industrial Age, and along with it the primacy of many of the industries that require factory workers. In many cases, robots took the place of people doing the most repetitive jobs. That certainly was the case in the automotive industry.

As the century wound down, so did the Industrial Age, and along with it the primacy of many of the industries that require factory workers.

The new jobs have been created in information- and entertainment-based companies—what we refer to as content industries—which require workers to create and manipulate data. These new-economy workers do not fit the traditional model of union members.

Consequently, the membership in trade unions is down and the number of nonunionized workers in small businesses, home offices, and fields such as financial services and high technology is up. In addition, globalization has moved hundreds of thousands of union jobs out of industrial nations to less-developed regions where workers earn much lower wages and benefits. A further strike against unions has been the anti-union policies instituted over the past two decades by world leaders such as former U.S. president Ronald Reagan and former British prime minister Margaret Thatcher.

Information Age workers generally do not fit the profile of union members. For one thing, Information Age workers make high wages. College graduates with a degree in computer programming can start at $50,000 (Can) per annum or more. Bright high-school kids with no university education at all can earn $100,000 (Can) a year if they understand how to put together and dismantle computer networks. Writers, animators, graphic designers, musicians, producers, and directors are all in demand to create content.

These workers are creative people, each one unique and each performing a different routine; they are certainly not interchangeable. They all bring a personal approach to their jobs, and the results of their work are not just measured by quantity (lines of code per hour, say) but also by the quality and distinctiveness that make their products competitive and valuable. In short, these folks aren't likely targets for unionization.

Government and private programs that cover all workers, not just those in unions, are now monitoring many of the working conditions and social agendas that unions had previously taken up. Government and private health care plans, retirement plans, unemployment insurance plans, and compensation for injury on the job have now become part of the fabric of life in the industrialized world. Similarly, the issues of workplace discrimination by gender, race, and ethnicity, which used to be taken up by unions, have moved onto the general agendas of governments, which deal with these issues for all citizens.

As a result, at the turn of the twenty-first century, the percentage of U.S. workers belonging to unions fell to only 13.5 percent, its lowest point in six decades.[14] Furthermore, most of these unionized jobs are in the public sector, which still has 37 percent unionized workers. If you take the public sector out of the statistics, the private-sector unionized workforce represents only 9 percent of workers, with strong bargaining leverage in only a handful of industries, such as aircraft, steel, and auto manufacturing.

The Growth of Global Corporations

As union power was eroded, large corporations were given free rein to move their labor-intensive operations to regions of the world that were less developed and had lower labor costs. At the same time, governments' appetite for anti-monopoly regulation was waning. For example, in the days of the coal and steel barons, governments were loath to allow a single company to dominate an important market, but Microsoft did just that in the last quarter of the twentieth century, and governments turned a blind eye.

In other sectors, particularly the entertainment industry, there was no single monopoly; instead, there was a rationalization of the previously free market into a global market with only a handful of companies controlling nearly all the global trade in music, movies, television programs, and books. In effect, entertainment companies have cornered the market by each offering a broad range of content products that are almost indistinguishable from the others in price, production value, and style. The high production values of today's content media, along with the high distribution costs, make it unprofitable to market anything but the most popular titles that appeal to the largest global audiences. Thus, the multinational content corporations are among the strongest proponents of globalization.

The multinational content corporations are among the strongest proponents of globalization.

These large multinationals have used mergers and acquisitions to quickly gain the channels necessary for vertical and horizontal integration of content creation, manufacturing, and distribution throughout the world. This growing appetite for mergers and acquisitions has resulted in a rash of mega-mergers by companies in the content fields. The growth has been further fueled by the convergence of content in digital forms that are now marketed and distributed through common digital networks, whereas the analog formats were previously available only in nonrelated industries, distribution chains, and retail outlets.

While content companies struggle to maintain control over the stories and songs they tell, they now need access to the digital distribution channels, which are controlled by telcos, cablecos, and ISPs. These distribution companies have trillions of dollars of network infrastructure in place, along with the workforces and corporate cultures that are needed for networked digital distribution.

Consequently, content production companies have attempted to align themselves with or join digital content carriage (distribution) companies in order to maintain pipelines to their customers. The predominant trend has been to merge with or acquire digital distributors rather than opt for contractual access, since contracts can be canceled or not renewed, providing little security for the future.

Anti-Client Mergers

The mergers and rationalizations among the content and telecommunications industries have been disadvantageous to clients. These mergers have as their goal the empowerment of a few large corporations with the necessary internal resources to control the global trade in entertainment, information, and culture.

On September 16, 2000, BCE (Canada's largest telecommunications company) acquired CTV and merged with Thomson Corp., making BCE a major player in the Canadian content arena. BCE chair Jean Monty noted at the time, "We want to be more than a network operator. We want to … provide some of its content."[15] Yet eight years earlier, BCE was touting the Stentor alliance of telephony carriers as its preferred instrument of entry into the Digital Age. The earlier emphasis was on providing digital networks—the information pipelines. But in less than a decade, BCE changed its fundamental corporate strategy and decided instead to focus on content. BCE's new focus on combining content with carriage illustrates the changing relationships between suppliers of infrastructure, content creators, and producers/publishers/aggregators throughout the industrialized world. Because of digital convergence, they are all vying for the same clients and the same transactions.

The disruptive technology of digitization has caused disintermediation at every level of commerce, culture, and government.[16] This is particularly true for the content industries because their products travel easily over the new distribution channels. Consumers use the Web to deal directly with suppliers, circumventing retailers, and content creators can distribute their works directly to their audiences, bypassing the distributors that were once their only conduit to commerce.

The Content Layer Cake

It wasn't always like this. In the twentieth century, a balance was established among three layers of content stakeholders:

1. composers, authors, screenwriters, playwrights, and recording artists
2. independent producers and publishers
3. major distributors able to access world markets

These stakeholders made up the three tiers of content value, in which each tier had a clear role to play and was interdependent of the others. Creators worked for or sold their work to production companies. These companies raised the production money and managed the making of programs, shows, records, and books. The production companies entered into deals with distributors, who made the content available worldwide.

By the late twentieth century, only those works with mass-market appeal merited entry into these distribution channels because the cost of marketing and distributing an item nationally and internationally had become too high for any but the most popular of works.

Only a few large companies could survive in the capital-intensive and risky business of physical product distribution.

In fact, the distribution costs were higher than the creation costs and frequently higher than the production costs. The payment advanced to an author, a recording artist, or a screenwriter might be in the tens or hundreds of thousands of dollars, while the production and distribution costs of books, CDs, and films ran into the millions and tens of millions. As a result, only a few large companies could survive in the capital-intensive and risky business of physical content distribution. These distributors became gatekeepers who decided whether a work would be available to a general audience or not.

The Top Layer: The New Media Conglomerates

The new breed of media conglomerate is no longer restricted to a single content industry, but can now capture once-distinct industries, such as print, television, music, and telecommunications, within the same organization. From the customer's point of view, this is not a good development because the merged entities have enormous power to limit product choices for audiences. Further, the larger the merged entities have become, the less inclined they have been to embrace new client priorities, particularly with respect to new options for consuming content online. The tendency to date has been for the major content companies to increasingly try to control every aspect of content creation and distribution. Retailing/distribution of content has been kept separate from the creation of content by anti-monopoly laws, but those laws are not being enforced online, allowing the major players to directly control and limit the options of every aspect of the content chain, up to and including the audience.

In January 2000, an event occurred that characterized the changing business environment: America Online (AOL) acquired Time Warner. The value of the transaction—more than $30 billion (US) in combined annual sales—received wide attention. It was significant that AOL gobbled up Time Warner, not the other way around. Time Warner, in the minds of many, was the archetypical twentieth-century content giant, yet it was absorbed into a relative newcomer on the business block that had only 15 percent of its sales. The merger highlighted the importance to Time Warner of accessing AOL's digital distribution channels. It also accelerated a merger mania that had been building in the marketplace.

Even though online distribution dramatically lowers the cost of distributing digital content, the cost of mass marketing and promotion continues to be a barrier for those content products that require a large international audience to repay their high production costs. It is expensive to set up a secure e-commerce site, and it is even more expensive to maintain and run it. The high production values that mass markets have come to expect from magazines, television programs, films, and music CDs must be reflected in the website's audio and visual presentations, and streaming these media-rich objects requires costly computer web servers and software.

What's more, netizens who log on to such sites have become fickle about how frequently the content needs to be changed (or "refreshed," in industry terminology) so that it stays in fashion. In addition, there is the need to cross-market and cross-promote web content using traditional billboard, newspaper, magazine, radio, and television media.

There is the need to cross-market and cross-promote Web content using traditional billboard, newspaper, magazine, radio, and television media to bring an awareness of the new media using mass media.

These requirements argue for the continued need for a few large multinational companies with sufficient resources to satisfy mass markets for music, literature, movies, and other forms of cultural entertainment. Consequently, the mega-merged behemoths will likely continue to dominate in mass entertainment, and the big will keep getting bigger in the content industries. Recent statistics bear out this trend. The ten largest Canadian companies in the combined television, film, and audio/visual industries had revenues of $213 million (Can) in 1988–1989. A decade later (1997–1998), the top ten's revenues were $839 million, an increase of 1,220 percent. In contrast, all the other companies in those industries had combined revenues of $415 million in 1988–1989, which grew to only $589 million in 1997–1998, a 41 percent increase. By the turn of the twenty-first century, the top ten companies had revenues exceeding the total revenues generated by all other companies in their industries.[17]

The top eight media companies account for almost all of the world's entertainment sales.

In the global arena, the trend is the same. The top eight media companies, listed in Table 5.2, account for almost all of the world's entertainment sales. Most of these companies have already been absorbed into larger cross-industrial companies. A snapshot of these merged companies paints a compelling picture of media and distribution integration. Each of the top eight has major content holdings and annual sales of at least $10 billion (US). Together, they account for a quarter trillion dollars in annual sales.

TABLE 5.2 THE TOP EIGHT MEDIA COMPANIES

Company	Annual Sales (US$)	Holdings
Sony	$58 billion	Columbia TriStar movies and TV shows; Columbia and Epic recording labels; PlayStation video game systems; TVs, VCRs, stereos, and other consumer electronics.
Vivendi/Universal	$42 billion	Universal Music Group and Universal Studios; CANAL+ (15 million TV subscribers in Europe; Vivendi Universal Publishing (formerly Havas); telecom Cegetel; 42 percent of USA Networks; 63 percent of Vivendi Environnement (the world's top water distributor); road and rail transportation.
AOL Time Warner	$36 billion	AOL; CompuServe; Netscape; Warner Bros.; Time Warner Cable; Warner Music; Time Warner publications.

Company	Annual Sales (US$)	Holdings
Walt Disney Company	$25 billion	ABC television network, broadcast TV stations, and radio stations; cable channels such as ESPN (80 percent ownership) and A&E (38 percent ownership); Touchstone Pictures, Hollywood Pictures, and Miramax Films; theme parks, including Walt Disney World and Disneyland; Walt Disney Internet Group.
Viacom	$20 billion	BET (Black Entertainment Television), CBS network, and television stations; production and syndication of TV shows through Paramount Television and CBS Enterprises; Paramount Pictures, the United Paramount Network (UPN), MTV Networks (MTV, VH1, Nickelodeon), Showtime Networks, and Comedy Central (50 percent ownership); Simon & Schuster publishing; Blockbuster video rental chain (82 percent ownership); dozens of Internet holdings; Infinity Broadcasting, with 185 radio stations.
Bertelsmann AG	$15 billion	Operations in nearly 60 countries engaged in publishing, music distribution, and broadcasting; Random House publishing; music company BMG Entertainment; 75 percent stake in Gruner + Jahr publishing (*Stern*, *Family Circle*); 67 percent ownership of RTL Group, Europe's top broadcaster.
The News Corporation Limited	$14 billion	Scores of newspapers (e.g., *The Times* of London) and book publishers (e.g., HarperCollins); FOX Broadcasting; Twentieth Century Fox; the Los Angeles Dodgers. Rupert Murdoch's corporation also owns 34 TV stations in the United States and cable and satellite operations in Asia, Australia, Europe, and Latin America.
BCE	$12 billion	Canada's biggest telecom company, with 80 percent ownership of Bell Canada, Bell Mobility, and Teleglobe global broadband network; 70 percent ownership of Bell Globemedia; broadcaster CTV; Internet portal Sympatico; and the *Globe and Mail* newspaper.

The next tier of companies, with familiar media names such as Quebecor, Thompson, Gannett, Pearson, Tribune, Knight Ridder, Hearst, Rogers, Dow Jones, and CanWest Global, are all in the game for rationalization, mergers, and acquisitions. These companies are likely to continue to be anti-client, restricting choice, driving prices upward, and relying on the products themselves to deliver enough EMOs to clients to keep their minds off their suppliers' shortcomings.

The Bottom Layer: Content Creators

Despite the concentration of power with large media conglomerates, the new digital distribution network enables content creators to directly access their audiences, sometimes much larger audiences than the major distributors could previously reach. Moreover, the cost of distribution has fallen to almost nothing for content that is delivered over the Internet. Consequently, creators are beginning to market, promote, and distribute their own literature, music, visual art, and moving pictures online. Recording artists such as Sting and Jane Siberry declare that the major record companies are their problem, not their solution, for reaching an audience. They and others like them have begun to market and distribute their works to online audiences through their own websites or through web hosting services.

A Cautionary Case History: The Music Biz

I experienced the transition of the entertainment business from a client-centered, touchy-feely affair to a supplier-focused, out-of-touch industry on the brink of self-immolation. In the 1970s I was a rock-and-roll star. My band, Lighthouse, garnered gold and platinum record album sales and performed throughout the world at events ranging from the Isle of Wight Festival in England to Expo '70 in Japan, with fill-in dates at Carnegie Hall and the Fillmore West in San Francisco. I was inducted into the Canadian Rock and Roll Hall of Fame.

I signed multimillion-dollar record deals and had a very good time. When I entered into my first negotiations in 1968, the record industry was at the tail-end of its heyday—a period that began with Thomas Edison's invention of the phonograph recording at the close of the nineteenth century.

Creators are beginning to market, promote, and distribute their own literature, music, visual art, and moving pictures online.

Like the motion picture industry, which had its beginnings around the same time, the record industry measures its success by the popularity of its artists and the stories they tell. And, like the motion picture industry, picking which artists and stories will catch the fancy of the public is the key to making a fortune.

But picking winners is very difficult. The record industry used to rely heavily on people known as A&R (artist and repertoire) guys, whose noses were in the street and whose guts guided their decisions. The heads of record companies would sign record contracts based on the pronouncements of their A&R people. The deal-making trigger was "I like the music. People will buy this record!"

I benefited from this sort of ad-hoc decision-making when I made my first forays into the pop music biz. My musical partner, Skip Prokop, was already a rock-and-roll luminary for his work with Peter, Paul and Mary, the Mommas and the Poppas, SuperSession, and his own band the Paupers. Skip arranged for the A&R guy at MGM records to listen to a demo we recorded in Toronto.

We flew to New York, played our music for the A&R guy at 10 a.m. in his Avenue of the Americas office tower, went out for lunch, and returned that same afternoon to be offered our first recording contract. The decision-makers at MGM had listened to our music, liked it, and believed that others would like it too and buy our records. *Badda bing badda boom!*

The people who made the decision had never been to business school, and none of them were lawyers. They were music aficionados who listened to music every minute of their spare time.

In the film business, the legacy of Louis B. Meyer and the other scions of the houses of popular celluloid taste operated similarly. Executives rose to the top because they could smell a hit, and they could do so because they were rooted in the same emotional experiences as the fans who bought records and tickets to the movies.

And then the earth moved. I remember the year as 1975, but the transition started earlier and took a while longer to take hold in some companies. All of a sudden, it seemed, none of us knew the decision-makers anymore. The A&R people were relegated to advising, not deciding. In their stead was a new layer of corporate executives, and all of them were MBAs or lawyers who knew nothing about hit records, but understood business. They knew how to minimize expenses and maximize efficiency, and above all they understood the new driving force in the entertainment business—namely, the Package.

The Package was a new concept to artists and their managers, who had grown up thinking that talent, timing, and good luck were the essentials for success. The problem with these elements was that not one of them could be quantified and justified in the new framework of business decisions (try to put *these* in a spreadsheet). But the Package was something that executives from outside the biz could understand.

The Package includes such quantifiable elements as market research, focus groups, image creation, branding, promotional plans, marketing plans, cross-promotion, cross-marketing, music videos, genre mapping into demographics (I remember when the word *demo* used to mean a rough version of a song), calculations of potential sales in each market segment, cross-collateralization of publishing income, recruitment of an experienced management team, and so on.

Don't get me wrong. The application of good general business practices is a positive development for conducting business in the entertainment industries. The problem is, the metrics of business need to be applied to products (recordings, movies, books) that have yet to be made, rendering the assumptions almost useless. For executives who have no sense of (and little regard for) their clients, the Package is a better predictor of success than nothing at all, but not by much. The result is that, although only five companies—Sony, AOL Time Warner, EMI, BMG, and Vivendi/Universal—control more than 90 percent of all worldwide record sales, they are unable to judge which products will be successful in the marketplace. In fact, less than 5 percent of the products they introduce make money ... even with great Packages! Can you imagine any other industry that could survive if only one in twenty product introductions was profitable?

Can you imagine any other industry that could survive if only one in twenty product introductions was profitable?

In the television and film businesses, the hit ratio is even smaller. Companies have been able to survive only because their few winners have become super-profitable, as a result of the supplier-centered strategy of maximizing income from publishing rights, spin-offs, sequels, and sales of branded apparel and toys.

But the movement of corporate focus away from client-sensitive executives has had serious and disastrous side effects for the record industry, which has been in crisis for several years. Witness the industry's underestimation of the popularity of services like Napster, which satisfy music lovers while disintermediating the record and music-publishing companies.

Music executives still want to believe they are selling plastic products (CDs), which are easy to quantify and audit and are subject to the transactional analysis taught in business school. The costs of raw materials and manufacturing are X; the costs of warehousing, distribution, insurance, losses owing to pilfering, and so on, are Y; and the costs of marketing, sales, retailing, promotion, and artist royalties are Z. Add them up in a spreadsheet and you get the cost of a record. Add your profit margin and you get the price to the consumer, right?

Not any more. When consumers buy a CD, they place little value on the physical product. Instead, what they value most is the *experience* of listening to music. The EMOs are working big time in the music business. Consumers buy music that makes them feel good. They are in control of which musical selections they play when they are feeling blue and which they play when they are about to paint the town red. The CD cover helps to induce an impulse buy but has no value thereafter. It's the musical experience that provides value for the listener. Music and movies are valuable to consumers because they provide emotional and visceral experiences, the very things that are not quantified by supplier-focused business frameworks. Consequently, when digital networks were introduced, music lovers quickly saw how they could get the experience without buying the physical product.

This sort of business upheaval is not uncommon when new and disruptive technology is introduced into the marketplace. It has been the subject of thousands of articles and has caused the re-engineering of just about every business that is operating in the twenty-first century. It has been called a paradigm shift, a new economy, a new currency, and a new age of information. But the record industry has refused to acknowledge that times have changed and that they must change their business practices as well.

The record industry has been unable and unwilling to understand its clients' point of view. The same executives who use focus groups and market research to justify their business decisions nonetheless refuse to acknowledge that their clients are uninterested in the products they have been peddling, now that an alternative is available.

The record industry business model is based on forcing customers to buy, on average, ten times as many products as they want or need. That's because the content package is a compilation of about fifteen songs bundled into a single music CD. The cost of manufacturing a CD with one or two songs on it, which is what record buyers listen to on the average CD (and on the radio), is the same as the cost of manufacturing a CD with fifteen songs. The recording artist is paid with a percentage of the retail price, not by the number of songs on an album. And it is the artist who pays the cost of recording the extra songs (recouped through record royalties). This means that it costs the record company only a few dimes to put the extra tunes on an album.

Consequently, the retail price point of a record, which by trial and error has been found to optimize at about $20 (Can) in North America, has been exchanged for about fifteen songs bundled into a physical CD.

Even before the advent of online music services, the industry knew that its CD products were not what customers wanted. The huge business of selling blank audio cassettes and cassette recorders allowed listeners to unbundle the songs from a CD, choose their favorite selections, and make their own music compilations.

So instead of taking advantage of the new digital networks as an opportunity to better serve their clients with unbundled songs, music industry leaders saw the new digital technology as a threat. They refused to make their music available online, at any price. And when music lovers opted for the new online services and portable players that circumvented the CD business entirely, industry lawyers branded their erstwhile customers as pirates and thieves.

Let's see how the record business stacks up against the new business rules.

1. Shift from internal to external focus.

Record producers have so far ignored this rule. The industry continues to navel gaze, considering only its traditional business of producing a physical product based on internal considerations. The industry considers external factors, such as the move to an information-based economy and client empowerment, evil forces to be fought in the courts and avoided.

2. Give clients more input and control.

Again, the record industry fails. Customers have strongly indicated that they want control of music programming. Alternative unbundled products are soaring in popularity while the industry clings to its outmoded model, which denies clients any input or control over how they select their individual music products or custom compilations.

3. Base pricing on client valuation.

Now that clients can separate the experience of listening to music from the physical product, their valuation of the product is lower than when they had to pay for manufactured plastic and distribution. Record companies still insist that the value of a song online should be the same as on a retail CD. Their online pricing has reflected the model of $20 (Can) per burned CD, even though the online customer is now absorbing the labor and costs of manufacturing (buying the blank CD and the manufacturing equipment—the computer and CD-RW drive). The record industry has failed to address this fundamental divergence of customer and industry valuation.

4. Motivate clients with emotion.

Clients have been motivated to turn against the record industry suppliers by negative media reports and the record industry's publicity campaign that blames consumers for the industry's problems.

5. Put yourself in your client's shoes.

The industry believes that empathizing with its clients would result in its downfall. Therefore, the industry bases its business strategy on creating a walled fortress within which the few major companies can control all distribution and pricing. There are essentially no free markets in the record business today. The industry model is so outmoded, in fact, that record companies continue to limit most songs to less than four-and-a-half minutes, a limit that is an artifact of the earliest phonograph recordings on wax cylinders or 78 RPM disks, which could not accommodate longer musical selections.

Sound like a recipe for disaster? Well, it is. Record sales have been falling 10 percent annually. The key reason is that new Internet technologies have cropped up, such as Napster (now defunct) and its offspring, which provide a catalog of collected music files and allow millions of users to transfer the files to their computers. The new services offer what the record companies do not: access to unbundled songs that users can stream, download, listen to, or burn onto their own CDs in whatever order and combination they want. Because the record companies have so far refused to license these services, users get the recordings as bootleg, generally without paying for them at all.

Napster had more than 10 million users signed up, validating the desirability of the new products and market. But instead of replicating its service or buying into it, the major record companies responded by taking legal action against Napster.

The music industry succeeded in shutting down Napster in 2001, but by 2002 a half dozen other royalty-free music distribution services had sprung up. The publicity of the court case made Napster and record piracy a newsworthy item, so now everyone knows about it and wants to try the new way of listening to music. Morpheus music-sharing software, one of Napster's progeny, had 71 million users nine months after Napster was shut down.

Instead of replicating its service or buying into it, the major record companies responded by taking legal action against Napster.

The problems of the record industry are not relegated to the Internet. The Associated Press reports that consumers get upset when music suppliers try to control transactions.[18] For example, Karen DeLise bought a Charlie Pride music CD, put it into her computer's CD drive, and tried to make a copy that she could listen to on her portable player, an activity that is legal. The copy didn't work because technology was embedded on the CD to prevent unauthorized copying and sharing of digital music. DeLise believed that it was reasonable to expect that the CD she had bought would work like the millions sold before it. So she filed suit against the record company in September 2001 (and won). This type of consumer action is increasing as record companies wage what they see as a war against thieving consumers who wish to have more convenient use of their products.

The heart of the issue is that record companies continue to use an internally focused, supplier-based strategy, even though other businesses have moved to external, client-based models. Worse, the record companies are doing so within the era of emerging music distribution on the Internet, the greatest client-empowering tool ever created. Their problems have been exacerbated by another important factor in their business: recording artists. The same internalized approach that discounts the primacy of clients also leads to the corporate marginalization of recording artists.

Relationships between recording artists and their labels have deteriorated to the point that big-name stars now band together publicly to rail against their companies. "This is a just cause," declared Billy Joel in March 2002 while performing before an audience that had paid up to $130 (US) to see him, John Fogerty, Sheryl Crow, Stevie Nicks, and the Eagles raise money for their new Recording Artists' Coalition. The negative public relations fallout for the record companies has reinforced consumers' general belief that record companies are ripping everybody off and profiting unreasonably from the sale of other people's music.

In the end, the big labels could end up losing their power while the recording artists become a marketing force on par with the entertainment conglomerates.

Many well-known recording artists, including David Bowie and Jane Siberry, have opted out of their record contracts and now sell their recordings directly to their fans from personal websites. Other artists, such as Alanis Morissette and Neil Young, stick with a major company but publicly advocate sharing music files online, since it helps to promote their concert performances and careers, whereas the record companies' approach to selling their songs online results in virtually no income to the artists because of the terms of their contracts.

In the end, the big labels could end up losing their power while the recording artists become a marketing force on par with the entertainment conglomerates, paying marketers to promote their music directly to their audiences and keeping the lion's share of the profits. That's what disintermediation is about. Remember, United Artists film company was started by Charlie Chaplin and his actor buddies, who felt they were getting a raw deal from the major film companies of the time.

But what will the new business model be for online music? Kevin Kelly, writing in the *New York Times,* puts it this way:

Copies are so ubiquitous, so cheap (free, in fact) that the only things truly valuable are those that cannot be copied. What kinds of things can't be copied? Well, for instance: trust, immediacy, personalization…. So while you can score a copy free of charge, if you want something authenticated, or immediately, or personalized, you'll have to pay…. A friend of a friend may eventually pass on to you the concert recording of a band you like, but if you pay, the band itself will e-mail it to you seconds after the performance.[19]

The record industry, with its vast resources, may yet be able to recover some market share in the emerging market for musical experiences. It is unlikely, however, that it will continue to maintain its stranglehold on the worldwide business. These companies committed the cardinal sin of underestimating the power of their clients and alienated them in the process. In fact, it may just be too late for the majors to recover from their folly, in which case they will fall on the scrap heap of commercial oblivion along with hundreds of other companies that didn't change with the times.

The Middle Layer: Producers and Publishers

The top layer of the content cake has become stronger as a result of mega-mergers, and the bottom layer is potentially stronger as a result of creators' new access to clients. Yet, the middle layer is languishing in the no-man's land of disintermediation. The potency and relevance that were once found in the middle tier are migrating upward to the large content conglomerates and downward to the creators. In the new content layer cake, *major distributors* are gaining power by merging and acquiring former middle-tier companies; *creators* are establishing distribution schemes to supply their works directly to their audiences; and *middle-tier content producers and publishers* are finding it increasingly difficult to stay in business.

Independent record, book, and television production companies are facing three basic business-strategy options:

1. be acquired by a top-tier company and cash out
2. merge with other like-sized companies to gain size and access to capital. This scenario might lead back to the first choice later on, with a bigger cashout.
3. re-engineer the business for online distribution so that it will be profitable when the Web becomes commercially viable. This option is viable only for those companies with enough cash reserves, a rarity in this tier.

Narrowcasting

Today, creators and producers who do not need or wish to address the large mass market are gaining access to alternative channels to reach their audiences. The specialty cable and satellite television channels have already proven to be such alternatives. Their programming frequently lacks high production values and sometimes panders to narrow and local interests (as in the bass-fishing channel or the Cantonese Chinese channel), but these alternatives to *broad*casting and mass markets are chipping away at the dominance of the mass-market networks.

On the Internet, the opportunity is greater for narrow, diverse, and local content. And the history of the Internet, unlike television, is based on peer-to-peer (P2P) communications, not one-to-many. Consequently, mass marketers are finding the Internet a difficult nut to crack when they try to impose their Industrial Age models on it.

Mass marketers are finding the Internet a difficult nut to crack when they try to impose their Industrial Age models on it.

The key for both local and global suppliers of content is to understand their audience-clients. While the central hump of the bell-shaped consumption curve will continue to attract the major distributors, the exciting growth is happening at the edges, where audiences are clamoring for content that is fresh and original, closer to its creators' intentions, and untainted by the lawyers and business execs whose atypical tastes govern the mass market.

In 1998, Professor Jerome Durlak and I reported on a music-on-demand trial we conducted for CulTech Research Centre, in consultation with the Canadian Record Industry Association.[20] Both multinational record industry majors (Sony, Polygram, Warner, EMI, and BMG) and independents (Attic, Anthem, Nettwerk, and Denon) supplied the music. Seventy-five record labels were represented in total, with 2,000 song titles from a wide range of musical styles, including jazz, classical, pop, urban, and country. We obtained licenses for the songs from SOCAN (distribution to the public right) and CMRRA (mechanical reproduction) and similar rights for the recordings from the record industry's licensing agent AVLA (Audio Video Licensing Agency). Custom software that we had created—the IVY music management system—automatically tracked and aggregated the usage data.

Listeners chose from a much broader range of artists and titles than they would normally get from a radio station or a personal record collection. The sixty-five suburban homes that participated in the trial listened to more than 700 titles in the six-month trial period. In the traditional record business, you would expect that the top ten titles accessed would account for the great majority of use, perhaps 90 percent or more. Instead, we found that the top ten play list represents less than 20 percent of the total plays. Even the top fifty titles cumulatively represent only 42.6 percent of the music played. All told, the home residents listened to more than 8,000 music sessions online in the period from August 1, 1997, to February 15, 1998. Table 5.3 provides an analysis of the frequency of play for the 729 songs they listened to.

TABLE 5.3 FREQUENCY OF PLAY OF TRIAL SONGS

Popularity	Percentage of Play Time
Top 10	17.5
11–20	8.6
21–30	6.5
31–40	5.3
41–50	4.7
51–729	57.6

Within a few years, online retailers such as amazon.com found similar results retailing CDs on the Web. The explosion in business was not with mass-marketed hits, which are available at traditional distribution outlets in any case, but with less readily available titles that are not normally stocked in retail stores. The evidence supports clients' demands for more product choice.

The system that we have grown up with favors promoting just a few hit records, films, television programs, and books. That's because the amount of shelf space in stores, television channels, and movie theater screens has been limited, and because it's too expensive to promote and distribute every title that gets produced. These are supplier issues, not client issues. Audiences have a much greater diversity in tastes—not only do tastes differ from one person to another, but each person has varying tastes at different times and in different contexts. You may like to wake up to rock or rap, unwind with cool jazz when you come home from work, and listen to classical music over a nightcap. Within any of these styles, you might sometimes feel like listening to mainstream artists and sometimes take a chance on music you've never heard.

The bottom line? Audiences have a much broader palate for content than the Industrial Age was able to deliver. Today, digital networks offer the potential for access to all the content ever produced. That's what clients want. And they are sure to get it sooner or later. Chances are it will be sooner.

The Staying Power of Mega-Mergers

The merged content companies are likely to hold together because it makes sense in a convergent world to treat content as a single entity rather than break it into its physical parts of books, CDs, television programs, and the like. The new way of looking at a piece of content is as a room with many windows. The content may be viewed (or "windowed") in different ways depending on whether you look through the DVD window, the book window, the music CD window, or the Internet window, but the content itself is indivisible.

Audiences have a much broader palate for content than the Industrial Age was able to deliver.

For example, *The Lord of the Rings* was a very successful book. The thing that was popular was the story, not the physical book, although it was the book that sold in bookstores. The story was then made into a successful movie. The soundtrack album with music from the film also told the story from a certain perspective and became a hit. A video game let players interact with the story in real time. Toy characters let fans interact with and fantasize about story characters.

Each of these products is part of what is known in the entertainment business as the "property" (short for intellectual property). And companies today want to control a property in all of its media manifestations, so that they can recoup any money they spent to acquire or develop it.

The merger of content companies with distribution companies has a different rationale. The largest mega-mergers have integrated digital distribution channels with content so that a single entity can guarantee (or own) a complete end-to-end chain of creation, production, and distribution. Yet many argue that these mergers are ineffective because the business of distribution is fundamentally different from the business of producing content.

As this book went to press, some of the mega-mergers between content and distribution companies were beginning to strain at the seams. If the new client's wishes are to prevail, the provision of content and distribution will most likely diverge, once again allowing customers to pick the method of delivery from a number of suppliers, just as they choose their content from various suppliers.

From a client's perspective, the greatest choice would come from competing content suppliers offered through competing distributors. This scenario would require that content and carriage be separated, as they are for analog content. Television gives a hint of how those services could be split. Cable, satellite, and terrestrial wireless television services all offer the same television programs, each package bundled and priced differently. In this example, there is still no free market, since the content and pricing are regulated by the CRTC in Canada and the FCC in the United States. Still, the client gets to choose not only the content but also the distributor. That's what choice and control are all about.

The Information Pipelines

The new client was born of the Information Age, which is enabled by the deployment of digital networks. The cost of building this infrastructure, of laying the fiber-optic cables and placing the microwave wireless equipment in strategic ground and space locations, is so high that companies have been careful not to move too quickly, lest their investments remain underused for a long initial period, with consequent financial losses. Based on optimistic projections of use and income, these companies have planned several times to accelerate the construction and deployment of high-speed networks to homes and offices, only to be let down because their business models were proven wrong by the marketplace.

In the early 1990s, most analysts predicted that interactive televisions, not computers, would be the information highways of the future. But the introduction of the World Wide Web in 1993 as a branch of the Internet, with its unlimited potential for images, music, and video, cast the die in favor of computer technology, not television. Soon, the race was on to build this infrastructure as quickly as possible. The next disappointment came in the mid-1990s, when telcos and cablecos planned to deploy high-speed (broadband) networks that could distribute television-quality signals using Internet technologies. The business plan was based on selling movies-on-demand, at about $8 to $10 per view. But trials showed that not enough viewers were willing to pay those prices when they could rent the same movies from their neighborhood video store for $2 or $3, and that the cost of technology to deliver hundreds of movies to a neighborhood (equaling the choice at a video store) was too high for the companies to make money, even at $10 per view. So, the plans for broadband were shelved in favor

> **In the early 1990s, most analysts predicted that interactive televisions, not computers, would be the information highways of the future.**

of medium-band technologies—cable and DSL modems—that could work with existing telco and cableco wiring. The consequence of this strategy is that today Internet access is faster than using a dial-up modem, but not nearly fast enough to deliver the multiple television-quality signals that will become the hallmark of the Information Age.

At the turn of the millennium, there was once again a flurry of activity to build high-speed connectivity, and this time it appeared that the stock markets would fund the deployment as part of the dot.com boom, when business plans no longer had to show quick profits. But the bubble burst on the tech sector and we are now back in a holding pattern, waiting for the Information Age to fulfill its promise to allow clients to communicate with their suppliers and with each other using video conferencing, video telephones, and other real-time moving images and sound.

Having been burned several times and with share prices at record lows (companies like Nortel and BCE that were driving the deployment have tanked on the stock exchange), infrastructure companies and their suppliers have become ultra conservative about building information superhighways, deciding instead to hold back development in favor of squeezing as much profit as possible from their legacy systems. Such a strategy is not in tune with the demands of new clients who want to feel good, be in control, and have lots of choices.

Bellheads, Netheads, and Cableheads

Clients are not alone in demanding the good stuff sooner. A schism has formed among digital infrastructure planners. The first camp, the "Bellheads," is led by the telephone companies. Bellheads believe that suppliers should use their existing "intelligent" telephone networks and their complex and expensive switching capacity to deliver information and entertainment. The telephone networks have the same basic architecture that Alexander Graham Bell and his cronies designed more than a hundred years ago. A pair of copper wires goes to each connected appliance (telephone or modem), and the communication takes place along an unbroken path made up of separate line segments connected for the duration of the communication session by switches.

Clients are not alone in demanding the good stuff sooner. A schism has formed among digital infrastructure planners.

The switching is done at large and expensive central offices, each of which handles all the calls traveling to and from a particular area, defined by the area code and the first three digits of the telephone number. The complexity of the switching network enables any caller to reach any receiver and allows the connected appliances to be relatively "dumb" and cheap (telephones) because the electronic smarts are in the network itself. These networks are very costly to build and maintain, as they include millions of switches that complete the circuits from one end of a conversation to another, and require a dedicated path that can carry only one message at a time to and from the appliances.

The second camp, the "Netheads," believes that using smart computers instead of telephones at the end of the communication lines eliminates the need for an expensive network to connect them. In fact, a relatively dumb and inexpensive network is both sufficient and more appropriate. The architecture Netheads favor is the same as that used for decades in computer local area networks: LANs. This type of network requires no central switching offices. Each connected computer is capable of being the sender, receiver, and controller of communications at the end of a mostly passive and inexpensive network.

Instead of connecting real circuits with complex switches, the computer LAN breaks all messages (voice, data, music, and video) into small packets of digital data, each of which has its own copy of the sending and receiving address, along with its position in the message stream. The packets from all messages commingle on the same cables and are sorted en route by (appropriately named) routers, which note their destination addresses and forward each packet to its eventual recipient, where it is reunited with its brethren, reassembled in the order in which it was sent, and delivered to the recipient. If this sounds like a familiar description of the Internet, it's because that's exactly what it is, hence the term Netheads.

The cable TV companies form a third camp. They had an early advantage in terms of infrastructure because their coaxial home connections carry a much higher capacity than telephone connections—more than 100 times higher. On the negative side, they had no way to switch or route the digital signals from one end of a communication to an arbitrary destination, so they have been building expensive switching-and-routing physical plants to make their network suitable for digital traffic.

The Network Backbone

All three camps agree (more or less) on one part of the ultimate design, the long-distance stretch known as the network "backbone." Digital backbones carry communications over the long hauls between cities and regions, known as the

Digital backbones carry communications over the long hauls between cities and regions, known as the Wide Area Network (WAN).

Wide Area Network (WAN). This portion of the infrastructure requires the highest communications capacity and the lowest maintenance costs. It is the equivalent of a superhighway and is similarly used only for long-distance communications, not for local traffic. The hardware technology uses fiber-optic cables, hair-thin strands of glass that cost almost nothing to make and require almost no maintenance because they don't rust and don't carry electrical signals. At one end, a light modulated by the digital signals is shone, and at the other end, the digital signals from the modulated light beam are recovered. For inaccessible regions with low population densities, it is cheaper to use wireless technologies, similar to those used to beam television signals from satellites to your home.

Even though all camps generally agree on the backbone, the Bellheads and the Netheads are split on which software transportation protocols should be used for routing the digital packets. Netheads believe that the entire system, end-to-end, should use the protocols of computer networks, essentially a scaled-up version of the Ethernet connections that are built into computers and used on local area computer networks (LANs) throughout the world. Ethernet products are standardized and produced in huge quantities because they are consumer items used in homes and offices. Therefore, they are inexpensive and easy to set up, and they don't require trained technicians for maintenance. Over the years, Netheads have developed advanced Ethernet equipment that can operate at the higher capacities needed on the WAN, up from the original few megabits per second (standard Ethernet) to 100 megabits per second (now available on most computers), to gigabits and even terabits per second. The beauty of using a single simple protocol is that all the equipment by different manufacturers can interoperate, eliminating the need for inefficient and costly translations from one digital protocol to another.

But Ethernets and the Internet were designed for sending data, not real-time signals like voice or video. One of the reasons why Ethernet equipment is inexpensive is that it uses simple protocols, with little redundancy or checking that all packets arrive at their destinations without errors. If a few text characters in your email arrive scrambled, it's no great inconvenience to have the message re-sent, even if it arrives a few seconds or minutes later.

On the other hand, telephone protocols like SONET were engineered to deliver what's known as QoS (quality of service), a kind of guarantee that the signals you send will arrive intact without errors. After all, it is very disconcerting if the sound of someone's voice is interrupted for a few seconds as a result of delays or errors in the transmission. The Bellheads maintain that QoS considerations dictate a continued use of their more costly telephone protocols and hardware, which means that Internet packets must be converted on the on-ramps to the telco backbones and then reconverted on the off-ramps.

The Netheads point out that the motivating factor for telcos is not really QoS but the investment that they have made in their infrastructure: trillions of dollars for the wires and associated electronics that compose the telephone networks. The cost of junking this gear and quickly converting the networks to more efficient and cost-effective Internet designs could bankrupt the telcos. To deal with the issue of quality of service, Netheads just increase the capacity of their networks, reducing the traffic jams that packets encounter and making delays and errors less likely. This approach is much less costly than the Bellhead solution.

Meanwhile, there remains the question of the last-mile (or first-mile) architecture—the communication links from each office or home to the fiber-optic backbone. There is no agreement about how these on-ramps and off-ramps to the information superhighway should be constructed. The telephone companies have an enormous investment in copper wires to homes and offices, so the Bellheads want to use them instead of spending an estimated $1,500 per home or office to lay a more modern connectivity infrastructure. Telcos have developed DSL (digital subscriber line) technology that allows digital Internet signals to travel on their designed-for-analog copper wire system by using DSL modems (modulator/demodulator) at each end.

There is no agreement about how these on-ramps and off-ramps to the information superhighway should be constructed.

The cablecos also use a type of modem to allow the digital Internet signals to travel along their designed-for-analog copper coaxial cables. These cable modems have a higher capacity than telephone wires but are not generally available at offices, since the cable TV business has been aimed at home television use.

The Netheads scratch their heads at these modem solutions, because the best architecture for the first and last mile, the one that carries the greatest capacity at the lowest maintenance cost, is the same as that used in the backbone—fiber optics. Fiber to the home and office is the wired solution that all three camps agree will eventually prevail, but the Netheads want it deployed right away, while the cable and telco interests want to stick with their short-term modem strategies.

With end-to-end fiber in place, it will be child's play to deliver multiple television-quality signals to each home or office. Applications such as full-motion video telephones, video conferencing, television programs, and movies on demand will dramatically change the way we live and work, but they cannot be made available to the general public until higher-capacity end-to-end fiber is in place.

The telcos and cablecos want to put off replacing their current networks as long as possible so they can get the most value from their already-paid-for physical plants. Therefore, today's infrastructure is based on this reality, not on the cornucopia of bandwidth and applications that were envisaged in the 1990s. As clients, we are still waiting for the major goodies to arrive.

There Is No Free Market

In addition to these squabbles, there are political and regulatory factors that greatly influence decisions about deploying broadband networks. The stakeholders' arguments have received a fair amount of media coverage, but the public is less aware of the behind-the-scenes regulatory actions, even though these probably have a greater impact on which infrastructure architecture will be deployed and how soon. These political machinations are supplier-driven leftovers of twentieth-century thinking.

Until recently, telecommunications companies were regulated monopolies. In each country or region of a country, exclusive rights were granted to telephone companies to provide services. Later, cable television companies were given the right to provide television services. The rationale was that the cost of deploying the infrastructure in each case was so high that it would not be financially viable for a company to provide it unless it was guaranteed exclusive rights to a customer base. In addition, the government could require that monopoly suppliers serve all taxpayers by making services available in every nook and cranny of the country.

In order to avoid the price gouging that normally accompanies monopolies, governments gave exclusive rights only to form the business, not to set pricing. Telecommunications and cable television pricing has been regulated (meaning approved) by government or quasi-governmental bodies where exclusive territories are granted. The system has worked pretty well, particularly because it has resulted in almost universal access to services, which would have been unlikely if companies had deployed infrastructure only to the most commercially advantageous (high population density) regions.

As alternative capacity has become available for long-distance (optical backbone) and television (satellite, terrestrial wireless) services, these sectors are gradually being deregulated, with competitive forces now at work to lower prices and offer differentiated products. But not everyone agrees that deregulation is fostering true free markets. Each of the legacy stakeholders has an enormous advantage in owning and operating a huge physical plant, built when they could not lose money doing so (because the government ensured it). So,

Not everyone agrees that deregulation is fostering true free markets.

although competition is now being encouraged, the cards are highly stacked in favor of those who are currently in control.

Local Service

The industrial competitive imbalance applies particularly to local service—the connection from each home or office to the backbone. Unlike long-distance connectivity, for which many companies can provide optical cables, only the local phone company and cable television company have a connection from the backbone to your home or office. Bob Frankston, inventor of the first spreadsheet program, VisiCalc, puts it this way:

> The crux of the matter is that those who are most supportive of an open marketplace confuse the removal of regulations with the creation of such a marketplace. By defining the "marketplace" in terms of telephony and television we have actually prevented a real free market because it cedes control over the key resource (connectivity) to those whose strongest incentive is to restrain trade. Naively "deregulating" without addressing this structural issue is little more than government-mandated restraint of trade.[21]

As long as the first mile of connectivity is a limited resource, those who have an interest in using it to prevent competition in services and content must not be given the ability to control it. A bifurcated marketplace of connectivity versus services/content is necessary in order to enable a true free market.

With a monopoly, companies can afford to invest big money in infrastructure, knowing that they will recoup their costs over the long haul. But now that governments are beginning to deregulate local telecommunications, telecom executives can no longer count on captive markets to recoup the costs of building new networks. The result of competition in long-distance telephone service has been a huge reduction in long-distance rates, which is good for clients but bad for shareholders of long-distance companies. Teleglobe, one of the major international long-distance companies, went bankrupt in 2002, dragging down the share price of BCE, which owned a chunk of the company. Others have gone under as well.

The consequence has been a slowdown in building the first- and last-mile links to the digital highways. Telcos and cablecos are loath to build the right networks for their clients because regulators (actually, deregulators) will force them to allow their competitors to use these data pipelines, even though their competitors are not funding the construction. And governments are wary of enforcing the deregulation that they tout, because so many citizens and corporations own stock in the telcos and cablecos that countries' entire economies could crash if these mega-corporations were to fail as a result of cheaper competition. And the competition most certainly would be much cheaper, because the newer and more capable fiber networks cost less than one-hundredth what the older technologies of coaxial cables and twisted copper wires cost.

Here's a simple example that puts things in perspective. A single telephone line service costs about $20 (Can) per month. That buys you 56 kilobits per second of bandwidth.[22] If you buy Internet service from the same telephone company, it costs about $40 (Can) a month for a digital connection that provides about twenty times the telephone bandwidth.[23] Not a bad deal, eh? Twenty times the bandwidth for just twice the price!

Let's look at it another way. If you could use your Internet connection for telephone conversations, you would get twenty lines for the same price as buying two lines of regular telephone service. Now here's the kicker. If a competitor were allowed to string new fiber to your home, it could probably deliver 1,000 times the bandwidth for about $5 a month (amortizing its cost over thirty years). That's right, a thousand times the capacity at a quarter of the price.

If a competitor were allowed to string new fiber to your home, it could probably deliver one thousand times the bandwidth for about $5 a month.

Since this result would be highly favorable to clients, and since we are supposedly in the midst of telecommunications deregulation, why isn't this solution available today? There are two main reasons: First, the scenario assumes that telecommunications will truly be deregulated and open to free competition, and second, the scenario assumes that telco competitors could connect to the long-distance backbones at reasonable rates. Both of these assumptions require strong political and regulatory will, which has not been forthcoming to date.

The argument against this scenario is that although it would be good for consumers and most businesses, it would be disastrous for telcos and cablecos. If you could switch to fiber optics, the first thing you would do is cancel your phone service and make all your phone calls on the big digital pipes. That's what companies and universities are beginning to do now within their internal campus networks. The next thing you would do is cancel your cable or satellite television service, because you could get full-motion movies, videos, and television programs on demand through your fiber connection, at a much lower cost than with your current cable and satellite TV providers, who must charge for sending their signals over much more costly infrastructures.

The cost differentials for a new, substitute telecommunications infrastructure are well documented and not based on conjecture or opinion. Alternative and competitive end-to-end broadband networks are being built every day by schools, municipalities, and consortia of businesses that are laying their own fiber, bypassing the entire legacy telecommunications system at a fraction of the cost.[24]

A Few Scenarios

So the big question is, Will the new client be in control of the information infrastructure rollout, with dramatic and disruptive effects, or will the legacy suppliers be able to maintain the status quo, with its stabilizing effect? The answer to that question will move billions into the pockets of some and out of the pockets of others.

Here are a few scenarios that could play out and change the balance of power between telecommunications suppliers and clients.

Scenario 1: Disruption, Then Rapid Growth

This scenario is close to the Nethead approach. Telcos and cablecos could bite the bullet and reset the valuation of their obsolete infrastructure to a realistic value, near-zero. Doing so would take a collective act of political will, not only by the telecommunications industry, but also by the public at large and its governments, since the shareholdings of telecom infrastructure companies would likely plummet. The possible outcome could be similar to the savings and loan crisis of the 1980s in the United States.

This scenario could trigger a short-term recession, but it would set the stage for tremendous and rapid growth and for entry into the heyday of the Information Age. Government intervention might be necessary to ensure a controlled environment for recovery, as, for example, the 1989 S&L bailout by George Bush Senior allowed a U.S. industry to write down its losses and get on with its business.

Roxane Googin writes, "Meanwhile, humanity stands on the threshold of building an omni-functional network that embodies the highest principles of democracy, expression and entrepreneurialism. Freedom-loving people should hold it dear. Should we delay its construction to preserve yesterday's moribund businesses? Must we endure permacession until the incumbent telcos have played their last card?"[25]

Scenario 2: A Middle Ground

Every new client, whether a student, patient, senior, or person with disabilities, would benefit from greater and cheaper bandwidth for communications and entertainment. However, many clients own shares in telecommunications infrastructure companies and would likely lose a great deal of money should these stocks fall. This situation argues for a solution that will change the telecommunications infrastructure more quickly than the incumbents would like but not as quickly or as disruptively as with Scenario 1.

In this scenario, many of today's telecom clients would become their own suppliers, by buying collectively. Condominium and apartment residents would make deals directly with content suppliers (television networks, web content aggregators) and bandwidth suppliers, disintermediating some of the current satellite and cable TV companies and eventually the local telephone companies. Cities and towns would follow suit, and the global village would be replaced by a large number of tribal villages, or local affinity groups, each with its own information infrastructure culture.

The global village would be replaced by a large number of tribal villages, or local affinity groups, each with its own culture.

This scenario is not as far-fetched as it may seem. The city of Chicago is building a fiber-optic infrastructure that will enable it to function as the Internet service provider (ISP) for all Chicago businesses and residents. Dozens of towns, cities, and regions across the United States and Canada have done this already.

In a typical arrangement, the municipality tenders contracts for building and managing the communications infrastructure. If they are competitive, incumbent cablecos and telcos can keep the business. If not, new entrants get the business (thus, free markets are affected by business Darwinism). The cost of mortgage payments for the legacy telco infrastructure would not factor into the cost of the new services, and the telcos would not have to finance the new construction.

Instead of trying to sell consumers interactive television boxes with built-in hard drives (personal video recorders) with a $1,000 price tag, the local telecom collective would finance broadband fiber-optic pipes to homes and offices, which might have the same cost but would be financed over a longer term (thirty years or so). The video-capable infrastructure would eliminate the need for costly video distribution systems within every home and even more costly video distribution systems on the wide area network. In essence, this is neither a Nethead nor a Bellhead scenario because it builds a new infrastructure *between* the network and the home/office. This option puts a new level of intermediary into the supply chain—the local community.

Here, the new clients will be in control of their content and communication: They will be able to negotiate with a much larger number of telecommunications intermediaries and content agents for customized services to suit their lifestyle and working needs.

Scenario 3: A Rearguard Action

This scenario is essentially Bellhead. It involves keeping a brake on deregulation and free markets and letting the Information Age unfold slowly and in an orderly manner. This option is basically status quo, and although it has some positive elements it can lead to long-term recession. We're currently living through the consequences of this strategy. Since the entertainment, information, and telecommunications industries have been driving most of the economic growth worldwide, clamping a lid on their expansion by limiting the natural exploitation of their best products and services dampens the entire global economy.

The reason companies such as Cisco and Nortel have lost so much of their value (and so much of investors' money) is that the projections they had made for selling their infrastructure components turned out to be wildly optimistic in the wake of the dot.com meltdown and its associated slowdown of infrastructure rollout.

When will things shake out and settle down? When will the new client reign supreme? The process will take time with any of these scenarios, up to five years for Scenario 1 and perhaps twenty years for Scenario 3. Scenario 2, the middle-ground scenario, would take a period that is, well, somewhere in the middle.

The same forces were at work at the turn of the last century **When will the new client** with the introduction of disruptive technologies, including automobiles, electricity, telephones, moving pictures, and sound **reign supreme?** recordings. It took a few generations (plus a stock market crash and two world wars) before things settled down to the relatively benign 1950s, when consumer confidence and business optimism were high and every kid expected to do better than his parents in every way. The same prosperity can be expected as we move ahead in the twenty-first century.

The Problem with Business Training

With all of these massive changes occurring in business, you might think that the academics who teach business would have changed their thinking in fundamental ways. Unfortunately, the underlying principles of Industrial Age business management are still being taught to aspiring entrepreneurs and executives. Central to this thinking is a concept of transactions that relies heavily on mathematical models and powerful computer-driven spreadsheets. The lack of client-centric approaches and recognition of EMOs is an anti-client force that needs to be corrected in the business community.

While researching this book, I interviewed many leaders of industry. They all accept the thesis that human activities can be reduced to transactional models. A student pays tuition and receives an education. Citizens pay taxes and receive protection, travel infrastructure, and social services. Renters pay rent for their apartments and receive shelter. People buy food and receive sustenance.

Most of these business executives studied business and hold master of business administration (MBA) degrees. The MBA has become the ante for sitting down at the gaming table of commerce. The number of MBAs has been increasing exponentially. In the United Kingdom, for example, MBA graduates are doubling every five years (from 4,000 in 1990 to 8,000 in 1995).[26] In the United States, the figures are increasing even more dramatically, as Table 5.4 reveals.[27]

TABLE 5.4 MBA GRADUATES IN THE UNITED STATES FOR SELECTED YEARS

Year	Number
1919	110
1949	4,335
1969	18,000
1979	40,000
1999	150,000

The reason for the popularity of the MBA degree is obvious. The average MBA graduate gets three job offers at starting salaries between $60,000 and $100,000 (Can) annually.

But for the past three decades, U.S. researchers have been tracking the utility of business schools that train MBAs and have come to the unexpected conclusion that these programs have been failures by their own standards of measurement. For example, although more than 2 million MBAs manage businesses worldwide today, the quality of business management hasn't improved since 1975, when MBA training became the norm in business. In fact, the MBA explosion has coincided with a marked decrease in the performance of corporations.[28]

Certainly, the quality of MBA graduates is very high. They share a keen interest in commerce, have lots of drive, and are very intelligent. Otherwise, they wouldn't make it through the educational sieve that sorts through dozens of applications for each available spot in an MBA program.

The problem lies in what is taught, or more precisely what is *not* taught. There is lots of math and lots of scientific analysis, but not much psychology, sociology, or humanities. In other words, MBA programs have a strong supplier focus that prepares graduates well for administering efficient organizations but doesn't teach them much about human behavior and the factors that motivate an organization's clients.

Our leaders of commerce are trained in the intricacies of statistical analysis and logical consequences. They are able to attack business problems of high complexity because they use computers to do the calculations and perform "what if" scenarios. The most complex tools of analytic and mathematical economics have been tamed from their wild origins in the hinterlands of brilliant professorial minds to become the house pets of mundane managers who need only be able to enter a few numbers into a spreadsheet.

But the reduction of commercial activities into equations that represent the values of sellers and buyers is incomplete. It lacks the difficult-to-quantify intuitive and emotional elements in decision-making known as "gut feel."

The visceral and emotional elements of life are difficult to measure in business models. Most businesspeople will tell you that emotions should play no role in commercial decisions. They advise that business should be driven by statistical analysis, projection of trend lines, and other data that can be easily gathered, graphed, and used in calculations.

The visceral and emotional elements of life are difficult to measure in business models.

Consequently, the founders of most of the Industrial Age's great wealth would find it difficult to achieve positions of power today, because they operated by the seat of their pants. They made their fortunes because they sensed opportunity and didn't question the emotional rush that led them to bet the farm on a hunch.

Before he was elected president of the United States, Woodrow Wilson was president of Princeton University when the idea for a master's degree in business was proposed, in 1910. At the time, he argued against the program, saying, "You wouldn't have universities teach business, would you?" This sentiment seems foolish today, but only if you fail to compare the success of European and American enterprises at the turn of the twentieth century with that at the turn of the twenty-first. For all the improvements in technology and business schooling, the success rate of businesses is lower today than it was then.

Capturing transactions only as those items that are easily quantifiable gives a distorted picture of what is taking place. For example, individuals with Internet access approach the Web as a market space.[29] They do research online before they buy, make purchase commitments, arrange financing, take delivery of digital products, and obtain follow-up service. The "commerce" in e-commerce encompasses all of these activities. However, when measuring business-to-consumer (B2C) e-commerce, sellers can easily identify and quantify only the transactional component, and this becomes the focus of most current e-commerce measurements.

Business's obsession with reducing entrepreneurial approaches to numerical analysis has had some bizarre outcomes. In 1982, Tom Peters and Robert Waterman, two consultants at McKinsey & Co., wrote *In Search of Excellence,* a book that became the bible for revamping businesses to be more globally competitive. One of the best-selling business books of all time, it detailed eight key elements for profitability, spurred corporate decentralization, and encapsulated modern corporate management.

Its eight basic principles were boiled down from a statistical analysis of forty-three large companies that were at the head of their corporate classes. The data provided clear direction to companies seeking success and transformed the authors into $50,000 per day consultants. Peters went on to be one of the cheerleaders of the new economy, and he predicted the changes necessary for businesses to operate successfully in the Digital Age.

Twenty years after the publication of the seminal book, in a stunning interview with *Fast Company* magazine Peters admitted, "We faked the data."[30] The seminal book upon which most modern companies have based their ethos was fraudulent. There were no data at the time to support Peters and Roberts's hypotheses. They now explain that there was just too much pressure to justify their industrial observations with statistical evidence. As it turned out, their informed hunches were correct, but no one would have given them credence without the numbers to back up their claims. So the authors came up with a list of companies that they instinctively felt were on the right track. Then they faked the statistics to mollify the business community.

In a follow-up interview with *USA Today*, Peters gave his advice for success in business: "Start by using common sense, by trusting your instincts.... I don't see any value in having a ton of data to see who pops out."[31]

Understanding the trends will help individuals and companies to steer the best course through the minefield of change.

The entrepreneurs who created enormous wealth from the innovations of electricity, automobiles, telephones, phonograph recordings, and moving pictures shared a quality that many of today's business leaders lack: the ability to envisage the forces that trigger clients to reach into their wallets and purses and part with their hard-earned money.

The anti-client trends discussed in this chapter will not halt the progress of the Information Age or its new client focus. Understanding the trends, however, will help individuals and companies to steer the best course through the minefield of change and find the swiftest path to the safer and more profitable landscape beyond.

The better we understand the new clients and adopt strategies that support them, the more successful we will be in our endeavors.

THE START OF THE
INFORMATION FAIRYTALE

T he future unfolds slowly, as an infinite series of seemingly unrelated events. The stock market declines five days in a row; the universe is found to contain millions of black holes; a war erupts on the other side of the world; a good friend loses her job; and so on. But with the benefit of hindsight, we can see that a few pivotal events have changed the course of human civilization: the invention of the wheel; the advent of the modern corporation; the fall of the Soviet Union; and the rise of the Internet.

The emergence of the new client falls into this category of catalytic events. Although the change was not obvious at first, the empowerment of clients at the expense of suppliers is now evident in hundreds of social, industrial, and political contexts.

The realignment of the client–supplier relationship is a consequence of new communications tools that are transforming the way we relate to each other and to our political, economic, and social institutions. Although we all fear the unknown, the result of this revolution in technology will lead to a more comfortable and people-friendly world than did previous upheavals because it builds on the two most distinguishing characteristics of humans: the ability to design and use tools and the ability to communicate complex ideas.

The changing relationship between clients and suppliers presents many new opportunities for entrepreneurs, governments, and other organizations to get in line with the new framework and prosper. Although it may be challenging to understand the framework, the results will be more than worth the effort. After all, most organizations are still struggling to understand how they best fit into the Information Age. As a result, those that adapt quickly will have a competitive advantage.

Although the framework is changing, the fundamentals are not. People are still people, and human nature will continue to drive transactions. The business advice my father gave me when I was a young boy is still the best advice in the Information Age: A good deal is one from which both parties emerge feeling upbeat and victorious.

The Information Fairytale

Once upon a time, there was a land with marvels beyond compare. Wondrous networks connected all parts of the realm, performing miraculous feats that allowed people greater productivity than their ancestors. Some of the networks were made up of wires that crossed the terrain, sometimes tunneling underground like worms and sometimes reaching across poles like giant spider webs. The wires crossed the oceans and the lakes as well, lying on the bottom like enormous sleeping sea snakes. Other networks had no wires at all, but instead used invisible waves to communicate messages between antennas, like electronic insects. Sometimes the antennas were on the ground and sometimes they were in space, hovering above the planet in fixed locations, like hummingbirds drinking from a flower.

The networks and communications between people proliferated beyond the wildest dreams of those who had lived only a few generations earlier. Whereas sending messages used to take many months by ground and sea transportation, it now became commonplace for people to send messages instantly to others thousands of miles away.

The networks were more than carriers of messages, though. All along their routes, they were connected to computing machines that sorted out which information was to go to whom, performing transformations on the information to make it more useful and enjoyable. The thousands of separate languages spoken around the world had previously prevented people from communicating with those outside their cultures. But the computing machines could now automatically translate their communications from one language to another, like the Babble fish in Douglas Adams's novel *The Hitchhiker's Guide to the Galaxy.*

The networks and computers allowed people to share more than ever before. They shared information; they chatted; they exchanged mail; they sent pictures and music to each other. The new networks were bringing people throughout the world together in ways they had never dreamed of. It seemed that the tribal associations of their ancestors were being replaced by a new global village in which every single human being could communicate with each other.

The sharing of information and communication made the people much more knowledgeable than ever before. Solutions to problems that had seemed intractable, such as curing human diseases, became commonplace. The increased importance of communications meant that a person's intellect and personality became more important than physical strength or endurance. And, because ordinary people were more informed, they became more powerful, equalizing the roles of those who had been in control with those who had been controlled.

It was the dawning of a new age.

NOTES

The End of the Industrial Fairytale

1. Katherine Mieszkowski, "Web Commerce as if Customers Mattered," *Fast Company* (November 1998).
2. The capitalization of U.S. Steel was $1.4 billion (U.S.) in 1901.
3. Douglas Goold, "Editor's Diary: The Steel Industry Isn't What It Used to Be, and Neither Are Its Unions," *Report on Business* (February 22, 2002).
4. The switch from mined fossil fuels to renewable energy sources such as solar, wind, and water will likely take place in the second half of the twenty-first century, when the world's supply of oil and gas runs out. See Paul Hoffert, Eric Hoffert, and Martin Hoffert, "Effect of Multimedia Telecommunications on the Global Environment," Proceedings of Multimedia '93 Conference, Calgary, March 1993.
5. The terms "Digital Age" and "Information Age" are often used interchangeably, but sometimes the former is used to describe the enabling tools while the latter refers to the result. The era of information dominance is a direct consequence of digital technology, particularly digital networks.
6. Cyveillance (www.cyveillance.com <http://www.cyveillance.com>), a company founded in 1997, provides "Extra-Site" e-business intelligence. For this study, Cyveillance analyzed Internet pages and examined links, tracking the frequency of unique URLs. More than 350 million links were analyzed over a four-month period.
7. eMarketer, from CyberAtlas.com (March 21, 2002). Online: http://cyberatlas. internet.com/big_picture/geographics/article/0,1323,5911_151151,00.html
8. Elaine Carey, "High-Tech Census Is a Net Gain for Statistics Fans," *Toronto Star* (March 10, 2002).

1 The New Age of Information

1. *Fast Company,* "Fast Talk: The State of the Customer Economy," *Fast Company* 50 (September 2001): 80. Online: www.fastcompany.com/online/50/fasttalk.html
2. UCLA Center for Communication Policy, *Internet Report: Surveying the Digital Future* (February 7, 2002). Online: www.ccp.ucla.edu/pages/internet-report.asp
3. Jakob Nielsen, *Designing Web Usability: The Practice of Simplicity.* Indianapolois, IN: New Riders Publsihing, 2000.

4. David Pogue, "DVD Players Under $100: What Price a Bargain?" *New York Times* (February 7, 2002). Online: www.nytimes.com/2002/02/07/technology/circuits/07STAT.html

5. Stanley Brown, *Customer Relationship Management: A Strategic Imperative in the World of E-Business.* Toronto: J. Wiley & Sons, 2000.

6. See Paul Hoffert, *The Bagel Effect: A Compass to Navigate Our Wired World.* Toronto: McGraw-Hill Ryerson, 1998.

7. John Sheridan, president of Bell Canada, responsible for Bell's wire-line, wireless, voice, data, IP broadband, and digital satellite TV services, was interviewed by the author on October 10, 2001, in Toronto, Ontario.

2 The New Business Rules

1. U.S. Department of Commerce, *Digital Economy 2000* (June 2000). Online: www.esa.doc.gov/de2k2.htm.

2. The inherent signal-carrying capacity of fiber optics and its low cost make it the information link of choice, except in areas where laying cable is too difficult because of local terrain or too expensive because of small populations separated by large distances. For the underlying science, see Paul Hoffert, Eric Hoffert, and Martin Hoffert, "The Effect of Multimedia Telecommunications on the Global Environment," in proceedings of Multimedia '93 conference in Calgary (March 1993).

3. Full-time workers make up about 75 percent of the workforce, down from almost 100 percent a decade earlier, according to the U.S. Department of Labour. Online: www.bis.gov/news.release/wkyeng.t05.htm.

4. Erik Brynjolfsson and Lorin M. Hitt, "Beyond the Productivity Paradox: Computers are the Catalyst for Bigger Changes," *Communications of the ACM* (Association for Computing Machinery), August 1998.

5. Patricia B. Seybold, with Ronni T. Marshak, *Customers.com: How to Create a Profitable Business Strategy for the Internet and Beyond.* New York: Times Business, 1998. See also Patricia B. Seybold with Jeffrey M. Lewis and Ronni T. Marshak, *The Customer Revolution: How to Thrive When Customers Are in Control.* New York: Crown Business, 2001.

6. Jennifer Gilbert, "A Dot.com That's (Holy Discredited Business Paradigms!) Doing Things Right," *Business 2.0* (August 2001).

7. *Fast Company,* "Fast Talk: The State of the Customer Economy," *Fast Company* 50 (September 2001):80. Online: www.fastcompany.com/online/50/fasttalk.html

8. Leslie Ellen Harris, *Digital Property: Currency in the 21st Century.* Toronto: McGraw Hill.

9. "Priceline Looms as Prized Catch in Buyout Deal," *Toronto Star* (March 11, 2002).

10. William G. Huitt. "Motivation" (January 10, 1998). Online: http://chiron.valdosta.edu/whuitt/col/motivation/motivate.html.

11. See A. Maslow, "A Theory of Human Motivation," *Psychological Review,* 50, 370–396; W. James, *Psychology: Briefer Course.* New York: Collier, 1892/1962; E. Mathes, "Maslow's Hierarchy of Needs as a Guide for Living," *Journal of Humanistic Psychology,* 21 (Fall), 69–72; C. Alderfer, *Existence, Relatedness, and Growth.* New York: Free Press, 1972.

12. Elliott Ettenberg, *The Next Economy: Will You Know Where Your Customers Are?* New York: McGraw-Hill, 2002.

13. Interview with David Siegel by Katherine Mieszkowski, "Web Sight—Let Your Customers Lead," *Fast Company* 33 (April 2000).

3 New Client Expectations

1. Ron Jette, "Are User's Content with Your Content?" in the Editors' Association of Canada newsletter, *Active Voice,* 22, 1 (February 2002).

2. Stanley Brown, *Customer Relationship Management: A Strategic Imperative in the World of E-Business.* Toronto: J. Wiley & Sons, 2000.

3. Liz Shahnan, quoted in Bryan Eisenberg, "CRM, Yes, But Don't Forget to MRC," *eCRM Insights,* reprinted from *ClickZ* (September 27, 2001). Online: www.ecrmguide.com/columns/article/0,,10383_891451,00.html

4. Christopher Fletcher and Isaac Ro, *Worldwide CRM Spending: Forecast and Analysis 2001–2005.* Aberdeen Market Analysis Service, November 2001.

5. Bryan Eisenberg, "CRM, Yes, But Don't Forget to MRC." ECRM Insights, reprinted from *ClickZ* (September 30, 2001). Online: www.ecrmguide.com/columns/article/0,,10383_891451,00.htm.

6. *Fast Company,* "Fast Talk: The State of the Customer Economy," *Fast Company* 50 (September 2001): 80. Online: www.fastcompany.com/online/50/fasttalk.html.

7. Philip Say, "Do You Know What Your Customers Experience?", *eCRM Insights* (August 28, 2001). Online: www.ecrmguide.com/columns/article/0,3376,10383_87411,00.html. Reprinted from *ClickZ.* Online: www.clickz.com/b2b_mkt/ b2b_mkt/article.php/836551

8. *Fast Company,* "Fast Talk: The State of the Customer Economy," *Fast Company* (September 2001): 80. Online: www.fastcompany.com/online/50/fasttalk.html.

9. The Gartner Group, Report, "The Emergence of CRM Infrastructures" (March 2001). Online: www.ecrmguide.com/columns/article/0,3376,10383.871301,00.html.

10. Personal email communication with author, 2002.

11. Brian Caulfield, "Facing Up to CRM." *Business 2.0 Inc.* (August 2001). Online: www.business2.com/articles/mag/0,1640,16663,FF.html

12. As reported by Julie Sloane, "Follow Your Customers," *Fortune magazine*, "Small Business" Issue (July–August 2001).

13. Bryan Eisenberg, "CRM, Yes, But Don't Forget to MRC." ECRM Insights, reprinted from *ClickZ* (September 30, 2001). Online: www.ecrmguide.com/column/article/0_10383_089141,00.html.

14. Ipsos-Reid, research poll, "Privacy Policies Critical to Online Consumer Trust," (February 28, 2001). Online: www.ipsos-reid.com/media/ dsp_displaypr_cdn.cfm?id_to_view=1171

15. Secure Socket Layer technology is available in the two most popular browsers, Microsoft Internet Explorer and Netscape Communicator.

16. John Schwartz, *New York Times* (September 25, 2002).

4 The New Clients

1. David Siegel, interviewed by Katharine Mieszkowski, "Web Commerce As If Customers Mattered," *Fast Company* 19 (November 1998). Online: www.fastcompany.com/online/19/webcomm.html.

2. Paul Sonderegger, in an interview with Mark Vigaroso in "What Shoppers Expect Today," *E-Commerce Times* (October 23, 2001). Online: www.newsfactor.com/perl/story/14157.html.

3. David Siegel, interviewed by Katharine Mieszkowski, "Web Commerce As If Customers Mattered," *Fast Company* 19 (November 1998). Online: www.fastcompany.com/online/19/webcomm.html.

4. Mark Vigaroso in "What Shoppers Expect Today," *E-Commerce Times* (October 23, 2001). Online: www.newsfactor.com/perl/story/14157.html.

5. Cyber Atlas Staff, "Car Shoppers Increase Use of the Internet." *E-Commerce News* (November 27, 2001). Online: www.internetnews.com/ ec-news/article/0,,4_929231,00.htm.

6. Cyber Atlas Staff, "Car Shoppers Increase Use of the Internet." *E-Commerce News* (November 27, 2001). Online: www.internetnews.com/ec-news/ article/0,,4_929231,00.htm.

7. Katharine Mieszkowski, "Web Commerce As If Customers Mattered," *Fast Company* 19 (November 1998). Online: www.fastcompany.com/online/ 19/webcomm.html.

8. Angel Martinez in "Fast Talk: The State of the Customer Economy," *Fast Company* 50 (September 2001): 80. Online: www.fastcompany.com/ online/50/fasttalk.html.

9. Cyber Atlas Staff, "Car Shoppers Increase Use of the Internet." *E-Commerce News* (November 27, 2001). Online: www.internetnews.com/ec-news/ article/0,,4_929231,00.htm.

10. Erick Schonfeld, "Corporations of the World Unite!" *Business 2.0* (June 1, 2000).

11. Bell Canada news release, Toronto (April 17, 2001). Online: www.bell.ca/en/about/news/releas/2001/pr_20010417.asp.

12. W3C develops free and open specifications, guidelines, software, and tools for the Internet.

13. Keith Bradsher, "Carmakers to Buy Parts on Internet," *The New York Times* (February 25, 2000): A1.

14. H. Dan Belser, "Cisco Chief: Future May Lie in Virtual Networks," *USA Today* (November 12, 2001). Online: www.usatoday.com/life/cyber/tech/2001/11/12/comdex-cisco.htm.

15. "Seller Beware," *The Economist* (March 4, 2000), 61–62. Online: www.economist.com.

16. Clinton Wilder, "Unload Your Surplus on the Web," *Informationweek* (August 30, 1999). Online: www.informationweek.com/750/trade.htm.

17. Katharine Mieszkowski, "Web Commerce As If Customers Mattered," *Fast Company* 19 (November 1998). Online: www.fastcompany.com/online/19/webcomm.html.

18. Jason Bater on 2000 CanWin website. Online: http://ace.acadieu.ca/polisci/aa/digagora/courses/pols1006/canwin/doc.html.

19. Lucy McCauley, "How May I Help You?: Unit of One," *Fast Company* 32 (March 2000): 93.

20. Elaine Bernard, speaking at the San Francisco Economic Summit, "San Francisco Sustainable Urban Growth: Challenges and Opportunities," Fairmont Hotel, San Francisco, April 17, 1996.

21. From the U.S. government website: http://egov.gov/about_us.htm.

22. Stephen Clift, paper delivered at the Gorbachev Foundation conference, "Technology and Democracy," in Boston, MA, December 1999. Online: http://publicus.net/present/agora.html.

23. Jeff Warren, "Point and Think," *The Globe and Mail* (March 2, 2002).

24. From a survey of 330 top government officials by the Pew Research Center for the People and the Press, in association with the National Journal and Congress daily, GovExec.com, April 17, 1998. The 330 government officials surveyed include 151 members of the Senior Executive Service, 81 members of Congress, and 98 presidential appointees.

25. Heather Scoffield, "E-Commerce Eluding Tax Net," *The Globe and Mail* (April 4, 2002): B1.

26. Julie Smyth, "71% Favour Charter Schools," *National Post* (September 8, 2001): A1.

27. At www.geneticalliance.org individuals can search for support groups and resources on almost any genetic condition.

28. Jupiter Communications, "Internet Health Commerce to Soar to $10 Billion, But Current Offerings Don't Deliver on Consumer Convenience," Press Release, January 26, 2000. Online: www.jup.com.

29. John A. Cutter, *The New York Times* (September 4, 2001). Online: www.informationweek.com/750/trade.htm.

30. Online: www.dyingwell.com.

31. From a transcript of PBS television program "Online Therapy" on *Healthweek*. Online: www.pbs.org/healthweek/featurep2_415.htm.

32. Katie Dean, "Docs Bid to Give You a Facelift," *Wired News* (May 19, 2000). Online: www.wired.com/news/print/0,1294,36344,00.html

33. André Picard, Public Reporter, "Bypassing their MDs, Canadians Go Online for Drugs," *The Globe and Mail*/CTV (March 2, 2002): A1.

34. Lucy McCauley, "How May I Help You?: Unit of One," *Fast Company* 32 (March 2000): 93. Online: www.fastcompany.com/online/32/one.html.

35. Online: www.iltech.org/faces_stories.htm.

36. UN Secretary Kofi Annan, in an address to a New York Internet conference, as reported in *Business Week* (August 8, 2001) in "Assistive Technology: New Gear for Disabled Web Serfers," by John M. Williams. Online: www.businessweek.com/bwdaily/dnflash/aug2001/nf2001088_451.htm.

37. Exceptions can be made only if an undue burden would be imposed on providing the service.

38. The proportion of baby boomers per population is highest in Canada and somewhat smaller in the United States and Europe. Their impact is similar throughout the countries that participated in World War II.

39. U.S. Census Bureau and the National Institute on Aging (NIA), *Report: An Aging World* (December 13, 2001).

40. David K. Foot with Daniel Stoffman, *Boom, Bust & Echo: How to Profit from the Coming Demographic Shift*. Toronto: Macfarlane Walter & Ross, 1996, p. 102.

41. A survey of adults 50 and older was conducted on the SeniorNet website from late February through early April 2000, in which 1,001 individuals voluntarily responded to a set of ten questions related to their use of the Internet.

5 The Anti-Clients

1. A full transcript of the television program is available at the PBS website: www.pbs.org/globalization.

2. Robert Hormats and George Soros, speaking at the World Economic Forum in Davos, Switzerland, January 1998. Online: www.pbs.org/globalization/view/html.

3. For more information on the IMF, see www.imf.org; for the World Bank, see www.worldbank.org/; and for the WTO, see www.wto.org.

4. S.P. Shukla, *From GATT to WTO and Beyond*. Working Paper No. 195. UNU World Institute for Development Economics Research (UNU/WIDER), August 2000.

5. Global Exchange, "World Bank/IMF Questions and Answers." Online: www.globalexchange.org/wbimf/faq.html.

6. Tom Baldwin, "New Allies Sought to Beat Genoa Generation." *The Times* (London) (August 28, 2001).

7. Jeff Warren, "Point and Think," *The Globe and Mail* (March 2002): 6.

8. Naomi Klein, "You Can Arrest Protestors, But You Can't Stop the Free Trade of Subversive Ideas," *The Globe and Mail* (June 7, 2002).

9. Alan Rugman is the Leslie Waters Chair of International Business, Kelly School of Business, Indiana University, and author of *The End of Globalization: Why Global Strategy Is a Myth and How to Profit from the Realities of Regional Markets* (New York: AMACOM, 2001).
   Karl Moore is a professor in the faculty of Management, McGill University, and co-author with David Lewis of *Foundations of Corporate Empire: Is History Repeating Itself?* (Harlow: Financial Times, Prentice Hall, 2000).

10. Michael Volpy, "Look Out, They're Back," *The Globe and Mail* (November 21, 2001): 11.

11. David Morris, "We Make the Rules and the Rules Make Us," speech delivered to the International Forum on Globalization, Washington, D.C., May 1996. Online: www.newrules.org/journal/why.htm

12. Marshall McLuhan wrote the liner notes for author Paul Hoffert's Violin Concerto. The notes contain the first published references to the four stages of introducing new transformative technologies.

13. Barry Wellman, "Little Boxes, Glocalization, and Networked Individualism," *Communications of the ACM*, December 2001.

14. U.S. Bureau of Labor Statistics. Online: www.bls.gov.

15. *Globe and Mail Report on Business* (September 16, 2000).

16. The author detailed this phenomenon in *The Bagel Effect: A Compass to Navigate the Wired World*. Toronto: McGraw-Hill Ryerson, 1998.

17. Statistics Canada, *Quarterly Bulletin from the Culture Statistics Program*, Vol. 12 (2). Ottawa: Statistics Canada.

18. Associated Press, "Women's Lawsuit Targets Technology," *The New York Times* (September 19, 2001).

19. Kevin Kelly, "Where Music Will Be Coming From," *The New York Times* (March 17, 2002). Kevin Kelly is the author, most recently, of *New Rules for the New Economy: 10 Radical Strategies for a Connected World* (New York: Penguin, 1999).

20. Professor Jerome Durlak is director of York University's New Media Laboratory and on the faculty of Bell H@bitat, the new media school of the Canadian Film Centre.

21. Bob Frankston, "Beyond Telecom" (October 30, 2001). Online: www.frankston.com/public/essays/BeyondTelecom.asp.

22. Regular analog telephone service is known in the biz as POTS (Plain Old Telephone Service). It supports a frequency range up to about 8 kHz (hi-fi sound goes to 20 Hz) and has a rather grainy resolution of 8 bits (music CDs use 16 bits of resolution). Nonetheless, the quality is appropriate for communicating human voice conversations.

23. Currently the bandwidth is asymmetrical, with about 300 kilobits per second available for sending and more than 1 milobit per second available for receiving information. This asymmetry works well for most Internet downloading but not very well for sending email attachments. It is not well suited to bi-directional video conferencing.

24. For details of these activities, see Paul Hoffert, *All Together Now: Connected Communities: How They Will Revolutionize the Way You Live, Work, and Play* (Toronto: Stoddart, 2000).

25. Roxane Googin, "How Networking Advances Screwed Up the Economy," in David Eisenberg's *Smart Letter* #64. Copyright 2001 by David S. Isenberg isen@isen.com. Online: www.isen.com.

26. As noted by Howard Davies, Deputy Governor of the Bank of England, in his Maurice Lubbock Lecture in Management Studies at Regent's Park College, November 14, 2001.

27. The MBA Portal. Online: www.pgmba.com/home/ecom.htm.

28. Thomas L. Mesenbourg, "Measuring Electronic Business: Definitions, Underlying Concepts, and Measurement Plans," U.S. Census Bureau, 1999. Online: www.census.gov/epcd/www/ebusines.htm

29. Thomas J. Peters and Robert Waterman, *In Search of Excellence: Lessons from America's Best-Run Companies.* New York: Warner, 1982.

30. Tom Peters, "Tom Peters's True Confessions," *Fast Company* 53 (December 2001): 78.

INDEX

Frankston, Bob, 185
free market, 184–187
free trade agreements, 35
Freemarkets.com, 104
freeware, 20
future, 196–197
Future Now, 61
Future Shock (Toffler and Toffler), 14, 157

G
Gartner Inc., 67
Gates, Bill, 119
General Agreement on Tariffs and Trade
    (GATT), 35, 147–148
General Electric, 97
General Motors, 103
Gerstner, Lou, 50–51
Gillette, 42
Gimenez, Auggie, 134
global village, myth of, 157–158
globalization, 144–160
Globe and Mail, 72, 132
Gorbachev, Mikhail, 34
Gorbachev Foundation, 112
government regulations, 73–74, 137–138,
    184
governments
    as clients, 145
    direct democracy, 113–114
    e-democracy, 114–115
    online, 108–109
    services online, 115
    as suppliers, 107–108, 145
    taxation, 115–117
    traditional *vs.* online, 110–111
Guns, Germs and Steel (Diamond), 123–124

H
hackers, 78
Hampton, Keith, 159
Harris, Lesley, 42
Harris, Mike, 111
Harvard Trade Union Program, 109
health care, 25, 124–138

*Health Information and Privacy Portability
    Act (HIPPA),* 74
Health on the Net (HON) Code of Ethical
    Guidelines, 128
HealthAllies.com, 131
Healtheon/WebMD, 127
Here2listen.com, 131
High Tech High, 123
Hilder, Paul, 113
Hisaura, Hiroki, 21
HitBox, 55
Hitt, Lorin M., 34
Hormats, Robert, 145
html (hypertext markup language), 100
Hyundai, 38

I
IBM, 50–51
in-person user tests, 69
In Search of Excellence (Peters and
    Waterman), 192
Inco, 103
individual user paths, 37
industrial convergence, 22–23
industrialization, 155–156
information pipelines, 179–189
information technology, 15–16
informed patients, 127–128
infrastructure, 31, 96, 179–189
Institute for Local Self-Reliance, 155
integrated sales channels, 87–89
integrity of information, 71
Intel, 130
Inter Net Economy: Technology and Practice
    (Choi and Whinston), 88
Intercom Ontario, 130–131, 135
internal focus, shift from, 32–33
International Bank for Reconstruction and
    Development (IBRD), 147–148
international commerce, 16
International Monetary Fund (IMF),
    147–148, 149–150
International Treaty and Arms Regulation
    (ITAR), 76